Kimmo Katajala, Maria Lähteenmäki (Eds.)

Imagined, Negotiated, Remembered

Mittel- und Ostmitteleuropastudien

herausgegeben von

Gerhard Besier und Katarzyna Stokłosa
Sigmund-Neumann-Institut für Freiheits- und Demokratieforschung
(Technische Universität Dresden/Syddansk Universitet Sønderborg)

Band 11

LIT

Imagined, Negotiated, Remembered

Constructing European Borders and Borderlands

edited by

Kimmo Katajala, Maria Lähteenmäki

LIT

The cover picture: excerpts of maps from the 16th to the 20th century.
Maps from the Nordenskiöld Collection, National Library of Finland.

Bibliographic information published by the Deutsche Nationalbibliothek
The Deutsche Nationalbibliothek lists this publication in the Deutsche Nationalbibliografie; detailed bibliographic data are available in the Internet at http://dnb.d-nb.de.

ISBN 978-3-643-90257-3

A catalogue record for this book is available from the British Library

Klosbachstr. 107
CH-8032 Zürich
Tel. +41 (0) 44-251 75 05
Fax +41 (0) 44-251 75 06
e-Mail: zuerich@lit-verlag.ch
http://www.lit-verlag.ch

LIT VERLAG Dr. W. Hopf
Berlin 2012
Fresnostr. 2
D-48159 Münster
Tel. +49 (0) 2 51-620 320
Fax +49 (0) 2 51-23 19 72
e-Mail: lit@lit-verlag.de
http://www.lit-verlag.de

Distribution:
In Germany: LIT Verlag Fresnostr. 2, D-48159 Münster
Tel. +49 (0) 2 51-620 32 22, Fax +49 (0) 2 51-922 60 99, e-mail: vertrieb@lit-verlag.de

In Austria: Medienlogistik Pichler-ÖBZ, e-mail: mlo@medien-logistik.at

In Switzerland: B + M Buch- und Medienvertrieb, e-mail: order@buch-medien.ch

In the UK: Global Book Marketing, e-mail: mo@centralbooks.com

CONTENTS

'Us' and 'Others' on Both Sides of the Post-War Borders

IMAGINED, NEGOTIATED, REMEMBERED – FOREWORD

This collection of papers explores the history of borders on the eastern and north-eastern frontiers of Europe from early modern times up to the second decade of the 21st century. The theme is based on the perception that without a long-term historical viewpoint it is not possible to analyse or reinterpret the formations and transformations of borders and border regions, for as the French historian Fernand Braudel has emphasised in his classic works The Mediterranean World (1949) and Civilization and Capitalism, 15th–18th Century (1979), the *longue durée* (Eng. long-term) perspective is *de rigueur* for understanding historical processes. The long-term perspective on the border issue becomes even more important because of the lively competition between the paradigms of primordialism, neo-perennialism and modernism in the discussion of the nature of pre-modern nations and states. An understanding of the differences and similarities between modern and pre-modern borders cannot be based on dominance of the modern view of the nation-state. The past must be respected and valued in its own terms and under its own conditions. The other starting point for this collection is an awareness of the idea that national histories – including border politics – form an important part of the collective memory of the peoples of Europe. This book offers twelve different ways of presenting and analysing European borders and at the same time twelve case studies on the history of the development of Europe. The nature and sense of a border will always be connected with concrete historical times and places.

The historical borders between states taken up in this collection are mainly physical ones, but they can also be considered immaterial, as expressed in the title of the book: constructs that are imagined, negotiated and remembered. This division between physical and immaterial borders has recently been described with the concepts of "hard" and "soft" borders. Borders exist not only physically in the terrain but mentally between groups of people: between Us and Others divided by a physical border and between Us and Others on the same side of the border, often in the borderlands. Soft borders can sometimes be extremely strict and "hard", however, as we can see from the papers by Jens Petter Nielsen/Konstantin Zaikov, Anna Laakkonen, Katarzyna Stokłosa, Gerhard Besier and Monica Andriescu in this volume. These soft borders, when one might even call them prejudices, construct the corresponding physical borders in an ideological manner. This implies that borders defined in the terrain often carry strong mental and ideological meanings. In that sense they are imagined and sometimes consciously constructed. This process of constructing imagined borders is handled in this volume especially in the papers by Kimmo Katajala, Laakkonen, Hallvard Tjelmeland and Besier. Not only are nations and nation-states imagined, but also the boundaries of pre-modern nation-states.

Borders in Europe have been negotiated on countless occasions in the course of time, leaving us with a body of collectively negotiated agreements that represent attempts to stabilize flexible, unstable and controversial borders between ruling classes, kinships, peoples and states. Throughout history, people have organized themselves into groups in order to optimize the realization of their common interests, as the Swedish social scientist Sven Tägil has argued. The politically negotiated borders of states have been marked and re-marked in the terrain, and also in peoples' minds. From the 15th to the 21st century peace treaties have been signed by local, regional and national negotiators after wars or non-violent actions. Probably the most famous politically negotiated European treaties are the Peace of Augsburg (1555), the Westphalian Peace Treaty (1648), the Congress of Vienna (1815), the Treaty of Versailles (1919) and the Congress of Potsdam (1945), a list to which we could add the non-violent Treaty of the European Union (1992). Besides these continentally important milestones, regional and local borders were also negotiated, leading Thomas M. Wilson and Hastings Donnan to argue that borders are political constructions of everyday life. The paper by Krom with which this anthology starts out presents in a concrete way the complex nature of late medieval and early modern borders. They were a mixture of alliances and vassalages of dukes and princes and their dominions, bound up with choices made by the people living in the borderlands.

These imagined and negotiated borders are also remembered. As Jens Lerbom shows in this book, remembering the border played an important role in solving many court cases in the early modern borderlands between the Swedish and Danish realms in present-day southern Sweden. As noted in Katajala's article, finding and explaining the "original" borders for the needs of the national collective memory has always been the task of historians in the young nation-states, just as it is the task of social scientists to study and explain such processes at present-day borders in the best possible manner. This process of explaining modern borders and their content is reconstructed in the papers presented here. Not all the experiences and recollections of borderland inhabitants live on in their memories, however, for people remember mainly intersubjective, shared experiences, which form ensembles in different layers.

The historically dominant continental treaties – alongside local, regional and supranational treaties – have also affected borderline demarcations in the eastern and north-eastern regions of Europe to a greater or lesser extent. The English Professor of regional studies Michael Keating has remarked that before the rise of the modern nation-state Europe had a highly differentiated political order. Power was fragmented territorially, among empires, kingdoms, principalities, cities and other self-governing entities, as well as functionally, among the political, religious and economic spheres. In the first main chapter of this collection the historians Mikhail Krom, Lerbom and Jukka Kokkonen analyse border demarcations during the pre-modern period in their case studies from Lithuania, Sweden and Finland, indicating in very concrete ways how complex the procedures involved in constructing a shared border can be and how many interest groups were sometimes entangled together in such a process. They also emphasize the importance of local actors by combining the macro-historical method with the grass-roots aspect in the context of early state building. Nielsen and Zaikov continue these discussions on state building by focusing on border demarcation issues between Russia and Norway in the 19th century and early 20th century, arguing that immaterial, "soft" borders can influence physical or "hard" borders and even make them harder, to such a degree that they change their physical appearance.

In the second main chapter, the historians Katajala, Maria Lähteenmäki, Olga Ilyukha and Laakkonen concentrate on one borderland, the historically controversial territory of Karelia located between Sweden/Finland and Russia/the Soviet Union, thereby opening the debate on identity building and political actions. They analyse the role of Karelia as a subject of historical research, how the closure of the border between Finland and the Soviet Union affected everyday life in the region and the way in which the people of Karelia on both sides of the border have established their Karelian identities. All the main actors in these articles are Finns: Finns writing histories of the borders and the Karelian borderlands and Finns crossing the border illegally after its closure when Finland gained independence in 1917. Similarly, the main actors in the writings of Ilyukha and Laakkonen are Finns, although the stage for their action is Soviet and Russian Karelia. The history of this borderland region would doubtless appear in a very different light if recounted from the viewpoint of the other main ethnic groups living in Karelia, the Karelians and Russians.

In the third main chapter of this book the historians Tjelmeland, Stokłosa and Besier open up new windows on the European border debates, the resulting political actions and their consequences after the Second World War. Political, socio-economic and cultural circumstances on the Norwegian/Soviet/Russian border and in the border regions were quite different from those on the borders between the former Eastern Bloc countries and Russia. The Norwegian-Russian boundary in the north is only about one hundred kilometres long, but the border issue is more politically and culturally charged than on the eastern borders of Europe. The researchers indicate that everyday life with its border crossings on the Polish-Russian, Polish-Ukrainian and Polish-German borders has been very active and diversified since the collapse of the Soviet Union in 1991, in response to the dynamic border policies adopted by the European Union in the 1990s and 2000s. Although the opening of the borders has not been a trouble-free process by any means, as there have been conflicts and power struggles, the open borders can be seen as having generated the potential for new kinds of trade and cultural interaction. The common open border policy has affected the internal politics of individual countries, as the historian Andriescu shows in her discussion of the politics surrounding the Hungarian minority in Post-Communist Romania and the struggle on behalf of the Hungarian identity, culture and language in the Romanian borderlands.

All the contributors to this collection are historians, mainly working at universities in Russia, Sweden, Finland, Norway, Denmark and Germany. The idea of producing the volume arose from an international conference "Imagined Borders in the European North" held at the University of Eastern Finland on 2nd December, 2010 in the framework of the project "Building Borders" (funded by the Academy of Finland) taking place in Department of Geographical and Historical Studies, and the Karelian Institute at that university, under the auspices of the "Europe Beyond the East-West Division" centre of expertise. We would like to thank all the participants in the conference as well as the contributors to this collection for their fruitful cooperation. The English language of the papers was revised by Malcolm Hicks (Krom, Kokkonen, Katajala, Lähteenmäki, Ilyukha, Laakkonen), Margot Hart (Nielsen, Tjelmeland) and Anna Fåhraeus (Lerbom), and translated by Andrew Smith (Stokłosa, Besier, Andriescu). Therefore, despite the editorial work, there may be some discontinuity in style, and especially in the spelling of the Russian names. The map in the paper by Krom was originally drawn by Viktor N. Temushev for the book Mikhail Krom: "Mezh Rus'iu i Litvoi [Between Rus' and Lithuania], Moscow 2010, and was reworked for this volume by Darya M. Sokolova and Andrei Y. Sokolov. All the other maps were drawn by Mr. Jussi Virratvuori, who was also responsible for the layout of the book. We wish to thank all the above people for their valuable work. Publication of this book was supported by the European Union Social Fund and the Regional Council of North Karelia. We are grateful to Professor Gerhard Besier for suggesting that the book should be published in the Mittel- und Ostmitteleuropastudien series produced by the respected publisher LIT-Verlag.

Joensuu, 15th May, 2012

Kimmo Katajala Maria Lähteenmäki

REFERENCES

1 On this discussion, see for example Anthony D. Smith, The Cultural Foundations of Nations. Hierarchy, Covenant, and Republic, Blackwell Publishing, Malden – Oxford – Carlton 2008, 1–11.

2 See The Contested Nation. Ethnicity, Class, Religion and Gender in National Histories. Stefan Berger/Chris Lorenz (eds.), Writing the Nation Series, European Science Foundation, Palgrave Mcmillan, London 2011.

3 A recent discussion about hard and soft borders has been presented in Madeleine Hurd, Constructing and Challenging Nordic Borders – Introduction, in Bordering the Baltic. Scandinavian Boundary-Drawing Processes, 1900–2000, Madeleine Hurd (ed.), Nordische Geschichte, band 10, LIT Verlag, Berlin 2010, 10. See also all the articles in the book.

4 See Benedict Anderson, Imagined Communities. Reflections on the Origin and Spread of Nationalism, Verso, London [3]2006 ([1]1983).

5 Sven Tägil, Introduction, in: Ethnicity and Nation Building in the Nordic World. Sven Tägil (ed.), Hurst & Company, London 1995, 1–7.

6 Thomas M. Wilson/Hastings Donnan, Nation, State and Identity at International Borders, in: Border Identities, Nation and State at International Frontiers. Thomas M. Wilson/Hastings Donnan (eds.), Cambridge University Press, Cambridge 1998, 19–21.

7 An application of the theory of social constructionism on the border studies see for example Klaus Eder, Europe's Borders: The Narrative Costruction of the Boundaries of Europe, in: European Journal of Social Theory 9 (2006).

8 See Peter Berger/Thomas Luckmann, The Social Construction of Reality: A Treatise in the Sociology of Knowledge. Anchor Books, New York 1966.

9 Keating Michael, The New Regionalism in Western Europe, Edvard Elgar, Cheltenham 1998, 16.

Constructing the Pre-Modern Borders

MIKHAIL KROM

CHANGING ALLEGIANCES IN THE AGE OF STATE-BUILDING: THE BORDER BETWEEN THE GRAND DUCHY OF LITHUANIA AND THE GRAND PRINCIPALITY OF MOSCOW

The shaping of the border between the biggest East European powers in the late Middle Ages, the Grand Duchy of Lithuania and the Grand Principality of Moscow, has usually been studied against the background of military conflicts and diplomatic relations between the two neighbouring countries. Scholars have exerted great efforts in order to locate the settlements mentioned in the Lithuanian-Muscovite peace treaties and to put them on a map.[1] But paying these diplomatic or geographical histories of the Russian-Lithuanian border their due, I would like to draw attention to some other important aspects of the problem which so far have been neglected by scholars.

First of all, it seems promising to regard the formation of the border between Lithuania and Muscovy as a part of the state-building process in Eastern Europe. Besides, it is essential to assess the impact of the borderland population's changing loyalties on shifts in the border itself in the course of time. In this article I will adopt a kind of double perspective, situating the events under review both in a macro-historical context of state formation and in a local context.

STATE-BUILDING AND THE EMERGENCE OF STATE BORDERS IN EASTERN EUROPE

The rivalry between the Lithuanian dukes and the Muscovite princes for dominance over Russian lands began in the second half of the 14th century, but at that time it did not involve any territorial claims or border issues. In 1368, 1370, and 1372 Algirdas, the Grand Duke of Lithuania (1345–1377), marched against Grand Prince Dmitry of Moscow (1359–1389). In these campaigns Algirdas sided with Prince Mikhail of Tver', his ally and father-in-law, who was competing with Dmitry for the grand-princely throne of Vladimir. Although Algirdas twice besieged the Muscovite Kremlin, he failed to derive any political gains from those raids.[2]

Hostilities were resumed in 1406 under Vytautas the Great, Duke of Lithuania (1392–1430), and Basil I, Grand Prince of Moscow (1389–1425) on account of Vytautas' conquest of Smolensk (1404) and pressure on Pskov (1406), and this situation lasted for three years.[3] By the time of Vytautas' death (1430) his sphere of influence in the Russian lands had reached its peak: not only had he conquered the towns of Smolensk and Viaz'ma but he had also forced Pskov and Great Novgorod to pay him indemnities, while the princes of the Upper Oka, Pronsk and Riazan' acknowledged him as their suzerain.[4]

But at the same time the territory controlled by the grand prince of Moscow expanded as well and his influence on the other Russian princes increased. By the mid-fifteenth century the two grand duchies, Lithuania and Muscovy, had become the strongest powers in Eastern Europe. The balance of forces was reflected in a peace treaty concluded on August 31, 1449 between Casimir, King of Poland and Grand Duke of Lithuania, and Basil II (Vasilii Vasil'evich), Grand Prince of Moscow. This is the first treaty between the two countries which has been preserved although in a later copy included in the *Lithuanian Metrica*.

The document proclaims "brotherhood and love, and eternal agreement" between the monarchs. It should be noted, however, that the text contains no description of the border: instead it lists a number of possessions belonging to Casimir and Basil II, with obligations to respect the rights of the other side to this or that town. Thus Basil II promised not to intrude into Smolensk, Liubutsk, Mtsensk or the outlying districts (*ukrainnyie mesta*) surrounding these towns,[5] while Casimir was to refrain from intruding into the town of Rzheva on the River Volga and the district around it.[6]

The treaty also confirmed protectorates for Casimir and Basil II over certain Russian principalities and cities. Thus the Grand Principality of Tver', formerly Moscow's principal rival, was referred to as being under Casimir's control or protection or literally, "on his side" while Grand Prince Ivan Fedorovich of Riasan' was referred to as Basil II's vassal or literally, "junior brother" and friend. Casimir promised not to offend Ivan of Riasan', although the latter was free to change his allegiance and to enter the grand duke of Lithuania's service.[7] Basil II also secured his suzerainty over certain borderland princes, such as Prince Vasilii Ivanovich of Tarusa and his kin. The city republics of Great Novgorod and Pskov were treated as Basil II's protectorates, and Casimir pledged to refrain from intruding into them or doing any harm to them. Moreover, even if the Novgorodians and Pskovites were to decide pledge allegiance to him, the king would have to refuse to accept them.[8]

The Muscovite-Lithuanian treaty of 1449 exemplifies a medieval type of agreement between two realms: instead of changing a previous border or establishing a new one, it delineated spheres of influence.[9] The "high contracting parties", i.e. Grand Prince Basil II and King Casimir, did not represent nation-states, but rather each of them was an overlord at the head of a complex network of autonomous and semiautonomous principalities, city communes and possessions of various kinds. Such a loose political organization was cemented by personal and collective oaths of allegiance to the sovereign. Since neither the Grand Duchy of Lithuania nor the Grand

Principality of Moscow constituted a homogeneous territorial unit, it is no wonder that for many decades they were separated not by a clearly demarcated borderline but by a broad buffer zone whose inhabitants could choose which sovereign to serve.[10]

The situation began to change in the reign of Ivan III, Grand Prince of Moscow (1462–1505). In 1478 he annexed Great Novgorod with its vast territories in the Northern Russia. Soon after that Ivan III assumed the title of the "sovereign of all Rus' (*gosudar' vsea Rusi*).[11] In domestic affairs, the new title reflected the growing power of the Muscovite ruler, who now claimed absolute and unquestioned authority in his realm. The idea of sovereignty marked the transition from a principality to an emerging nation-state.

In foreign relations, the new title of Ivan III implied his claims to all Russian lands, including those which had formerly been incorporated into the Grand Duchy of Lithuania. In 1485, Ivan III conquered the Grand Principality of Tver'. The new acquisitions brought Muscovy into closer contact with the Lithuanian realm, and the buffer zone started to shrink. In the late 1480s, the border disputes between vassals of Ivan III and Casimir grew into a Muscovite-Lithuanian war (on the role of local princes in the origins and outcomes of this military conflict, see the following section). Ivan III won this undeclared war, as in winter 1493 his troops occupied the town of Viaz'ma, the centre of the principality of the same name, and some principalities in the upper Oka region also passed under his control.

It is significant that the peace treaty of 1494, which put an end to the war, provided a much more detailed description of the border than had the previous treaty of 1449. Listing the recent acquisitions of Ivan III, including Great Novgorod and Tver', the agreement specifies that the borders of these formerly independent territories with Lithuania should be preserved as before (*a rubezh...po staromu rubezhu*).[12] Special attention to territorial issues can also be discerned in the detailed lists of possessions held by each of the sides after the war, in which the area of the recent military conflict – the principality of Viaz'ma and the upper Oka region – was demarcated especially meticulously. Thus the treaty secured Ivan III's title to the newly conquered towns of Viaz'ma, Kozel'sk, Liudimsk, Serensk, etc. and confirmed his patrimonial rights to Aleksin, Tarusa, Venev and Obolensk, which had already been parts of the grand princely domain.[13] The main participants in the disputes over the upper Oka district, the local princes of Odoev, Vorotynsk, Peremyshl' and Belev, were explicitly referred to in the treaty of 1494 as belonging to the Grand Principality of Moscow.[14]

On the other hand, the text of the agreement contained a list of possessions of the Grand Duchy of Lithuania in the disputed area, including Smolensk, Liubutsk, Mtsensk, Briansk, Serpeisk, Mosal'sk, Dmitrov and other towns and rural districts.[15] The buffer zone between the neighbouring realms remained, but in 1494 it contracted to the tiny principality of Mezetsk, the possessors of which could declare allegiance to either the Lithuanian or the Muscovite sovereign.[16] On the whole, the treaty of 1494 is the first document which provides sufficient information for a reconstruction and mapping of the Muscovite-Lithuanian border (see the map).

The text of the next agreement between the Grand Principality of Moscow and the Grand Duchy of Lithuania, namely the truce of 1503, is even more lengthy. Not only did it fix the new acquisitions of Ivan III made during the war of 1500–1503 but it also listed *all the possessions* of both sides in the borderlands, including dozens of cities, towns, rural districts (*volosti*), and even villages.[17] Since then all subsequent Muscovite-Lithuanian treaties followed the same pattern and contained a full description of the border. The peace treaty of 1508, for instance, which put an end to the short military conflict of 1507–1508, mentioned all the possessions of the Grand Duchies of Lithuania and Muscovy on both sides of the border, notwithstanding the fact that the gains and losses of the two parties in the war of 1507–1508, and therefore the changes in the border, were insignificant.[18]

Thus we may conclude that the *state border* between the Grand Duchy of Lithuania and the Grand Principality of Moscow had come into being by the beginning of the sixteenth century. As a definite borderline replacing a vast buffer zone between the two rival duchies, it was a by-product of the state formation process, which entailed the integration of semiautonomous principalities and independent city republics into the territory of an emerging state. This process took place in both countries, the Grand Duchy of Lithuania and Muscovy alike, but in different ways and at different speeds.

The Muscovite way of state-building implied the extensive use of military force and coercion. The new-born Muscovite state did not tolerate any forms of autonomy or self-government, as the fate of Great Novgorod and Pskov clearly shows. The Grand Duchy of Lithuania developed towards a *Ständestaat*, and its rulers actively used privileges as a means of integration within the realm.[19] In the initial phase until the beginning of the sixteenth century, the Muscovite strategy proved to be more effective in terms of expanding its territory westwards at the expense of the Grand Duchy, but starting from the second decade of the sixteenth century the Lithuanian policy began to bear fruit and the Muscovite advance was arrested.

This is, of course, a rough outline of the processes that took place on the two sides of the Muscovite-Lithuanian border. In order to fill out this scheme with facts, we need to consider the crucial phases of border formation in some detail. Special attention will be paid to the role of the borderland population like princes, townsmen and nobles. Were these people merely victims of the clashes between the rival powers or they could really affect the course and outcome of events?[20]

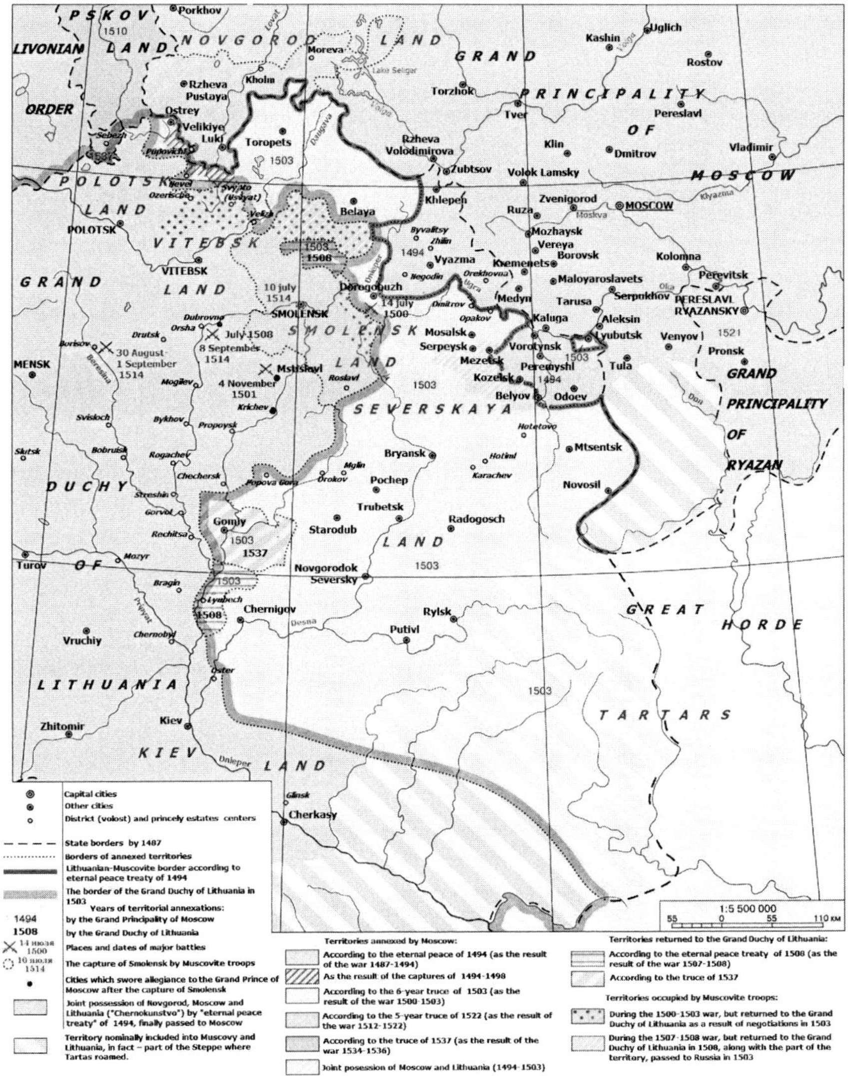

Map 1. *The Muscovite-Lithuanian border at the end of 15th and in the first fhird of 16th century*

LOCAL PRINCIPALITIES AND THE LITHUANIAN-MUSCOVITE BORDER

The eastern borderlands of the Grand Duchy of Lithuania in the fifteenth century comprised a host of principalities varying in origin and legal status. In the north, between Toropets and Rzheva on the upper Volga – the latter belonged to the Muscovite domain – there was an appanage of the ruling dynasty with its centre in the town of Belaia, where the local princes were descended from the grandson of Algirdas, Prince Ivan Vladimirovich.[21] The principality of Belaia bordered in the south on Viaz'ma, the patrimony of the Viazemskii princes, the Riurikids, who were a branch of the Smolensk princes, while further south, in the upper Oka basin, there were many tiny principalities whose owners descended from the Chernigov branch of the Riurikid dynasty. The most important of these, the princedom of Novosil', which was a mere name at the time under consideration here, had split into the principalities of Odoev, Vorotynsk and Belev by the beginning of the fifteenth century. Two related but rival princely clans, the Odoevskis and the Vorotynskis, contested the title of Prince of Novosil', which carried with it the notion of seniority within the family. Meanwhile both clans maintained contract-based relations with the grand dukes of Lithuania, a tradition that goes back to the reign of Vytautas, although the earliest extant agreement to his effect dates from 1442 or 1447, having been concluded between Prince Fedor Lvovich Vorotynskii – who styled himself as Prince Novosil'skii and Odoevskii – on the one hand, and Grand Duke Casimir on the other.[22] The agreement defined the mutual obligations of the contracting parties: Prince Fedor promised loyalty and obedience to the grand duke, while the latter was to protect him and treat him honourably. In the event of Fedor's death his sons were to inherit his patrimony and to conclude the same agreement with the grand duke. The latter was also to play the role of an arbiter in internal disputes involving the princes of Novosil' but if he refused to observe the contract, they were free of any obligations.[23]

These agreements were renewed several times up to the 1480s, the heads of the two rival houses of the princes of Novosil' (i.e. the Odoevskii and Vorotynskii families) making separate contracts with Casimir, although the texts of agreements themselves were absolutely identical.[24] The neighbours of the princes of Novosil' in the upper Oka region, the princes of Mezetsk and Mosal'sk, did not enjoy the same privileged status. They had never concluded contracts with the grand dukes of Lithuania, and they were actually treated not as autonomous princes but rather as major landowners with hereditary rights over their lands (patrimonies).[25]

Finally, the south-eastern part of the Lithuanian borderlands in the mid-fifteenth century was formed by the vast possessions of recent Muscovite refugees: Prince Ivan Andreevich Mozhaiskii, cousin of Basil II, and the latter's nephew Prince Ivan Dmitrievich Shemiachich. Both had fled to Lithuania in 1454 because they belonged to clans who had lost out in the recent Muscovite internal strife. As close relatives of the Grand Prince of Moscow and his rivals, they were generously remunerated by the Grand Duke of Lithuania, Casimir. Ivan Mozhaiskii was granted the towns of Starodub and Gomel with their adjacent areas, while Ivan Shemiachich received Novgorod-Severskii. Thus the vast Severskaia territory[26] was divided between two Muscovite refugees, although, like the appanage of the Belskii princes mentioned above, this territory was considered to be part of the grand-ducal domain and the princes remained only the holders of the lands granted to them by the grand dukes.

Thus the eastern Lithuanian borderlands in the mid-fifteenth century looked like a patchwork of appanages, semiautonomous principalities and patrimonies, which were loosely connected to the core of the Grand Duchy. It is no wonder that this heterogeneous conglomeration could not withstand pressure from the neighbouring realm, the Grand Principality of Moscow, which had been successfully consolidated under Ivan III (1462–1505).

As border conflicts had become more frequent, it appeared that the grand duke of Lithuania was unable to protect his vassals. Under these circumstances the local princes behaved differently: some of them went over to the stronger side, i.e. that of Ivan III, while others passively followed the course of events. Quite predictably, the princes of Novosil', who enjoyed a certain degree of autonomy, were the most active. Prince Semen Yur'evich Odoevskii was the first to pledge allegiance to Ivan III, doing so before autumn 1473, when the chroniclers recorded Prince Semen's death in a skirmish with the townsmen of Liubech, who thus took revenge for the preceding Muscovite raid upon their town.[27] Three of the sons of Semen Odoevskii – the Princes Ivan, Vasilii and Petr – may have accompanied their father in deserting the Grand Duchy of Lithuania for Moscow, or else they may have followed his lead later, but in 1487 they were definitely referred to as being in the Muscovite camp, as the Lithuanian ambassador complained in October 1487 about their raid on the town of Mezetsk, the patrimony of the princes of the same name.[28] None of them was bound by an agreement with the grand duke of Lithuania, and so they felt free to choose another sovereign.

It is important to note that Semen Odoevskii's brother, Prince Ivan Yur'evich, and the latter's sons (Mikhail and Fedor) retained their allegiance to King Casimir. Thus there was a bitter split within the clan of the Odoevskii princes, cousins who were vassals of different sovereigns and were engaged in fighting each other. Finally these family conflicts grew into an undeclared war between the two neighbouring realms.

Towards the end of the 1480s defections to Moscow had become a widespread phenomenon among the princes of the upper Oka region. The Princes Ivan Mikhailovich Vorotynskii and Ivan Vasil'evich Belevskii declared allegiance to Ivan III in 1487, and they were followed by Prince Dmitrii Fedorovich Vorotynskii in 1489.[29] The latter's change of allegiance meant that family feud had now split the clan of the Vorotynskii princes, because Dmitrii's brother, Prince Semen Fedorovich Vorotynskii, remained a faithful vassal of Casimir until the latter's death in 1492.

It was the grand prince of Moscow who reaped the greatest benefit from the rivalry between the border princes, for he successfully extended the territory of his realm in the 1480s and early 1490s with the help of his new vassals, without resorting to his own military forces. When Prince Dmitrii Vorotynskii went over to Ivan III's side in 1489, for instance, not only did he hold the town of Kozelsk, which had recently been given to him by King Casimir, but he also seized a part of his brother Semen's patrimony as well as towns and rural districts such as Serensk, Byshkovichi and Nedokhodov that belonged to other landowners.[30]

It was only in August 1492, after the death of Grand Duke and King Casimir that Ivan III seized the opportunity to intervene in the border disputes and send his troops into the upper Oka region. Simultaneously, his vassals, Prince Ivan Vorotynskii and the sons of Semen Odoevskii, acting on Ivan's orders, conducted a raid on Mosal'sk, burned the town and captured the local princes.[31] The Muscovite predominance in the border area was now so evident and impressive that new defections followed. The Princes Andrei and Vasilii Belevskii, Mikhail Mezetskii and Semen Vorotynskii swore fealty to Ivan III at the end of 1492.

It is significant that Prince Semen Vorotynskii, when changing allegiance from Lithuania to Moscow, sent a message to the new grand duke, Alexander, explaining the motives for his action. First of all, he reminded the Lithuanian ruler of the fealty he had shown to the late King Casimir in return for his protection, but the latter had neither protected Semen's patrimony nor had he compensated him for the lands he had lost. Moreover, when Alexander ascended the Lithuanian throne, Semen Vorotynskii had hoped that the new sovereign would grant him a town as compensation for his losses. He had wanted to renew his agreement with the grand duke, but none of these hopes had come true. In his disappointment, Prince Semen declared himself free of any obligations to the grand duke and went over to the side of Ivan III.[32]

Prince Vorotynskii's declaration graphically demonstrates the decay of the vassalage system in the Grand Duchy of Lithuania, in that the grand dukes had stopped concluding agreements with their vassal princes after the 1480s, while Ivan III, in accepting the allegiance of the Odoevskii and Vorotynskii princes, did not sign any contract with them either, as he regarded them not as vassals but simply as subjects. Thus the concept of vassalage gradually disappeared on both sides of the border.

The Lithuanian-Muscovite peace treaty of 1494, which crowned Ivan III's success, clearly reflected the role of the local princes, whose support had predetermined Moscow's victory. It is instructive that the border principalities of Odoev, Vorotynsk, Peremyshl', Belev and Viaz'ma, whose owners had – voluntarily or under compulsion – pledged allegiance to Ivan III, were finally confirmed as new Muscovite acquisitions in the treaty of 1494, while the towns where Ivan III had failed to find support – e.g. Mtsensk, Liubutsk and Mosal'sk – were restored to the grand duke of Lithuania.[33] The most dramatic fate befell the princely town of Mezetsk, which, as already mentioned above, was divided between princes loyal to Muscovite and Lithuanian sovereigns.[34] As a result, the district of Mezetsk remained the only border area which was not delimited in 1494 (see the map 1).

The "eternal peace" between Muscovy and the Grand Duchy of Lithuania, concluded in 1494, lasted only six years, and a new war broke out in 1500. As before, Ivan III incited the border princes to defect from the Grand Duchy of Lithuania and promised to act as their "protector". What was new in this carefully rehearsed drama was the attempt to use a religious factor as a *casus belli*. At the end of 1499 Prince Semen Belskii, who ruled over the tiny principality of Belaia in the north-eastern sector of the Lithuanian frontier, went over to Ivan III. Explaining his defection in a message to the grand duke, Semen mentioned that he had fallen into disgrace with Alexander, having rebelled against the latter's alleged attempt to convert some Orthodox princes to Catholicism by force.[35] In April 1500 the Princes Semen Mozhaiskii and Vasilii Shemiachich, the mightiest lords in the land of Severskaia located in the south-east, on the edge of the Steppes, also swore allegiance to Ivan III, and the Muscovite chronicles refer to the same motive for their defection: the religious persecutions of Orthodox people.[36] Ivan III willingly accepted the princes and approved of their alleged motives for leaving the Lithuanian camp. In fact he made a formal protest against the persecution of Orthodox believers in the Grand Duchy of Lithuania, declared war on Alexander and sent his troops to protect his new vassals.[37]

Scholars have found that an attempt to enforce a union between the Orthodox and Catholic churches really did take place in the Grand Duchy of Lithuania at the end of the fifteenth century, but it was only a short-lived episode which did not affect the mass of the Orthodox population that constituted a majority in the Lithuanian realm even though it was ruled by a Catholic dynasty.[38] Thus there is no doubt that the attempt to implement such a church union in that neighbouring country was used by Ivan III as a pretext for violating the peace treaty of 1494. What really deserves our attention, however, is the clearly expressed intention, so typical of an early modern state, to justify a military campaign by the necessity to defend the people's faith. Rhetoric of that sort was to become commonplace in Muscovite diplomacy during the sixteenth century, but on the local level, in the borderlands, such propaganda was of no use, as the population was much the same in ethnic, cultural and religious terms on both sides of the emerging boundary.

The truce of 1503 was the last triumph for Ivan III. Having defeated the Lithuanian army in a battle on the Vedrosha River on July 14, 1500, the Muscovite troops, assisted in some places by Ivan's new vassals, occupied a vast territory that included dozens of towns and rural districts. According to the armistice concluded on April 2, 1503, the Muscovite-Lithuanian border was moved further westwards, by a distance of 25 to 90 km in the north and 180 to 500 km in the south[39]. In the subsequent decades, however, the Muscovites encountered growing resistance on the part of the Grand Duchy of Lithuania and its inhabitants. As a result, the Muscovite-Lithuanian border had become stabilized by the 1520s. To understand why, we should examine the changes in both the structure and attitudes of the population on the eastern frontier of Lithuania in the first third of the sixteenth century.

THE NOBILITY, PRIVILEGED CITIES AND STABILIZATION OF THE MUSCOVITE-LITHUANIAN BORDER

The severe blows that the Grand Duchy of Lithuania suffered at the end of the fifteenth century from the ascending Muscovite power produced a paradoxical effect on the former's state-building. On the one hand, Lithuania lost vast territories on its distant eastern periphery, but on the other hand, being deprived of these lands that were loosely connected with its core, the Grand Duchy had become more consolidated during the reign of Sigismund I (1506–1548) than ever before. The formation of the two main privileged social groups (*stany*, *Stände*), i.e. the townspeople and the nobility (*szlachta*), contributed greatly to the unity of the state.[40]

As for the principalities within the Grand Duchy of Lithuania, only a few of them remained after 1503. Those which survived (e.g. those in Mstislavl', Pinsk, and Slutsk) could not compare with the upper Oka or "Northern" (*Severskie*) principalities either in size or in degree of autonomy. They were much closer to the centre of the Lithuanian state both geographically and politically, and supreme administrative and judicial control over these principalities rested with the grand duke.

Meanwhile, the majority of the early sixteenth-century princes in the Grand Duchy could not boast any sovereign rights, not to mention any "autonomy". It was actually only the princely title that distinguished them from the rest of petty nobles. Many of them, like the Mosalskii or Kroshinskii princes, had lost their patrimonies in the eastern borderlands, which had been annexed by the grand prince of Moscow and had received areas of land in other parts of the Lithuanian realm in compensation.[41]

The same fate befell the boyars (the local nobility) of the Briansk district, which was conquered by the Muscovites in 1500, whereupon more than twenty boyar families left their native lands and were recompensed for their losses later by the grand duke of Lithuania.[42] Thus various elite groups, including impoverished princes, local boyars and servitors of various ranks, gradually melted into a noble class known as the *szlachta*. This process was judicially formalized and accelerated by the promulgation of the First Lithuanian Statute in 1529. In the third part of the law code entitled "On the liberties of the *szlachta* and the growth of the Grand Duchy", the various ranks of the nobility – princes, lords (*pany horugovnye*), boyars and urban servitors (*meschane*) – were treated together as a unified privileged category of *szlachta* and the grand duke promised to preserve the rights and liberties of "the whole of the nobility" (*vsia shliakhta*) as granted by his predecessors and by himself. He also promised not to elevate commoners to higher positions than noblemen have (*ne shliakhtu nad shliakhtu ne maem povyshati*).[43]

The formation of a unified privileged estate in the realm, one which brought together Catholic lords (*pany*), Orthodox princes and petty nobles from the eastern periphery (boyars), a group that some scholars have labelled "the political nation" of the Grand Duchy,[44] probably prevented this multiethnic and multi-confessional state from disintegration.

The loyalty of the Orthodox princes and nobility to the Grand Duchy was put to a severe test during the revolt stirred up by Prince Mikhail Glinskii in 1508. A favourite of the late Grand Duke Alexander who died in 1506, Glinskii fell into disgrace with the new sovereign, Sigismund I. In an attempt to restore his dominant position in the realm by force, he incited a rebellion and unleashed a civil war in the Grand Duchy. Being himself a Catholic, Glinskii tried to play on the religious feelings of the Orthodox population by spreading rumours that the Lithuanian government wanted to convert "Rus" to the "Polish", i.e. Catholic faith. But neither such tricks nor the military intervention of Grand Prince Basil III (Vasilii Ivanovich) of Moscow, who allied himself with Glinskii, was of any help to the latter. It is significant that many Orthodox princes, such as Konstantin Ostrozhskii and Fedor and Semen Chartoryiskii, took part in the campaign against Mikhail Glinskii and the Muscovite troops. As the failure of the whole enterprise became evident, Glinskii with his kin and a handful of followers left for Moscow.[45]

Thus the rebels and their Muscovite allies failed to win sympathy with their Orthodox "brethren" among the princes and nobility of the Grand Duchy of Lithuania. The same attitude was taken by the city communes that found themselves in the border zone after 1503. Unlike the small princely towns of the upper Oka region or the Severskaia (Northern) lands mentioned above, whose fate had been decided by their owners, the large cities preferred to take their destiny into their own hands. As a rule, they enjoyed rights and privileges conferred on them by the grand dukes of Lithuania, beginning with Vytautas the Great. Thus Polotsk, Vitebsk, and Smolensk had grand-ducal regional charters, in effect codices of local common law.[46] Also, the Polotsk urban community received the Magdeburg Law as a privilege in 1498, which established a city government after the German pattern: a mayor, two burgomasters and twenty councillors – to whom the merchants, artisans and similar categories within the urban population were henceforth subordinate.[47] Minsk also received a Magdeburg charter in 1499.[48]

These charters contained impressive lists of benefits, rights and privileges guaranteed to the inhabitants by the grand duke. The townspeople of Polotsk and Vitebsk even had a right to demand the replacement of a governor if he did not please them: "if they do not like their governor and denounce him before us," the Vitebsk charter reads, "then we will give them another one according to their will".[49] These urban communities were very active in upholding their rights and remonstrating with the grand duke over every case of the governor's abuse of power.[50]

It is no wonder that the larger cities, being firmly entrenched in the political system of the Grand Duchy of Lithuania, were reluctant to surrender when Muscovite armies appeared near their walls. This became evident during the Muscovite-Lithuanian wars of the first decades of the sixteenth century, when Polotsk, for instance, withstood three severe sieges, in 1507, 1513 and 1518, while Vitebsk was besieged twice, in 1513 and 1516, not to mention devastations of its environs in 1518, 1520 and 1535. Nevertheless, both cities remained loyal to the Grand Duchy of Lithuania. Muscovite troops besieged the city of Smolensk four times between 1502 and 1514, but it was only in July 1514, after the fourth siege, when they were in a hopeless position, that the citizens surrendered their town to Basil III.[51] It is instructive that, in response to demands from the inhabitants, the Muscovite sovereign issued a charter to Smolensk confirming all the privileges conferred on the city by the grand dukes of Lithuania, but annulled this document later after the discovery of a pro-Lithuanian conspiracy in Smolensk in autumn 1514.[52]

The capture of Smolensk remained the only serious success of Basil III, in spite of further military efforts. By 1522, when an armistice was finally signed, the border between the two rival states had been stabilized, and a new war waged in 1534–1537 caused only minor corrections in the border.[53] From that time on the Muscovite-Lithuanian boundary remained unchanged for several decades.

CONCLUSIONS

For several reasons the history of how the Muscovite-Lithuanian border was shaped in the course of the fifteenth and early sixteenth centuries may be of some interest for scholars engaged in border studies. First of all, this gradually emerging border did not reflect any original ethnic differences or religious divisions among the local population. Moreover, even when the boundary was clearly established, as in 1503, it did not become a cultural or religious dividing line for the ordinary people of the borderlands unlike the elites in Moscow or Vilnius. It was only later, after it had become stabilized in the 1520s, that it served as a watershed between different political cultures, which in turn engendered further differences between the two neighbouring countries, quite noticeably at the end of the sixteenth century.

Thus the formation of the border in this area was primarily a political process and a part of state-building. The two ascending great powers of Eastern Europe, the Grand Duchy of Lithuania and the Grand Principality of Moscow, in their rivalry and expansion, put an end to a patchwork of independent and semiautonomous principalities, appanages, patrimonies and city communes which had formed a buffer zone between them for most of the fifteenth century and replaced it with two state territories divided by a carefully delimited border.[54] But, as I have attempted to show, the shape of this border at any given moment between 1449 and the 1530s was determined to a very significant degree by the attitudes of different layers of the borderland population: the princes, nobility and townspeople – who could really make a choice between the two rival sovereign powers.

REFERENCES

1 The basic works are Jan Natanson-Leski, Dzieje granicy wschodniej Rzeczypospolitej. Część I. Granica moskiewska w epoce jagiellońskiej, Lwów – Warszawa 1922, and an unpublished dissertation by Nina Shelamanova, defended in 1971, see the abstract: Nina B. Shelamanova, Obrazovanie zapadnoi chasti territorii Rossii v XVI veke v sviazi s ee otnosheniiami s Velikim kniazhestvom Litovskim i Rech'iu Pospolitoi, Moscow 1971. The mapping of borderlands between the Grand Duchy of Lithuania and Muscovy has been continued by Byelorussian historians, see Viktor N. Temushev, Gomel'skaia zemlia v kontse XV – pervoi polovine XVI v. Territorial'nye transformatsii v pogranichnom regione, Moscow 2009.

2 A short account of these events in English can be found in Zigmas Kiaupa, The History of Lithuania, Vilnius 2002, 69–70. For more details, see Edvardas Gudavičius, Lietuvos istorija: nuo seniausių laikų iki 1569 metų, vol. 1, Vilnius 1999; I will cite the Russian translation of Gudavičius's book: Istoriia Litvy s drevneishikh vremen do 1569 goda, vol. 1, Moscow 2005, here: 140–144.

3 Gudavičius, Istoriia Litvy, Loc. Cit. (Note 2), vol. I, 212–214.

4 For a brief survey of Moscow's growth between 1380 and 1462, see Robert Crummey, The Formation of Muscovy 1304–1613, New York – London 1987, chap. 3, 56–83.

5 Lietuvos Metrika (henceforth LM). Knyga Nr. 5 / Egidius Banionis (ed.), Lithuanian Metrica, Book of Inscriptions no. 5 (1427–1506), Vilnius 1993, no. 78/1, 131.

6 Ibid., 131–132.

7 Ibid., 132; 133.

8 LM, bk. 5, 132; 133.

9 The transition from jurisdictional to territorial sovereignty, to use Peter Sahlins' terminology (see Peter Sahlins, Boundaries: The Making of France and Spain in the Pyrenees, Berkeley etc. 1991, 93), was rather slow in early modern Western Europe as well. On the particular situation in France, see Bernard Guenée, Des limites féodales aux frontières politiques, in: Pierre Nora (ed.), Les lieux de mémoire: La Nation, vol. 2, Paris 1986, 11–33.

10 The state of confusion which was typical of border relations in this buffer zone is well illustrated by the fact that some rural districts (*volosti*) of Great Novgorod paid regular taxes to the grand dukes of Lithuania. This situation persisted until the conquest of Novgorod by Ivan III in 1478. For more details, see Valentin L. Yanin, Novgorod i Litva: pogranichnye situatsii XIII–XV vekov, Moscow 1998, 5–22.

11 According to Anna L. Khoroshkevich, this title was used for the first time in domestic affairs in 1479; see her Russkoie gosudarstvo v sisteme mezhdunarodnykh otnoshenii kontsa XV – nachala XVI v., Moscow 1980, 85. Recently Alexander Filiushkin has questioned such accuracy in dating the adoption of the new title: in his view it was a long process which lasted from the 1470s to the 1490s: Alexander I. Filiushkin, Tituly russkikh gosudarei, Moscow – St. Petersburg 2006, 65.

12 LM, bk. 5, no. 78/2, 134.

13 Ibid., 135.

14 Ibid., 135.

15 Ibid., 134.

16 Ibid., 135.

17 The text of the truce of 1503 see in: Sbornik Imperatorskogo Russkogo istoricheskogo obschestva (henceforth Sb. RIO), vol. 35, St. Petersburg 1882, 398–402, esp. 399–400.

18 The peace treaty of 1508 see in: Akty, otnosiaschiesia k istorii Zapadnoi Rossii, sobrannye i izdannye Arkheograficheskoi komissiei (henceforth AZR), vol. 2, St. Petersburg 1848, no. 43, 53–56.

19 On the social and political development of the Grand Duchy of Lithuania in the 15th and 16th centuries and the formation of classes (*stany, Stände*) see M. K. Liubavskii, Litovsko-russkii seim, Moscow 1901; Michail M. Krom, Die Konstituierung der Szlachta als Stand und das Problem staatlicher Einheit im Grossfürstentum Litauen (15./16. Jahrhundert), in: Jahrbücher für Geschichte Osteuropas, 42 (1994) 4, 481–492; Jūratė Kiaupienė, Lithuanian Society between Vytautas and the Union of Lublin, in: Zigmantas Kiaupa, Jūratė Kiaupienė and Albinas Kuncevičius, The History of Lithuania before 1795, Vilnius, 2000, 161–204.

20 In the following sections I will draw on the findings presented in my book: M. M. Krom, Mezh Rus'iu i Litvoi. Pogranichnye zemli v sisteme russko-litovskikh otnoshenii kontsa XV – pervoi treti XVI v. 2d ed. Moscow 2010. Three chapters from the 1st edition of the book (1995) are also available in English translation, see M. M. Krom, Between Rus' and Lithuania: The West Russian Lands in the System of Russo-Lithuanian Relations at the End of the Fifteenth and in the First Third of the Sixteenth Centuries, in: Russian Studies in History 40, no. 4 (Spring 2002), 9–93.

21 The standard reference book on genealogy of princes in the Grand Duchy of Lithuania is Józef Wolff's work: Kniaziowie litewsko-ruscy od końca czternastego wieku, Warsaw 1895, on Belskies see: ibid., 3.

22 LM, bk. 5, no. 136, 247–248. The date of the document is contradictory: it refers simultaneously to the year of 1447 and to the 5th indiction which corresponds to 1442. The most recent publisher of the document, Egidius Banionis, has adopted the year of 1447, while the traditional date (more plausible, in my opinion) is 1442. For a critical analysis of alternative dates for the document, see Krom, Mezh Rus'iu i Litvoi, Loc. Cit. (Note 20), 47–48, footnote 22.

23 LM, bk. 5, 247.

24 On 21.04.1459 Prince Ivan Yur'evich Novosil'skii and Odoevskii, also acting in the name of his cousin's sons, Princes Fedor and Vasilii Belevskii, made an agreement with Casimir, Grand Duke of Lithuania and King of Poland (LM, bk. 5, no. 137, 254–255). On 10.04.1483 a contract was concluded between Casimir and Princes Dmitrii and Semen Vorotynskii (sons of the above-mentioned Prince Fedor Vorotynskii) who was also acting in the name of their nephew Prince Ivan Mikhailovich, see AZR, vol. 1, St. Petersburg 1846, no. 80, 100–101.

25 On the status of the Mezetskii and Mosal'skii princes see Krom, Mezh Rus'iu i Litvoi, Loc. Cit. (Note 20), 59–64.

26 Literally, the "Northern land"; the term goes back to the time of Kiev' hegemony in the Rus'ian lands and means "located to the north of Kiev".

27 See an entry for 1473 in Russian chronicles: Polnoe sobranie russkikh letopisei (henceforth PSRL), vol. 18, St. Petersburg 1913, 247; PSRL, vol. 25, Moscow 1949, 301.

28 Cf. Sb. RIO, vol. 35, 3–5.

29 Cf. Sb. RIO, vol. 35, 1 (footnote); 3; 4; 8.

30 Ibid., 47–48; 51; 54.

31 Ibid., 73.

32 Ibid., 84.

33 Cf. LM, bk. 5, 134–135.

34 Ibid., 135.

35 Sb. RIO, vol. 35, 295.

36 Cf. PSRL, vol. 8, St. Petersburg 1859, 239; PSRL, vol. 12, St. Petersburg 1901, 252; PSRL, vol. 28, Moscow – Leningrad 1963, 333.

37 Cf. LM, bk. 5, 148-149; PSRL, vol. 8, 239.

38 See, e.g.: Boris N. Floria, Popytka osuschestvlenia tserkovnoi unii v Velikom kniazhestvie Litovskom v poslednei chetverti XV – nachale XVI veka, in: Slaviane i ikh sosedi, no. 7, Moskau 1999, 40–81.

39 For a list of the Muscovite acquisitions of 1503, see: Sb. RIO, vol. 35, 399–400.

40 This is the main argument of my paper: Krom, Die Konstituierung der Szlachta als Stand", Loc. Cit. (Note 19).

41 On the changing conditions of Orthodox princes in the Grand Duchy of Lithuania at the beginning of the 16th century see: Krom, Mezh Rus'iu i Litvoi, Loc. Cit. (Note 20), 124–136.

42 Cf. ibid., 234; Append. II, 264–267.

43 Cf. Pirmasis Lietuvos Statutas, Stanislovas Lazutka (ed.), vol. II, part 1, Vilnius 1991, 108; 112; 114.

44 Cf. Jerzy Suchocki, Formowanie się i skład narodu politycznego w Wielkim Księstwie Litewskim późnego średniowiesza, in: Zapiski Historyczne, vol. 48 (1983), 31–78.

45 For more details on Glinskii's revolt and its failure, see: Krom, Mezh Rus'iu i Litvoi, Loc. Cit. (Note 20), 141–150.

46 The extant texts of these charters date back to the early 16th century, when they were confirmed by grand dukes Alexander and Sigismund I, respectively, see AZR, vol. 1, no. 204, 351–353 (Vitebsk, 1503); ibid., no. 213, 359–363 (Smolensk, 1505); ibid., vol. 2, no. 70, 86–90 (Polotsk, 1511).

47 For the text of the Magdeburg charter issued to Polotsk by Grand Duke Alexander on 7.10.1498, see: Russkaia istoricheskaia biblioteka (henceforth RIB), vol. 27, St. Petersburg 1910, no. 176, 701–706.

48 For the text of the Magdeburg charter issued to Minsk by Grand Duke Alexander on 14.03.1499, see: RIB, vol. 27, no. 202, 739–746.

49 AZR, vol. 1, 352. Quotation from Carolyn Pouncy's translation of this article of the Vitebsk charter which appeared in: Krom, Between Rus' and Lithuania, Loc. Cit. (Note 20), 32.

50 For numerous cases in which cities tried to rid themselves of their governors, see Krom, Between Rus' and Lithuania, Loc. Cit. (Note 20), 37–41.

51 For a survey of the major events in the course of the Muscovite-Lithuanian wars of the first third of the 16th century, see: Krom, Mezh Rus'iu i Litvoi, Loc. Cit. (Note 20), 207–227.

52 This unique document dated 10.07.1514 has been preserved in the Russian archives; see its publication in Sobranie gosudarstvennykh gramot i dogovorov, vol. 1, Moscow 1813, no. 148, 411–413.

53 On the war of 1534–1537, see: Mikhail Krom, Starodubskaia voina (1534–1537). Iz istorii russko-litovskikh otnoshenii, Moscow 2008.

54 It should be noted that neither the Grand Duchy of Lithuania nor Muscovy possessed a "normal" border in the south, even in the mid-16th century. There was only a steppe frontier that was vulnerable to Tartar raids.

JENS LERBOM

THE SPACES AND BOUNDARIES OF THE REALM: SWEDEN IN THE EARLY MODERN POPULAR MIND

The formation of exact territories was one of the dimensions of the European state-building process. The boundaries that divided the medieval realms were porous and the sovereignties or kingdoms often overlapped on the peripheries. The early modern period saw an increased intent on the part of the ruling class to control and delineate their territories.[1] Territories in themselves gradually became part of national identities. The territorialization process included the emergence of cartography and the "historicization" and "mythologicization" processes, in which the memories and history of a community are linked to specific places in the natural and cultural landscape.[2]

The territorialization of the Swedish realm fits well into this process. In the late Middle Ages Sweden was imagined as a realm consisting of territories where the King exercised his judicial and administrative power.[3] The borders of the realm were in the Middle Ages already perceived, albeit imaginary, as lines separating Sweden from the surrounding realms.[4] The territory of Sweden was also "nationalised" over centuries. In the late middle ages it was portrayed as a "fruitful" and "beautiful" land created by God. From the 16th century and onwards the Swedish realm was symbolised in cartography, royal titles and provincial coats of arms. This was, in the intellectual discourses in the 18th and 19th centuries, followed by an incorporation of the natural and cultural landscapes of Sweden into the imagination of what it meant to be Swedish.[5]

The political and cultural territorialization of Sweden is, however, usually interpreted from the perspective of the intellectual and political elite. The aim of this article is to analyse how Sweden and its borders were perceived on the popular level of society, a subject that is still partly unexplored.

REACHING THE VOICES OF ORDINARY PEOPLE

The following analysis is based on the records of six county courts of southern Sweden from the first half of the 17th century. Until 1658, these counties shared a border with Denmark and the Danish provinces of Halland, Skåne and Blekinge.[6] Because the courts on the border as well as the people living there will necessarily need to deal with border related issues, the borderlands are regarded in here as zones where the cultural meanings of borders are produced.[7]

I have searched for words, expressions and narratives that can be linked to the people's thoughts about the concepts of territory and borders. The aim is not to explore the existence of territorial expressions in the court protocols but rather to question how popular these expressions really were. This problem has been a subject for discussion for a long time and the presented views differ from each other. Carlo Ginzburg states that the thoughts and meanings of the peasants of the early modern Europe are always filtered and therefore distorted by the scribes connected to the ruling classes. Peter Burke argues along similar lines and suggests that a historian with the ambition to investigate popular culture has to peel back layers of stereotyped narratives the elites have more or less consciously created in order to reach the source materials and therefore the core of the popular thought. This core can, in effect, only be reached indirectly.[8]

A different perspective has been presented by Nathalie Zemon Davies, Peter Sahlins and Stuart Caroll. They argue that texts purporting to reproduce "popular" narratives must be regarded as the result of an interaction between senders, intermediaries and the addressee. The narratives, albeit stereotyped, had to be accepted as "true" in the sense that they would seem reasonable and legitimate for the people involved.[9]

The contents of the court protocols are of course a result of what the court clerks chose to record and write down. Everything that was uttered cannot have been noted down. At the same time, one has to remember that the proceedings in the courts were something that had great importance in the collective popular memory of the court district. The notes of the clerk and the narratives of those involved in the court cases could not differ too much without losing their legitimacy for the people.[10] This means that the narratives in the court records, in effect, reflect both the individual and the collective imagination. What was said at the courts should be regarded as a collective repertoire of words, expressions and narratives which were understandable and meaningful to all those involved in the case regardless of their social status.

SWEDEN AS REALM AND FATHERLAND

The people at the borders were, of course, well aware that they lived in something which was referred to as Sweden in their narratives. They talk about how they themselves or others have arrived "here in Sweden" or that something has occurred "in Sweden". Denmark is described in the same manner. One typical testimony that reflects this was given by Karin Gudmundsdotter, a woman who was prosecuted for adultery in the Västbo district court on 2nd October 1635. She had made an agreement with the man she had had an illegitimate relation with and now she testified, inter alia, that:

Map 2. *The Swedish Realm and its conquered areas 1561–1700*

> If I stay in Sweden, Anders would give me 200 coins of copper. If I reside in Denmark, he would give me Danish money. [She also confessed that] when the district court was assembled at that time in Sweden a Swedish man came to her in Denmark and told her not to come to the district court [...] when Anders had pleaded not guilty.[11]

Karin speaks about Sweden and Denmark as two territorial units and that she had moved from one to the other. Aside from Denmark, people described the world outside Sweden as "abroad", "foreign country" or the "land of the enemy".[12] These words, phrases and narratives do not say, however, that much about how Sweden was perceived more than that it was considered a territorial entity. There is a need to look closer at what connotations and synonyms people attached to the concept of Sweden.

Both Sweden and Denmark were also described as people's birthplaces. The courts regularly noted people's territorial descent by phrases like "Olof Börjesson, born as a child here in Sweden" or "came before the court a Danish woman, Johanna Nielsdotter, born as a child in Denmark and the county of Torna in [the town] Lund".[13] People themselves could describe their descent in the same way. In June of 1643 a deserted farmhand Bengt Månsson was asked by the court of Västbo where he came from and he stated that he was "born as a child in Denmark".[14] In another case, written down in the court rolls of the county of Sunnerbo, a group of farmers, who described the circumstances in a case of manslaughter, told the court that the man who had been killed had "told them that he was born as a child in Sweden in [the town] Vadstena".[15]

Aside from referring to Sweden as a birthplace there are two other common parallel uses of the concept in the protocols. That is Sweden as a realm and Sweden as a fatherland. The realm was particularly associated with royal sovereignty and jurisdiction. In a case recorded at Allbo district court in 1649 one of the involved farmers stated that: "Although Her Majesty [Queen Christina] is not present in this part of the country Her majesty nevertheless has sovereign power and authority over all the realm, the land and its people."[16]

Several testimonies reflect how people imagined the connection between the realm and how it could fall into disagreement and discord with other realms and that enemies of the realm could harm its subjects. One example of this is a case where a Swedish sheriff had captured a Swedish runaway on the Danish side of the border without special permission. The court of Västbo stated that this behaviour was a "bad example between the realms that could cause dissension in the future".[17]

The realm was consequently something the subjects were expected to be loyal to and ready to serve. This loyalty and sense of duty were considered important for both the collective and the individual. We see this when the commoners in the county of Västbo stated that they were "faithful inhabitants of the Swedish realm". Similarly, a young man Carl Persson, who had been pardoned from a death sentence, promised that he would be willing to risk his life for "the Swedish realm".[18] There are also examples of how rumours about disloyalty to the realm were taken to court. This was the case when the sheriff of the county of Sunnerbo, Per Olofsson was acquitted from accusations that he had helped the Danish enemy during the Kalmar War (1611–1613). The court and several witnesses stated that Per "had never been unfaithful to the Swedish realm". Others, who were convicted by the courts, could lose their right to reside in the realm. That was the case with "Malin Finnish, an old vagrant woman" who was expelled from the realm by the court of Sunnerbo in 1619 because she was suspected of witchcraft and that she, "as tartars [i.e. gypsies] tend to do", had lied to many people.[19]

The people in the border areas seem not to have attached any emotions to the realm. They never describe the realm as "dear" to them. They don't "long" for it and it is neither a "home" nor a birthplace. Those kinds of emotional connotations are instead attached to the fatherland.

Previous research has indicated that the concept of the fatherland was invoked by the rulers in relation to political crises.[20] It is believed that the concept had no major significance and it has been observed that the usage of the concept did not spread to the lower strata of society but was used only by the representatives of the subjects at the Swedish diets from the 17th century and onwards.[21] These claims must be to some extent corrected.

It is true that the rulers demanded loyalty of their subjects on certain occasions. So did the County Governor Konrad von Falkenberg at the court of Södra Möre in March 1644 when he as a consequence of the month old war with Denmark demanded that the inhabitants of the county should show "fidelity, and obedience to [their] gracious superiors and the fatherland", something the commoners "with their hands raised" promised.[22]

The concept of the fatherland could, however, be invoked by the authorities in less dramatic contexts. In 1624, the governor of the Kronoberg province urged in connection with a case where the local bailiff was accused of corruption that the common people of the county of Allbo should show fidelity to "our dear beloved fatherland".[23] Yet another example comes from an account in May, 1656, when the district judge and the lay members of the court of the Västbo district court stood up and admonished the audience to obey the authorities whose power "had been set by God the Almighty to rule over us and our dear fatherland".[24]

But, the concept of the fatherland was also invoked by the people themselves in several ways. It was common in the appeals of exiles who wanted to return to Sweden. One example of this is to be found in the district court of Kinnevald in 1621, where the exile Måns Gudmundsson: "begs the King for mercy and [...] [he has] a good testimony from the common men that he has never done them no harm and that [he] is a brave, honest and manful soldier [...] now he offers to risk his life and blood for the crown of Sweden and the fatherland as long as he lives."[25]

There are several similar statements in the archives. In September 1625, the man killer Carl Persson, who had made an agreement with the victim's family in Sunnerbo County, promised that he would be willing to serve the King and the fatherland, if he was pardoned.[26] The exile Nils Abrahamsson, who had also killed a man, came before the court of Kinnevald in June 1642, and begged the court that they would allow him to return "safely back home to his fatherland again".[27]

Consequently, people could be seen as both offending and as abandoning their fatherland. One of these was the killer Per Birgersson. In 1612, according to several witnesses in the Kinnevald's district court, he had deserted to the Danes in the Kalmar War and betrayed his fatherland.[28] In a short note recorded in the protocols of Sunnerbo district court in 1629 it was stated that a farmer, in order to avoid being recruited to the army had "abandoned his fatherland".[29]

The concept of the fatherland also occurs as a part of narratives which are not directly connected to either personal or political crises. In the already mentioned case about a man who had been shot to death in the parish of Hallaryd near the border, three farmers testified that he had not only told them that he was "born as a child in Sweden" but also that he had been released from prison in Copenhagen and had wanted to "once more return to his fatherland".[30]

What did the concept of the fatherland mean to ordinary people? In the learned Swedish discourse from the 16th century and onwards the concept had two meanings. On the one hand, it could be synonymous with the political, or the "great" fatherland (*patria juris/civitatis*), which was Sweden as a community where people enjoyed civil rights and obligations. At the same time there was an idea about the local, natural or "small" fatherland (*patria loci/naturale*) which was synonymous with the home county or parish. It was essential that the people were expected to have a feeling of loyalty to both. The people should identify and associate the "great" fatherland with civic solidarity and emotional sentiments to a place where they were born, to their parents and kindred.[31]

It is clear that people in the border areas did not associate the fatherland with their region or their local societies. When people talked about their own or others' local communities they used the term "father district" (*fädernesbygd*). When the district court of Konga in 1634 asked from the present commoners about the origins of a fallen German soldier, "nobody knew where he was born because he had not told anybody about his relatives or father district".[32] Two brigands, who were condemned to death at the court of Sunnerbo in 1651, had been "inconstant towards their proper father district in Denmark".[33]

The idea of the fatherland was also something that possessed the people, individually or collectively. An example of this is during the breakout of the Kalmar War in 1611. The commoners of the county of Kinnevald demanded that vagrants along the border should be pardoned so that the enemy would not tempt them to harm "their own fatherland". In 1624, the commoners in the Allbo district court promised the County Governor, who suspected them of illicit trade, that they were faithful to the King and to "our dear beloved fatherland". Some individuals, like the farmer Jon, had "escaped his fatherland" while Per Torsson, who had fled because of a conviction of adultery, wanted to "willingly [return] to his fatherland again" in 1637. The same observation can be made in relation to foreigners. Peder Gärt, a Danish man, was due to his disorderly way of living in Sweden "banished to his fatherland Denmark".[34] Similarly, though less harshly, the commoners of the Sunnerbo district court appealed to the Göta High Court that a Danish woman who had been sentenced to death should be released and permitted to "return from here to her fatherland again".[35]

There was a similar expectation in relation to the realm. As an individual one had a duty to be faithful, to protect, serve and risk one's life for the fatherland. A testimony by the murderer Håkan Nilsson reflects this. He had killed a man and fled to Denmark where he was recruited to the Danish troops by force to be a pathfinder during the war 1643–1645. He fled from Denmark and told the court that he would sooner be punished "here in Sweden rather than be the pathfinder of the Danes and do harm to the fatherland".[36] There are several similar examples. In 1625, the relatives of a slain man struck a deal with the killer. They told the court of Sunnerbo that the murdered, because he was young and healthy, could serve the King and the fatherland. The deserted Swedish farmer Sven Svensson, who had been taken by the Danish army, voluntarily returned to Sweden although he knew he could be punished for a sexual crime because, as he said he "didn't want to raise arms against the fatherland".[37]

Several statements in the court protocols also reflect the opposition position. People could make the choice to refuse to serve and even raise arms against the fatherland. A murderer, Per Birgersson, had "assisted the enemy and betrayed his fatherland". An "old deserted soldier Löving Nilsson" had "never had a willingness to serve the crown or the fatherland".[38]

As already said, people's perceptions of the fatherland overlapped with their understanding about the concept of the realm. But there is also something we could describe as emotional connotations attached to the fatherland. This contradicts previous interpretations that emotional sentiments attached to the "great" fatherland, i.e. the realm, reached broader layers of society rather late in the history.[39]

The fatherland was something within which the people could enjoy peace and safety. Per Torsson, whose brother spoke for him at the Konga district court in June 1637, would, if he was allowed to return to "seek peace" in his fatherland. The killer Nils Abrahamsson wanted to return from exile and "come safely home to his fatherland again".[40] As we can see from this last quotation, the fatherland was compared to "home". This home was not only a birthplace but also populated by kindred and friends. The farmer Bengt Enersson from the parish of Långsjö, who had been arrested in the Danish province of Blekinge in 1618, told the court of Konga that when he had been released he had returned "home".[41] The perception that one's country was populated by friends and kindred can be illustrated by a case at Konga district Court in June 1643. A Danish woman, Anna Hansdotter, was described as a "poor stranger without friends or relatives here in Sweden".[42]

Moreover, people were expected to love their fatherland. In 1624, in a court meeting the commoners in the Allbo district described the fatherland as something they not only collectively possessed but also that it was "dear" to them.[43] The commoners could also, as was the case in the Västbo district court in January 1656, in their answer to a royal decree about a forthcoming diet, that they in addition to their faithfulness to the King would not "omit anything that the fatherland's needs, honour and welfare would require".[44]

THE BOUNDARIES OF THE FATHERLAND

As mentioned, previous research has shown that already in the Middle Ages the Swedish rulers imagined that the boundaries of the realm were clearly demarcated though there were no obstacles to the contacts between peoples in practice in the border areas. There is convincing empirical evidence that the political interest from the central power coincided with the material interests of regional and local societies on how the boundaries were imagined at a popular level. In fact, the borders could not be physically marked on the terrain without the knowledge and active participation of the inhabitants living near the borders. Borders were, in the minds of ordinary people, not diffuse zones: they were imaginary lines between realms.[45]

The court protocols confirm this further. The most obvious testimony of the interests of commoners in borders is to be found in everyday border disputes. In 1636, the farmers of Hinneryd parish demanded more boundary markers after a dispute with some farmers from the parish Knäred on the Danish side of the border. They considered that the distance between the existing markers was too long. The problem, according to them was that "the farmers are not quite sure if they are right or wrong. Therefore more markers and testimonies about the border are needed so that each country and realm knows its rights".[46] In a similar case, at the Konga district court in 1643, a Danish farmer complained that a Swedish farmer had ruined his fence. According to the Swede, the fence was situated on the Swedish side of the border. As in Hinneryd, the court found that it was too long a distance between the boundary markers and decided that "some trustworthy men" from both sides of the border should determine where the border exactly situated.[47]

In certain cases the farmers could, if necessary, invoke written proofs about the border. That was the case in northern Halland in the 1640s, where the farmers made references to the Danish border commission of 1555.[48] The local sheriff Jacob Broddesson did the same in October 1650 in the Sunnerbo district court, when he presented a list of landmarks ratified in the meeting of kings at Flabäck in 1603 as evidence in a border dispute between Swedish and Danish farmers.[49]

However, it is important to underline that the people in the border areas talked about and related themselves and others to the border in everyday contexts. This did not only happen in connection to land disputes. The border of the realm was in the peoples' minds a territorial designation only. In the testimonies, it's commonly called simply "the border" and it was something where different kinds of events took, had taken, or would take place. Common terms to describe the border were "at", "close to", "next to", "beyond" or "within".[50] The border was not necessarily "Swedish" but it could be referred to as the "Danish" border which is, for example the case in a statement in Allbo district court in March 1613 that addressed some people "living at the Danish border".[51] People also talked about how others or they themselves had crossed the border onto Swedish or Danish ground.[52]

Added to this, one aspect of how the ordinary people understood the border must still be studied. It was not only a political and material reality that divided the realms, but it also separated judicial entities. The latter dimension emerges in several ways. In 1618, for instance, the Konga district court decided that two captured Danes should be escorted in chains to the nearest border marker and then be deported "over the border".[53] A more macabre expression of this was the location of executions. There are several records which show that executions were carried out at the border. For instance, as recorded in Sunnerbo district court in 1650, "a Danish person Gunne in Sjuhult", who had lived in Sweden but had committed serious crimes, was executed and "broken on the wheel at the border".[54]

It was as important to know on which side of the border crimes had been committed, as it was to know where the boundaries of landed properties coincided with the borders of the realm. In 1648, at Kinnevalds district court there were discussions about on which side of the border marker a manslaughter had taken place.[55] Twelve years earlier, at Konga district court, a case concerning an assault where a farmer from the parish of Tving in the Danish province Blekinge accused a Swedish farmer of having "crossed the border mark onto Danish ground" and beaten him with a hatchet. The court was unsure whether the assault had taken place on the Swedish or Danish side of the border and ordered "three old men who remember when the border marker was examined last" to appear for consultation before they could solve the case.[56]

Finally, overlapping with the political, material and judicial dimensions of people's perceptions of the border, there is evidence of an early cultural discourse – even if it is vague and fragmentary. From the northern part of medieval Sweden there are several examples of how people used rhymes to remember the names and situations of border markers. These rhymes were transmitted from generation to generation.[57] I have not found any border rhymes in the court protocols but there are other examples of how the border was "culturally" made a part of people's everyday lives. One example is that individuals could be given epithets that alluded to the border. This was the case, for example, in a testimony given in Konga district court in 1629, in connection to the farmer Åke Gudmundsson who was accused of illegitimate relations with a "public border harlot by the name of Sigrid".[58]

The border could, as it seems, also be a location where people performed symbolic acts. An example of this is recorded in early 17th century Stockholm. In connection with an exchange of prisoners one of the attendants observed:

> When prisoners are exchanged at the border, then should each one confess how he has behaved himself. Then Carnaschij took Arvid by his hand when he stepped over to the Danish side of the border and Arvid crossed to the Swedish side and said: there are rumours about me of infidelity with another man's wife in Stockholm, but I beg, so help me God, that I am free from her and God will be my judge on judgement day.[59]

A similar case was recorded in the Södra Möre district court in 1643. Two thieves who had escaped to Denmark from Sweden wanted to reconcile with the plaintiffs. They met on a small islet "on a fishing lake where the border between Sweden and Denmark runs". Despite the fact that there were no visible border markers on the islet the thieves handed parts of the stolen goods over an imaginary borderline.[60]

CONCLUDING DISCUSSION

In the 17th century, Sweden was perceived as a clearly demarcated territory on a grassroots-level. It was the territory where the King exercised his political and judicial power. That is not surprising and fits well into previous interpretations.[61] But Sweden was also perceived as a fatherland where descent, kinship and friendship were emotional components. In that respect, Sweden was at the same time on a popular level an imagined political, judicial and cultural territorial community. The "local" and the "great" fatherland had obviously merged into one entity.

The question is then, when and why these sentiments had spread among the wider audience? Anthony D. Smith has suggested three types of pathways to nationalism. He speaks, first, about a "lateral" process, that is when nations are constructed from "above" by elite groups. Sweden is believed to be an example of this. Second he writes about "vertical" or "popular" nations formed from "below", like Finland. Third, according to Smith, there are "migrative" nations, such as the United States.[62]

Territories are not be regarded as frozen demarcated spaces where humans act. Territories are, in words and deeds, socially and historically constructed and often the result of a political exercise of power.[63] One explanation could then be that using effective propaganda the rulers of Sweden managed to plant their imagined territorial ideas in the minds of their subjects. It is impossible in this context to date the popular construction of the ideological Sweden and its borders. In the former research, the birth of the concept "Sweden" in the popular minds is seen as a result of, to quote Smith, a lateral process. However, I will tentatively discuss another slightly different interpretation.

As shown above, previous research concerning how the Swedish realm was demarcated, has pointed out that the borders of the realm were constructed, not by force but as a result of a dialogue grounded in mutual interests. My survey has confirmed this further and added that the border was important to the ordinary people because it also demarcated Sweden in legal terms. This is obvious. Aside from the monarchy, the law was seen as the foundation of society by the common people. The Law was ancient and given by God. The law could not in itself be unjust or bad. Injustice could only take place if people had forgotten the law or for some reason misinterpreted or refused to obey it.[64] Perhaps then we must see the territorialization of Sweden not as lateral or as vertical, but rather "reciprocal", and maybe as a consequence a product of a long, dynamic and non-linear process of negotiations between, and shared experiences of, rulers and subjects within an existing political framework.

REFERENCES

1 Benedict Anderson, Imagined Communities. Reflections on the Origin and Spread of Nationalism, London 1983, 19 f; Anthony Giddens, Sociology, Cambridge 1989, 303; Peter Sahlins, Boundaries. The making of France and Spain in the Pyrenees, Berkeley 1989.

2 Anthony D. Smith, The Cultural Foundations of Nations. Hierarchy, Covenant, and Republic, London 2008, 35.

3 Harald Gustafsson, Gamla riken, nya stater. Statsbildning, politisk kultur och identiteter under Kalmarunionens upplösningsskede 1512–1541, Stockholm 2000, 307.

4 Olof Holm, Den norsk-svenska riksgränsens ålder och hävd. En studie av rikssamlingsprocesser och gränsbildning i mellersta Skandinavien, in: Collegium Medievale. Interdisciplinary Journal of Medieval Research 16 (2003); Kimmo Katajala, The Origin of the Border, in: Harald Gustafsson/ Hanne Sanders (eds.) Vid gränsen. Integration och identiteter i det förnationella Norden, Uddevalla 2006, 86–106.

5 Patrik Hall, Den svenskaste historien. Nationalism i Sverige under sex sekler, Stockholm 2000, 16–17; Jakob Christensson, Landskapet i våra hjärtan. En essä om svenskars naturumgänge och identitetssökande, Lund 2002, 12; Mattias Legnér, Fäderneslandets rätta beskrivning. Mötet mellan antikvarisk forskning och ekonomisk nyttokult i 1700-talets Sverige. Helsingfors 2004; Torbjörn Eng, Det svenska väldet. Ett konglomerat av uttrycksformer och begrepp från Vasa till Bernadotte, Uppsala 2001.

6 The counties are Konga, Sunnerbo, Kinnevalds, Allbo, Södra Möre and Västbo. The court protocols are in the archive of Göta High Court (Göta Hovrätt) in the regional archive of Vadstena, Sweden.

7 John W. Cole/Eric R. Wolf, The Hidden Frontier. Ecology and Ethnicity in an Alpine Valley, New York 1974; Anssi Paasi, Territories, Boundaries and Consciousness. The Changing Geographies of the Finnish-Russian Border, Belhaven studies in political geography, Chichester Wiley 1996; Hastings Donnan/Thomas M. Wilson, Borders. Frontiers of Identity, Nation and State, Oxford 1999, 64.

8 Carlo Ginzburg, Osten och maskarna. En 1500-talsmjölnares tankar om skapelsen, Stockholm 1996, 9; Peter Burke, Folklig kultur i Europa 1500–1800, Stockholm 1983, 82–85.

9 Natalie Zemon Davis, Fiction in the archives. Pardon tales and their tellers in sixteenth-century France, Cambridge 1987, 3–6; Peter Sahlins, Unnaturally French. Foreign citizens in the Old Regime and after, Ithaca, N.Y. 2004; Stuart Carroll, Blood and violence in early modern France, Oxford 2006, 23, Harald Gustafsson, Att draga till Malmö och skaffa sig rätt. Undersåtar, överhet och identitetsföreställningar i skånska suppliker 1661–1699, In: Fredrik Nilsson/Hanne Sanders/ Ylva Stubbesgaard (eds.), Öresundsgränser. Rörelser, möten och visioner i tid och rum, Malmö 2007, 78–115.

10 Erling Sandmo, Voldssamfunnets undergang. Om disiplineringen av Norge på 1600-tallet, Oslo 1999, 38–40.

11 Västbo district court 02.–03.10.1635 fol. 31, Regional Archive, Vadstena. Göta Hovrätt. Advokatfiskalens arkiv (GHA) sign. EVIIAAAC vol. 8.

12 Västbo district court 18.5.1620, GHA EVIIAAAC vol. 6; Sunnerbo district court 19.09.1625 fol. 34v–35, EVIIAAAD vol. 11; Kinnevalds district court 02.11.1635 fol. 13v–14; Konga district court 11.06.1639 fol. 79f, EVIIAAAD vol. 12.

13 Konga district court 01.06.1640 fol. 9f, GHA EVIIAAAD vol. 12; Sunnerbo district court 15.05.1632 fol. 2v–3, EVIIAAAD vol. 11.

14 Västbo district court 02.–03.11.1643 fol. 25, GHA EVIIAAAC vol. 8.

15 Sunnerbo district court 14.05.1628 fol. 6, GHA EVIIAAAD vol. 11.

16 Allbo district court 22.06.1649 fol. 11v–12, GHA EVIIAAAD vol. 15.

17 Västbo district court 18.06.1640 fol. 2–4, GHA EVIIAAAC vol. 8. See also Kinnevalds district court 20.04.1620 fol. 11v, EVIIAAAD vol. 7; Västbo district court 30.05.1655 fol. 65f and 26.05.1657 fol. 31, EVIIAAAC vol. 9.

18 Nils Aschan, Ur Sunnerbo härads domböcker, In *Hyltén-Cavallius föreningens* årsbok 1935, 17; Sunnerbo district court 19.09.1625 fol. 34v–35, GHA EVIIAAAD vol. 11; Västbo district court 25.1.1655 fol. 5, EVIIAAAC vol. 9; Sunnerbo district court 19.09.1625 fol. 34v–35, GHA EVIIAAAD vol. 11.

19 Sunnerbo district court 12.00.1619 fol. 100v–101, GHA EVIIAAAD vol. 6. See also Kinnevalds district court 04.05.1612 fol. 6, GHA EVIIAAAD vol. 1; Sunnerbo district court 15.05.1632 fol. 2v–3, EVIIAAAD vol. 11; Sunnerbo district court 11.08.1636 fol. 38v–39, EVIIAAAD vol. 12; Konga district court 01.06.1640 fol. 11v, EVIIAAAD vol. 12; Kinnevalds district court 19.10.1655, 13f, EVIIAAAD vol. 19.

20 Mats Hallenberg, Kungen, kronan eller staten? Makt och legitimitet i Gustav Vasas propaganda, in: Börje Harnesk (ed.), Maktens skiftande skepnader. Studier i makt, legitimitet och inflytande i det tidigmoderna Sverige, Umeå universitet, Umeå 2003, 38; Börje Harnesk, Konsten att klaga, konsten att kräva. Kronan och bönderna på 1500- och 1600-talen, in: Börje Harnesk (ed.), Maktens skiftande skepnader. Studier i makt, legitimitet och inflytande i det tidigmoderna Sverige, Umeå 2003, 68; Joachim Östlund, Lyckolandet. Maktens legitimering i officiell retorik från stormaktstid till demokratins genombrott, Lund 2007, 96.

21 Johan Holm, King Gustav Adolf's death. The birth of early modern nationalism in Sweden, in: Linas Eriksonas/Leos Müller (eds.), Statehood before and beyond ethnicity. Minor states in Northern and Eastern Europe, 1600–2000, New York 2005, 113, 127, 129–130 Anders, Claréus, Primitiva bönder? Något om allmogens syn på statsmakt, politik och nation under 1700-talet, in: Åsa Karlsson/ Bo Lindberg (eds.), Nationalism och nationell identitet i 1700-talets Sverige, Uppsala 2002, 45.

22 Södre möre district court 26.–27.03.1643, unpag. GHA EVIIAAAE vol. 5.

23 Allbo district court 02.09.1624, 34f, GHA EVIIAAAD vol. 8.

24 Västbo district court 20.05.1656, 28–29, GHA EVIIAAAC vol. 9.

25 Kinnevalds district court 01.02.1621 fol. 3f, GHA EVIIAAAD vol. 1. Similar cases are to be found in Kinnevalds district court 19.03.1611 fol. 2f, EVIIAAAD vol. 1; Sunnerbo district court 19.09.1625 fol. 34v–35, EVIIAAAD vol. 11; Konga district court 13.06.1637 fol. 59f, EVIIAAAD vol. 12; Sunnerbo district court 25.03.1644 fol. 3, EVIIAAAD vol. 14; Kinnevalds district court 11.10.1644 fol. 10v, EVIIAAAD vol. 14; Kinnevalds district court 07.06.1650 fol. 8f, EVIIAAAD vol. 15.

26 Sunnerbo district court 19.09.1625 fol. 34v–35, GHA EVIIAAAD vol. 11.

27 Kinnevalds district court 07.06.1650 fol. 8ff, GHA EVIIAAAD vol. 15.

28 Kinnevalds district court 05.04.1612 fol. 6, GHA EVIIAAAD vol. 1. See also Allbo district court 26.01.1647 fol. 3f, GH EVIIAAAD vol. 14; Kinnevalds district court 29.05.1648 fol. 5v, EVIIAAAD vol. 15; Södra Möre district court 16.09.1652, EVIIAAAE vol. 8

29 Sunnerbo district court 21.10.1629 fol. 15, GHA EVIIAAAD vol. 11.

30 Sunnerbo district court 14.05.1628 fol. 6, GHA EVIIAAAD vol. 11.

31 Bo Lindberg, Den antika skevheten. Politiska ord och begrepp i det tidigmoderna Sverige, Stockholm 2006, 143–144.

32 Konga district court 11.11.1634, unpag. GHA EVIIAAAD vol. 9.

33 Sunnerbo district court 07.10.1651 fol. 33–34, GHA EVIIAAA vol. 16.

34 Kinnevalds district court 19.03.1611 fol. 2f, GHA EVIIAAAD vol. 1; Allbo district court 02.09.1624 fol. 34f, EVAAAD vol. 8; Sunnerbo district court 21.10.1629 fol. 15, EVIIAAAD vol. 11; Konga district court 13.06.1637 fol. 59v. EVIIAAAD vol. 12. See similar formulations in Sunnerbo district court 12.01.1652 fol. 18, EVIIAAAD vol. 17; Södra Möre district court 16.09.1652, EVIIAAAE vol. 8; Västbo district court 20.05.1656 fol. 28–29, EVIIAAAC vol. 9

35 Sunnerbo district court 12.01.1652 fol. 18, GHA EVIIAAAD vol. 17.

36 Kinnevalds district court 11.10.1644 fol. 10v, GHA EVIIAAAD vol. 14.

37 Kinnevalds district court 01.02.1621 fol. 3f, GHA EVIIAAAD vol. 1; Sunnerbo district court 19.09.1625 34v–35, EVIIAAAD vol. 11; Sunnerbo district court 25.03.1644 fol. 3, EVIIAAAD vol. 14.

38 Kinnevalds district court 04.05.1612 fol. 6, GHA EVIIAAAD vol. 1; Allbo district court 26.01.1647 fol. 3f, EVIIAAAD vol. 14.

39 Ole Feldbæk (ed.), Dansk identitetshistorie. Bd 1, Fædreland og modersmål 1536–1789, København 1991, 156–157.

40 Konga district court 13.06.1637 fol. 59f, GHA EVIIAAAD vol. 12; Kinnevalds district court 07.06.1650 fol. 8ff, EVIIAAAD vol. 15.

41 Konga district court 29.01.1619 fol. 23f, GHA EVIIAAAD vol. 3.

42 Konga district court 15.06.1643 fol. 9, GHA EVIIAAAD vol. 14.

43 Allbo district court 02.09.1624, 34f, GHA EVIIAAAD vol. 8.

44 Västbo district court 25.01.1655 fol. 5, GHA EVIIAAAC vol. 9.

45 Holm, Den norsk-svenska riksgränsens ålder, Loc.Cit. (Note 4.), 202–205, Katajala, The Origin of the Border, Loc. Cit. (Note 4), 104–105, Stefan Persson, Gränsbygd och svenskkrig. Studier i Blekinges, Skånes och Hallands östdanska historia, Lund, 2007, 196–197, 216–218.

46 Sunnerbo district court 21.06.1636 fol. 15f, GHA EVIIAAAD vol. 12.

47 Konga district court 15.06.1643 fol. 7, GHA EVIIAAAD vol. 14.

48 Persson, Gränsbygd och svenskkrig, Loc. Cit. (Note 45), 214.

49 Sunnerbo district court 29–31.10.1650 fol. 48vf, GHA EVIIAAAD vol. 16

50 See e.g. Kinnevalds district court 04.05.1612 fol 6, GHA EVIIAAAD vol. 1; Konga district court 29.01.1619 fol. 23f, EVIIAAAD vol. 3.

51 Allbo district court 01.03.1613 fol. 7, GHA EVIIAAAD vol. 2.

52 Sunnerbo district court 26.01.1648 fol. 4v, GHA EVIIAAAD vol. 15; Allbo district court 27.01.1647 fol. 4f, EVIIAAAD vol. 14; Sunnerbo district court 29.10.1651 fol. 48v, EVIIAAAD vol. 16.

53 Konga district court 20.11.1618 fol. 78v, GHA EVIIAAAD vol. 3.

54 Sunnerbo district court 29.10.1650 fol. 50vf, GHA EVIIAAAD vol. 16.

55 Kinnevald district court 29.05.1648, fol. 5v, GHA EVIIAAAD vol. 15.

56 Konga district court 11.06.1639, fol. 84, GHA EVIIAAAD vol. 12.

57 Holm, Den norsk-svenska riksgränsens ålder, Loc.Cit. (Note 4), 146–148.

58 Konga district court 27.4.1629 fol. 177, GHA EVIIAAAD vol. 9.

59 Folke Sleman (ed.), Stockholms stads tänkeböcker från år 1592. del III. 1600, Stockholm, 1953, 130–131.

60 Södra Möre district court 26.10.1643, GHA EVIIAAAE vol. 4.

61 In particular Gustafsson, Gamla Riken, Loc. Cit. (Note 3), passim.

62 Anthony D. Smith, "History and national destiny. Responses and clarifications", in: Nations and Nationalism (2004) 1–2, 197–198.

63 Lefebvre, Henri, The production of space, Oxford 1974 (^{2}1991), 48–49; Sack, Robert David, Human territoriality. Its theory and history, Cambridge 1986, 19; Paasi, Territories, boundaries, consciousness, Loc. Cit. (Note 7), passim.

64 Aron Jakovlevič Gurevič, Categories of medieval culture, London, 1985, 154, 157, 162, 165; Österberg, Eva, Folklig mentalitet och statlig makt. Perspektiv på 1500- och 1600-talens Sverige, In: Scandia (Lund), 58 (1992), 97, Harald Gustafsson, The Eight Argument. Identity, Ethnicity and Political Culture in the Sixteenth-Century Scandinavia, In: Scandinavian Journal of History 27 (2002) 2, 97–98, Harnesk, Konsten att klaga, Loc. Cit. (Note 20), 62–65.

JUKKA KOKKONEN

BORDER PEACE AGREEMENTS: LOCAL ATTEMPTS TO REGULATE EARLY MODERN BORDER CONFLICTS

The concept of *grensefred* in Norwegian, *gränsfred* in Swedish, *rajarauha* in Finnish and *grænsefred* in Danish, implies a separate local agreement entered into by a population in a border area with the corresponding population on the other side of the border in order to prevent an outbreak of hostilities between them in the event of war or the threat of war between their two countries. A literal translation of this concept into English would be "border peace", and it is referred to in the following by the terms "border peace agreement" or "local peace agreement". Regional or local agreements of this kind were concluded on numerous occasions in the Late Middle Ages or Early Modern times in peripheral border areas in Europe, mostly in Scandinavia but also in the British Isles.

In spite of periodic wars or violent conflicts, the ideal state of affairs was seen to be peace between the two parties. On the border between the Swedish and Russian realms a state of peace and harmony was commonly referred to as "trust" (Sw. *förtroende*), "neighbourly concord" (*nabolig sämja*), "neighbourly friendship" (*nabolig vänskap*) or "border concord" (*gränssämja*).

The border peace agreement procedure is examined in this article through two key issues. First of all, the aspects that were usually agreed on, and secondly, who actually had an interest in these contracts. One important process of change that took in the European sphere was that referred to as state building, which occurred at the beginning of the Early Modern Era. As is well known, this was when central powers began to emerge and become more powerful, at the expense of other actors. At the same time, these began to take a tougher grip on their distant subjects and the use of the systems that prevailed. This also seems to have been the case with border peace agreements. The areas under examination here are European border regions, mainly in Scandinavia, but also the border between England and Scotland in the British Isles. All of these areas were characterized by frequent wars and the need for local peacekeeping. It should be mentioned that the British Isles and the border peace agreements there have not previously been studied in parallel with Scandinavia. This article covers the time from the Late Middle Ages to the Early Modern Age, i.e. from the 1490s to the beginning of the 19th century. The research method is comparative, involving a search for what united the border areas mentioned above, and also what distinctive features they had. The article is based mainly on modern research literature, but at suitable points – mainly for the Swedish-Russian border region – it reverts to primary data.

THE MAINTENANCE OF MUTUAL PEACE AT TIMES OF WAR OR THE THREAT OF WAR

The chief importance of a border agreement lay in the guarantee and enforcement of security on both sides of the border. The population of the area through which the border ran concluded a mutual agreement to maintain peace and mutual assistance in that area in spite of the fact that the realms to which they belonged were at war with each other or moving towards such a situation. The aim was to prevent all forms of looting or destruction of property, loss of human life or other manifestations of violence or revenge. Lying behind these ideas in many cases were previous experiences of states of war, especially what we now refer to as guerrilla warfare. The security pledges also extended to the movements of actual military units, in that the parties to the agreement asserted that they would not take part in military operations that were mounted by the armies of their own country.

The consequence of the practice of agreeing over borders was that when the peasant farmers of the border regions were forcibly conscripted into their respective armies they would do everything in their power to resist involvement in the hostilities. Under the defence obligations written into medieval law the peasants were obliged to take part in operations to defend themselves and their kin against enemy attacks, but only in their home district. Therefore they felt entitled to protest as soon as they were marched beyond the boundaries of this district.[1] Another aspect of the agreement was that if one party was likely to come under attack it would be warned of this in good time, so that the people concerned would have a chance to flee, taking their relatives and valuables with them.

The problem was, however, that the people issuing the warning could find themselves in trouble with their own military authorities.[2] In the early 16th century, in fact, Swedish-Danish border peace agreements included a promise on both sides to provide military assistance to the other, which meant that they were in great danger of punishment or disciplinary measures on the part of their own military leadership. Collaboration of this kind was evident between the inhabitants of Småland in Sweden and the neighbouring Blekinge, belonging to Denmark (see map 2, page 33) in 1542–1543, when the peasant uprising known as the Dacke War was taking place in the former area.[3] Those who refused to take part in the peasant army in order to provide aid across the border were threatened with very serious reprisals.[4]

In the majority of cases these local peace agreements were of considerable practical significance. The only major instance of the infringement of such an agreement was on the eastern border of Sweden during the Great Northern War, concerning an agreement between the province of Kajaani (comprising the town of Kajaani and the parishes of Paltamo and Sotkamo) on the Swedish side and the Lapland parishes (Russ. *Lopskie pogosty*) and the district of Repola on the Russian side. There had already been some disturbance of the peace in the borderlands on account of cross-border raids and conditions were in any case extremely difficult because of years of crop failure and the protracted war between Sweden and Russia. Eventually the peace agreement over the border broke down entirely when a large consignment of cloth (frieze) was confiscated from four merchants who were Russian subjects at a point close to the town of Kajaani. Even the authorities in the area were of the opinion that the cloth should be returned to its rightful owners, but this was not done. The consequence was a large-scale and highly destructive attack on the province of Kajaani and those regarded as having perpetrated this injustice by Russian merchants supported by Russian forces, chiefly Cossacks and Kalmucks.

This "Frieze War" was in effect an act of vengeance for the infringement of common law. The Russians felt that there had been a severe breach of trust that justified them in seeking revenge and breaking the local peace agreement and the sacred rites surrounding it in order to do so. But once vengeance had been extracted, the Russians – the merchants, that is – returned to the area with the request that the border peace agreement should be re-established.[5]

AGAINST OUTLAWS, BANDITS AND RAIDERS

Another provision of border peace agreements connected with general security and its enforcement was joint action against bandits and raiders – a universal curse of borderlands. A great deal of very useful cooperation existed in this respect, on the Swedish-Russian border and elsewhere in Scandinavia, and similarly on the border between England and Scotland in the British Isles. As the borders in question were for practical purposes open everywhere and almost unsupervised, it was extremely important for each country that outlaws and criminals should not be able to seek protection and form a base for their operations on the other side of the border. The border, open and unguarded as it may have been, still prevented the authorities of each country from entering the other for the purpose of apprehending criminals. This would have led straight away to a diplomatic or military incident. One early mention of such cooperation against bandits and raiders is to be found in a truce signed between the then Danish province of Skåne and Sweden on 24th March 1381.[6]

The fear of attacks from bandits hiding in the nearby forests was a very common part of the everyday reality for people living in border areas, especially as these bandits were extremely cruel, indulging in robbery, arson, torture and murder. They were "men of the forest" who lived beyond the bounds of organized society and held both the authorities and their laws and citizens' obligations in scorn. It was in general difficult to eradicate them, as their raids took place suddenly and unexpectedly and could be aimed at the inhabitants of their own country as well as those on the other side of the border.

Also, these activities were usually clearly linked to other problems and misfortunes occurring at the same time, such as years of famine, wars and increased pressure from the authorities in the form of taxation and/or conscription. In the spirit of their border agreements, the people on the two sides would inform each other of the movements of bandits and arrange joint expeditions to eliminate them. Sometimes the Crown supported such efforts by providing arms and equipment and sending soldiers to guard the inhabitants. Bandits who were captured were either killed or handed over to the authorities of their own country to be punished.

One particularly common means of killing bandits on the Swedish-Russian border, as also on the English-Scottish border, was by drowning, as this had a certain symbolism attached to it.[7] The severe punishment meted out to these bandits reflects in general terms the importance that the people of that time attached to peace and its preservation – even if harsh means were called for. Those active on the Swedish-Russian border were referred to as "robbers" (Finn. *rosvot*, Karelian *rosboinikat*, *rosvoniekat*, Russ. *razboikniki*).

PEACEABLE MEANS OF RESOLVING CONFLICTS AND CRIMES

One integral part of the spirit of harmony and good neighbourliness implied in these border agreements was the procedure for resolving conflicts and crimes in a peaceable manner. This was looked on as an essential for the general preservation of peace, as especially in times that were critical as far as foreign relations were concerned, even a fairly minor misunderstanding could assume such proportions that it could endanger the security of the whole community.

On Sweden's eastern border the most common causes of such conflicts were economic in origin, involving matters such as the use of fishing grounds, forests or hunting rights close to the border, and also reindeer herding in the areas further north. Swidden cultivation was for a long time the predominant means of growing crops along the eastern border, and disagreements over this practise were constantly being mentioned in documents produced on the Swedish side from one decade and century to the next.[8] Lying behind these complaints were in many cases uncertainties as to where the border lay, in spite of the closer attention that was being paid to the maintenance of its markers in the terrain.

In the case of the Swedish-Russian border there were certain local procedures that were used for settling disputes of this kind, particularly the appointment of arbitrators, the conducting of surveys of the border area and the referral of cases to the courts. Serious conflicts were resolved from the 17th century onwards through diplomatic channels in Moscow and Stockholm, which meant, of course, that these essential local issues took on a marked national significance. It was in fact typical of the local border areas in pre-Modern times that their inhabitants began to "nationalize" their grievances and disagreements with their neighbours across the border in order to gain support for their cause from their own authorities.[9]

On the other hand, there were some places where problematic issues were resolved in the Late Middle Ages and Early Modern times actually on or close to the border itself. This applied not only to Sweden's eastern border with Russia but also to other borders in Scandinavia and that between England and Scotland. Here again it was characteristic for differences to arise between border inhabitants over economic questions and for these to be resolved in the framework of certain established institutions, customs and places.[10]

BORDER TRADE AND COMMUNICATIONS

Another major sector covered by peasant peace agreements was that connected with guaranteeing the livelihood of the inhabitants. As very considerable volumes of trade took place over borders, commitments were made to keep international trade and other connections open at times of war or the threat of war. Indeed, it can be said that cross-border trade was the one thing that, in spite of the conflicts, wars and other divisive issues that arose from time to time, created a sense of mutual dependence and belonging together between the two sides, and thereby a desire for peace and unanimity.

In all parts of Europe where local border agreements of the type considered here were entered into in Early Modern times, the status of commerce, both informal trading[11] and official cross-border trading, was considerable. This was the case on the border between Sweden and Russia, and also on that between England and Scotland in the British Isles and between Denmark-Norway and Sweden over extensive areas, e.g. between Ångermanland, Medelpad, Hälsingland and Dalarna in Sweden and Jämtland and Härjedalen in (Denmark-)Norway on an east-west axis and between the southern provinces of Sweden, Småland and Västergötland, and the eastern Danish[12] provinces of Halland, Blekinge and Skåne on a north-south axis.[13] Peace and trading contacts were clearly linked together in those areas.

The securing of international trade and communications in fact already had far-reaching historical roots well before Early Modern times. It is known that there was a demand in the Bronze Age, especially on the part of the elite, that the international exchange network should function properly at all times where ready-made bronze and its constituent metals, copper and tin, were concerned, because those were produced in only a few areas.[14]

As for the peace agreements of the Middle Ages, they would appear in our present understanding to have been to a great extent a matter of ensuring freedom of trade and movement. International trade at that time was very much based on proclamations of freedom of trade and the networks resulting from these.[15] This feature was well to the fore in the Late Medieval truce signed between the Christian Kingdom of Castile and the Moorish Caliphate of Granada. One clause that was repeated constantly was that merchants should be granted freedom of passage across the border. In fact, their passage was not entirely free, since they still had to pay the appropriate customs duties and were allowed to trade only in those items of merchandise that were not prohibited under the importation or exportation laws.[16] Cross-border trading rights were also included in the treaties and truces signed between Sweden and Denmark from the Late Medieval period onwards, notably those of 1381 and 1508.[17]

In the case of Sweden's eastern border the Crown was aware of the positive repercussions of border trade, so that it was also prepared to condone the illegal aspects that generally went with it. Attempts were made to regulate exports of important raw materials and certain critical products. At the same time trade was steered – at least in principal – towards legal market places and traffic turned away from dubious routes and byroads and onto the main thoroughfares, in accordance with the mercantile economic policy observed at that time – as was also the procedure in the other border areas examined here. But in spite of this, all kinds of illegalities, including smuggling, were rife. The principal issue, however, was regarded as being the livelihood of the border inhabitants and their ability to pay the taxes demanded of them, so that their failure to observe the letter of the law and statutes in every detail could be overlooked.[18] The general importance of trade on the eastern border was also reflected in the fact that the Swedish-Russian peace treaties always guaranteed subjects of both realms the right to pursue trade freely provided they fulfilled certain obligations.

Cross-border trade in Early Modern times was especially important for the Russian subjects living in the border area. The merchant class among them was referred to in the Swedish documents with the epithet *köpryssar*, "Russian traders". The movement of these people was taken as some kind of unofficial indicator of the state of Swedish-Russian relations, i.e. as soon as there were less Russian traders than usual to be seen on the Swedish side of the border it was known or suspected that there was friction between these two realms.

Admittedly the Swedish Crown also harboured the constant fear that these Russian traders might also indulge in all manner of intelligence and spying activities on behalf of their own government in between their commercial endeavours. That may well have been the case in many instances. Indeed, similar fears were also expressed elsewhere, e.g. King John III of Sweden suspected during the war of 1563–1570 that the Norwegian peasants coming into Sweden were observers and spies sent by the Danish authorities rather than actual merchants intent on selling their wares.[19]

AGREEMENTS IN THE BORDERLANDS BETWEEN ENGLAND AND SCOTLAND

England and Scotland were still separate kingdoms in the Middle Ages and at the beginning of Early Modern times, and a chronic state of war prevailed between them that lasted from 1333 to 1502. No permanent peace was achieved during that time, but there were some intervals characterized by periodic truces or temporary abstinences from warfare.[20] These were in some respects similar to the local border agreements concluded in Scandinavia, as will be seen in the discussion below.

Peace gradually came to the English-Scottish borderlands in the course of time, however, so that a firm truce was concluded in 1500, followed soon afterwards by a Treaty of Perpetual Peace in 1502, one of the provisions in which was that King James IV of Scotland should marry Margaret Tudor, daughter of King Henry VII of England. This union of the two dynasties did indeed come into effect and was to exercise a substantial influence on the later pattern of nationhood in the British Isles. The eventual outcome was a personal Union of the Crowns of England and Scotland in 1603, with the consequence that the military border and all the systems that accompanied it disappeared and the borderland peripheries began to be linked more closely to the single central administration.[21]

It was nevertheless several decades into the 17th century before this personal union between England and Scotland succeeded by dint of stringent measures in rooting out the ancient tradition of banditry in the border area. The restoration of peace in the area in this sense also owed much to the fact that the union had brought the perpetual state of war and the tradition of resorting to violence to an end. The bandits that operated in the borderlands were customarily referred to as "reivers", or "border reivers", from the Old English verb *reive*, "to plunder",[22] and bore a great resemblance to the "robbers" that were the scourge of the border between Sweden and Russia.

AGREEMENTS ON THE BORDERS BETWEEN SWEDEN AND DENMARK-NORWAY

In the Late Middle Ages and Early Modern times Sweden had two neighbours on its western land border, Denmark and Norway, who as a consequence of a personal union that lasted from 1380 to 1814 were subject to a common ruler, the King of Denmark. Initially all three formed the Late Medieval Scandinavian Union of Kalmar, but this began to crumble on account of disputes between the parties. Wars broke out between them from time to time from the 15th century onwards, leading to a struggle for mastery over the Scandinavian region. During the 17th century Sweden achieved a dominant position in the region when it succeeded in pushing the Danes back from the land boundary in the south to the other side of the Sound. In all the wars of that period it was the population of the Swedish-Danish-Norwegian borderlands who suffered most. Therefore it was natural that they should have concluded local peace agreements for their own protection.

The oldest known Swedish-Danish border agreement dates from 1505 and concerns the Blekinge and Göinge areas of Denmark[23] and those of Möre, Värend and Finnveden in Sweden.[24] The wording of the agreement has been preserved in its entirety to the present day and comprises nine points, four of which were concerned with security matters. It is also evident from this wording "They reached agreement as well now as before" (*sig forbwndith i mellom sa nw som til foren*), that similar agreements had been made by the population on the two sides of the border at earlier times of crisis but these older documents have evidently not survived. The 1505 agreement was first drawn up by representatives appointed for the purpose at a "provincial assembly" (Sw. *landsting*) at the church of Hjortsberga in Blekinge on the Danish side and then ratified by the *landsting* of Vaxjö on the Swedish side.

These county councils were important instruments of self-government that have been regarded as one essential feature of the "communalism" that characterized peasant life. There was one point in the agreement, however, which sets it apart from other comparable documents and their provisions, namely, that each "province" (Sw. *landskap*) committed itself to paying its taxes "to the same lords as before". This may be interpreted as a declaration of loyalty from each side to its own authorities and an assertion that the peace concluded between them did not carry any separatist implications.[25]

The local agreement procedures that applied on the borders between Sweden and Denmark-Norway were quite genuinely a matter of tradition, as every war that took place in the 16th and 17th centuries led the population of the border region to seek protection by this means.[26] The last mention of such an agreement, concluded by one parish in Småland and two in Skåne, was in connection with the war of 1676–1679, although admittedly the nature of the agreements had altered considerably by that time. Lars-Olof Larsson states that the Swedish-Danish agreements from the Late Middle Ages and the beginning of Early Modern times are very much more precise in their provisions and broader in geographical extent than those concluded in the same region later in the 17th century.[27]

AGREEMENTS BETWEEN SWEDEN AND THE GRAND DUCHY OF MUSCOVY/THE TSARDOM OF RUSSIA

As elsewhere in Scandinavia, the problem with the Swedish-Russian borderlands is that there is no single source or archive in which all the known border agreements are gathered together. It is nevertheless possible by employing a variety of sources to compile a series of such agreements made during the period from the Late Middle Ages to well into Early Modern times. An agreement applying to the Swedish eastern border is generally referred to in Sweden with the term *gränsfred*, "border peace", or *gränssämja*, "border harmony", which may be regarded as synonyms.[28]

The Finnish word for "border", *raja*, was certainly in existence in the 16th century,[29] so that it may be assumed that the corresponding word for "border peace", *rajarauha*, would also have been in use at an early stage. In practice, it is mentioned at least in 1849, in connection with a Kullervo ballad in Elias Lönnrot's edition of the national epic, the *Kalevala*.[30] The oldest mention of a local "peace", *frijdh*, connected with the present area of Finland dates from the Late Middle Ages, around 1490, when the inhabitants of Ii, Kemi and Liminka complained to the Privy Council in the following way:

> The people of Tornio travel to Lapland, trade there and make peace with the Russians, showing no concern for us poor men. When we poor men have made peace, it has been on behalf of the whole of Norrbotten.[31]

It is clear from the way this is phrased that the border agreement procedure had been in use in the area prior to that time. It was chiefly intended as a means of safeguarding trading interests, as a few decades later, in 1555, Olaus Magnus described in his celebrated *Historia de gentibus septentrionalibus* how the "Russians" would come to the Midsummer Market in Tornio in huge numbers to trade their goods.[32] The agreement must thus have to a large extent resembled those drawn up in Europe in medieval times for the protection of the freedom of trade and communications. The Russians concerned in this case were presumably Karelians, but as such they, too, would have been subjects of the Grand Duke of Muscovy and in that sense "Russians".

Sweden and Moscow/Russia confronted each other in the common border areas in nine wars between the end of the Late Middle Ages and the beginning of the 19th century. The sequence began soon after the Principality of Moscow had overthrown the trading republic of Great Novgorod (*Veliky Novgorod*) in the 1470s and inherited its territorial demands with respect to Sweden – and with them the border conflicts. Soon after this the Kingdom of Sweden also began to increase in power, breaking away from the medieval Union of Kalmar in the early 1520s and setting about creating a centralized administration headed by the Vasa dynasty.

From around 1560 onwards Sweden entered into a period of territorial expansion in the Baltic region at the expense of neighbouring states. The series of wars with Russia came to an end in 1809, when Finland was separated from its centuries-old connection with Sweden and became an autonomous Grand Duchy within the Russian Empire. The constant skirmishes, wars and times of persecution have nevertheless left their mark not only on the historical sources but also on Finnish folklore.[33]

The present area of Northern Finland was where the most vehement border disputes between Sweden and Russia took place, since it was there, and also in present-day Eastern Finland, that western-based colonization had penetrated over the boundary laid down in the Treaty of Nöteborg (Finn. *Pähkinäsaari*) concluded between Sweden and Novgorod in 1323. Even in the 17th century the Russians still held on to the notion that their rights had originally extended as far as the Gulf of Bothnia, as it was reported that "they say that the land and water where we live belongs to them",[34] whereas the Swedes demanded on the strength of a forged copy of that same treaty that the border should run through the sources of the rivers Iijoki and Oulujoki, i.e. close to the present Finnish-Russian border. The result was a conflict that manifested itself in numerous raids and incursions in the course of time, reaching its peak in a period of guerrilla warfare that exhausted both sides in the course of the war between Sweden and Russia in 1570–1595, in spite of the fact that the two realms had been at war for the same reason in 1495–1497 and again in 1555–1557. These events had left an indelible mark on the collective memory of the people of this area, so that they wished to avoid any repetition in the future. One way of ensuring this was to enter into local border peace agreements.

Other means were also used to control the scope of the hostilities during the long war of 1570–1595, including periodic truces, which have often been referred to erroneously in earlier research as border peace agreements. The term "truce" (Sw. *stillestånd*, *vapenvila*, Finn. *aselepo*) was understood as being an agreement by which hostilities that had already begun were suspended for a specific length of time or indefinitely. Often they were suspended for the time required to negotiate over a lasting peace or to allow the two sides to gather strength in order to resume the battle since wars seldom continued all year round.

We are still talking, of course, of the medieval way of waging war and limiting its repercussions. There were some respects, it is true, in which a border agreement resembled a truce, since both were intended to regulate the scope of hostilities and the related violence, but they differed in that a truce was an instrument used by the Crown authorities and commanders in a war to bring operations to a halt for a certain time, whereas a peace agreement was a local instrument for preventing the outbreak of hostilities in a given area. In fact, it was typical of that particular war that over-active Crown representatives such as bailiffs or the commanders of troops at the local level would negotiate a truce without consulting the Crown or the supreme command responsible for the conduct of the war. The consequence was that the Crown had to intervene in such projects from time to time, imposing prohibitions on those who perpetrated them, or at least threatening to do so, if they were unable to adapt to its plans or accept the overall notion of centralized development of the realm.[35]

The tradition of border agreements gained in prominence during the 18th-century wars between Sweden and Russia, those of 1700–1721, 1741–1743 and 1788–1790. Then these procedures were firmly in the hands of the Crown, the same also being true on the other side, in Russia. One could very well speak in these cases of "Crown-led peace agreements", as these local agreements were made with permission from the Crown or even commissioned by it, so that the Crown representatives at the parochial, provincial or national level were often implicated in their finalization in some way. By this time the Crown had perceived the importance of these agreements as means of defending the more distance parts of the national territory and the people living there.

The last effort at reaching a border agreement between Sweden and Russia took place in the war of 1788–1790, when the Governor of the province of Oulu at the time offered his counterpart in Petrozavodsk the opportunity to conclude such an agreement, the draft of which has been preserved. If it had come into force, it would have covered the vast administrative areas of the province of Oulu and the *Gouvernement* of Olonets (Petrozavodsk). The Russians nevertheless turned the offer down, as they regarded the Swedes as having begun the war and as having attacked them in the rear as Russia was engaged at the same time in a war with the Ottoman Empire in the south.[36] Certain customs connected with the border agreement tradition came to the fore in connection with the war of 1808–1809 which led to Finland's incorporation into the Russian Empire as an autonomous Grand Duchy. These were observable in the same areas as had suffered most from the hostilities of earlier centuries.[37]

Conditions at the latitude of Kuusamo in the present-day region of Northern Finland were exceptional relative to the other parts of the eastern border. For a long time there was no national boundary at all from this point onwards until the very north of Lapland, even though the principles for defining such a border had been laid down in the Treaty of Teusina in 1595. The process of marking the border in the terrain had nevertheless come to a halt at Kuusamo on account of differences in opinion between the Swedish and Russian border commissars and the work had never been completed during the period of Swedish rule in spite of periodic attempts to do so. The official border thus came into being only at the beginning of the Grand Duchy period, when it was easier to reach agreement since both parties were subject to the same ruler, the Emperor of Russia and Grand Duke of Finland.[38]

Under Swedish rule the local people had had two main means of seeking protection. Firstly, they regularly paid taxes to the Russians even though they were subjects of the King of Sweden. This "Russian tax", or "border peace tax", was felt to be as a compensation for the preservation of peace in the area, and also for the fact that the inhabitants exploited nearby areas on the Russian side of the border.[39]

This somewhat unusual solution was not entirely unique in the world as similar situations have been reported on the Swedish-Norwegian border, on the borders of the Byzantine Empire with the lands of the nomadic peoples of the steppes and between the Spaniards and American Indians in the New World.[40] The second means open to these people was to conclude local peace agreements. This is known to have happened, for example, in the war of 1700–1721 when an agreement was made between the priest in Kuusamo and the Russian tax collector, or as he was called by the local people *dansikka* (Russ. *danshchik*). In many cases it was the priest's house that served as the place for cultivating mutual relations.[41] Thus the procedures for reaching local peace agreements would appear to have been in the hands of local representatives of the central power from a fairly early stage even in this area.

THE BORDER PEACE AGREEMENT – A LOCAL INSTRUMENT OF PEACE

Another term frequently used for a border peace agreement in Norwegian, Swedish and Danish research is "peasant agreement" or "peasant peace" (*bondefred* in Norwegian, Swedish and Danish, *talonpoikaisrauha* in Finnish), a concept which is not actually mentioned in the sources dating from the Middle Ages or the early 16th century but is to be found later. Erik XIV of Sweden, for example, complained in his letter to the bailiff of Sunnerbo in March 1564 that he had heard it mentioned that the peasants of the district had "concluded a treacherous peasant peace" (*upprättat en förrädelig bondefred*) with the district of Göinge in Denmark and called for them to be punished.

Similarly, a century later, in 1676, two parishes in Skåne and one in Småland decided to enter into "a general, firm and powerful peasant peace according to custom" (*efter plägsed [...] en allmännelig, säker och kraftig bondefred*).[42] The concept came into the historical literature in 1864, when C. F. Allen published his work *De tre nordiske Rigers Historie* at a time when Denmark was at war with Prussia and Austria, so that he was attempting to arouse support for his country by evoking a Scandinavianist spirit and speaking of "peasant agreements" and the "general sympathy for one another" shown by the peasant populations on the two sides of the Swedish-Danish border.

As a concept, "peasant peace" is somewhat misleading and is frequently used wrongly. Interpreted literally it would mean an agreement concluded by the peasants themselves, probably unbeknown to the Crown or its representatives. There are indeed indications that this may have been the case in some instances, e.g. in the Swedish-Danish wars of 1611–1613 and 1676–1679. On the other hand it is known that the clergy were crucially involved in local peace agreements in the same area during the same century.[43] It is also possible to see the term "peasant peace" as a derogatory reference to a local agreement on the part of those in power, as was the case in the above quotation from King Erik XIV. As the king gained in power and the state-building process advanced, the Crown was inclined to take a dim view of activities that were not initiated by it or did not serve its interests.

On the other hand, the upper strata of society in general – the local aristocracy, bishops and priests and the merchant class – would very often be involved in local attempts at reaching border agreements, because they wanted to secure their own interests, largely economic ones. If we look at the oldest known agreement concluded on the Swedish-Danish border, dating from 1505, we see that the most influential political, economic and religious figures in the area, including both the bishop and a local aristocrat by the name of Erik Trolle, were actively involved in the process alongside the peasant farmers themselves. The same was true five years later, when a similar project was backed by two leading clerics, the Bishop of Växjö in Värend and the Archbishop of Lund in Skåne. The aim was to avoid the detrimental effects of war, the destruction and looting and the interruption of border traffic and trading. The bishops owned property in the border region, as also did the Trolle family, who had acquired an "agricultural" empire running into hundreds of farms on both sides of the border.[44] A similar desire on the part of the aristocracy to protect its financial interests in the border region could also be seen in connection with the war of 1563–1570.[45]

Exactly the same situation prevailed on the border between England and Scotland at the beginning of Early Modern times, since the power of the English in the border region rested with the local aristocratic families. The borderlands on both sides were divided into three administrative and military areas, or "marches", each governed by a specific official known as "the warden of the march", chosen from among the local aristocratic families. The "west marches" on the English side were in the hands of the Dacre family, or more correctly the "Dacre of the North", who wielded considerable economic power, controlling a network of estates, castles and tenant farms in the extreme north of England. Later, when the process of state building had advanced in England under the Tudors, the Crown began to look on these aristocrats – including the Dacres – as posing a threat to them on account of their administrative, military and economic power.[46]

As a state of war was still the rule rather than the exception on the English-Scottish border at the beginning of Early Modern times, the Dacre family was obliged to protect its property from the destruction and plundering that this entailed, and the method that they chose for the purpose was the maintaining of peace with the "Scottish foe". This ploy nevertheless came to the attention of the Crown, which saw in it an opportunity to intervene and restrict the power of the border aristocrats. The outcome was that William Dacre and his uncle were put on trial for treason on the orders of King Henry VIII, on the grounds of having aided and abetted the Scots, who were "enemies of the King", and having arranged secret meetings to conclude private treaties with them. The specific purpose of these was stated to have been "to arrange mutual immunity from raids and invasions for the lands and tenants of each party". This was clearly a case of "border peace", although one of the consequences was that the other administrative sectors of the border area, the "middle and east marches" had to suffer invasions by the Scots.

The eventual result of the trial, however, was that Lord Dacre was acquitted but forced to pay severe fines and dismissed from the office of "warden of the west marches", although the Crown still availed itself of his services and knowledge in the administration of the Scottish border region. Steven G. Ellis regards Lord Dacre's position and connections with the Scottish court and border community as having been such that he could easily have entered into arrangements of a kind that the English Crown could have interpreted as acts of treason.[47]

In the case of local border agreements it is indeed more justifiable to speak of "border peace", for such an agreement applied to a certain geographical area as a whole and all sectors of its population. Amongst the modern Swedish historians, the term "border peace" has been favoured by Karl Bergman, Mathias Cederholm, Lars-Olof Larson, who has done extensive work on the Early Modern period and on the history of Småland, and Stefan Persson.[48] The same holds good in the case of the eastern border of Sweden with Russia, both for the above reasons and because contemporaries spoke of the agreements in this way, for the first time in connection with the Swedish-Russian war of 1656–1658 and thereafter on a regular basis.

THE EMERGENCE OF THE BORDER AGREEMENT PROCEDURE AND PRECONDITIONS FOR IT

Wars were carried on at two levels in the Europe of the Middle Ages and Early Modern times: (1) between Christians and "pagans" (Muslims), and (2) as internal conflicts between Christians. In the case of the latter, the medieval Roman Catholic Church attempted to limit the sufferings of local populations in the course of these feudal wars by means of various ecclesiastical peace movements, e.g. *Pax Dei*, *Treuga Dei*. It was in the church's interests to restore peace in the spirit of the ideology that it proclaimed. Meanwhile the secular authorities took steps to ensure peaceful conditions by proclaiming peace within their countries and passing laws to this effect. This was true in Sweden, for instance, where a number of laws were promulgated that referred specifically to the establishment of peaceful conditions: commercial peace, church peace, peace at home, peace in the law courts, peace for shipping and peace for women, for example. In this way the Crown began to surround its citizens with a "security network" of circles within which peace was legislated for, to combat all those situations in which they might be threatened with violence.

By the Late Middle Ages and Early Modern times power in the nations of Europe had begun to be concentred in certain princely families, just as the concept of a realm, began to assume a more concrete form, i.e. by gaining a territorial dimension, rather than the abstract meaning that it had had in a medieval context. One consequence of all this was that the number of conflicts arising for territorial, dynastic, hereditary or despotic reasons began to increase, leading to wars that impinged most on the border areas and their populations, in the form of insecurity, destruction, taxation, plundering and violence. It was in this situation that the practise of concluding local peace agreements grew up, presumably following the example of the church's peace movements and the secular legislation for peace in given sectors of everyday life.

The first mention of such an agreement being concluded in the present-day area of Finland dates from 1490 and the first in what is now southern Sweden from 1505, although in both cases there is a specific reference to the procedure having been resorted to earlier. If we were to set a date for the origins of this custom in Scandinavia and also on the border between England and Scotland it could well be placed in the Late Middle Ages. Border peace agreements were a means by which local inhabitants could gain some protection and security in the face of disputes and conflicts to which they were not a party in any other sense, and the preconditions that led to them were an insecure position and weak defence brought about by the open and usually unsupervised nature of borders at that time. These local agreements were also means by which the inhabitants could protect their essential connections, in particular their cross-border trade connections. In this respect they also resemble the medieval truces and treaties, which similarly set out to guarantee the continuity of peaceful contacts.

As soon as the custom of concluding local peace agreements became established it came under attack from the central authorities in the various countries concerned. It was able to adapt to this situation, however, so that it altered according to the requirements of the surrounding society. In the case of the Kingdom of Sweden three phases can be recognised in the attitudes of the Crown to border agreements. The first was the period of fairly unrestrained activity in the Late Middle Ages, up to the year 1521 when Sweden left the Union of Kalmar and began a state building process under the Vasa dynasty. At this stage other sectors of the population were involved in the local agreements as well as the peasant farmers.

The second phase, from 1521 until around the beginning of the 17th century, was the time when the Crown prohibited all forms of freely organized activity on the part of the peasants as being contrary to the spirit of a centralized, hierarchical state. Regional and local agreements on the maintenance of peace were not consistent with the notion of a strengthening of central power and the building of the state. Wars were still conducted in the old medieval manner, however, and were regulated by truces. The third phase, which lasted from around the beginning of the 17th century until 1809, was that of local but Crown-led peace agreements.

The Crown finally realized that local peace agreements could be of some benefit to it if it could keep a tight enough hold over them. By this time they had become an important element in the management of crises on the eastern border of the Swedish Realm with Russia. Stefan Persson similarly speaks of the "dualist principle" that motivated them on the Swedish-Danish border, by which he means that local peace agreements served the needs of both the border communities themselves and the central government. Although the latter was often opposed to local agreements, they were still of significance because they protected the subjects in the border communities, the resources obtainable from them and the national territory itself from enemy activities.[49]

REFERENCES

1 A. G. Fontell, En blick på Österbottens tillstånd år 1571 samt gränsfejden 1573–1585, in: Valan. Album utgifvet af svenske österbottningar 1, Helsingfors 1881, 41; Werner Tawaststjerna, Pohjoismaiden viisikolmattavuotinen sota. Vuosien 1570 ja 1590 välinen aika, Historiallisia Tutkimuksia 1, Helsinki 1918–1920, 482; Halvdan Koht, Norsk bondereising. Fyrebuing til bondepolitikken, Oslo 1926, 137–141; Armas Luukko, Pohjois-Pohjanmaan ja Lapin keskiaika sekä 1500-luku. Pohjois-Pohjanmaan ja Lapin historia 2, Oulu 1954, 731; Mathias Cederholm, De värjde sin rätt. Senmedeltida bondemotstånd i Skåne och Småland, Studia historica Lundensia 14, Lund 2007, 140.

2 Tawaststjerna, Pohjoismaiden viisikolmattavuotinen sota, Loc. Cit. (Note 1), 482; Koht, Norsk bondereising, Loc. Cit. (Note 1), 135; Lars-Olof Larsson, Gränsfred i krigstid, in: Populär Historia 8/2002, 50; Lars-Olof Larsson, Arvet efter Gustav Vasa. En berättelse om fyra kungar och ett rike, Stockholm 2005, 182; Kimmo Katajala, Viipurin Karjala rajamaakuntana. Viipurin läänin historia 1534–1617, in: Yrjö Kaukiainen (ed.), Viipurin läänin historia III. Suomenlahdelta Laatokalle, Porvoo 2010, 129–130.

3 Lars-Olof Larsson, Historia om Småland, Växjö 1974, 108–109; Larsson, Gränsfred i krigstid, Loc. Cit. (Note 2), 50; Kenneth Johansson, "The lords from the peasants or the peasants from the lords". The Dacke War and the concept of communalism, in: Kimmo Katajala (ed.), Northern Revolts. Medieval and Early Modern Peasant Unrest in the Nordic Countries. Studia Fennica, Historica 8, Helsinki 2004, 59, 70; Cederholm, De värjde sin rätt, Loc. Cit. (Note 1), 140.

4 Larsson, Gränsfred i krigstid, Loc. Cit. (Note 2), 48.

5 Jukka Kokkonen, Rajaseutu liikkeessä. Kainuun ja Pielisen Karjalan asukkaiden kontaktit Venäjän Karjalaan kreivin ajasta sarkasotaan (1650–1712), Bibliotheca Historica 79, Helsinki 2002, 157–172.

6 Folke Lindberg, Bondefreder under svensk medeltid, in: Historisk Tidskrift [Sverige] (1928), 3.

7 Letter from the border commissars Hans Munck and Andreas Bureus in the border village of Porajärvi to Helge Jespersson, Commandant of Kajaani Castle, 13.9.1620. Gränshandlingar 1617–1621. Muscovitica. Riksarkivet, Stockholm; George Fraser MacDonald, The Steel Bonnets. The Story of the Anglo–Scottish Border Reivers, London 1989, 127. On one occasion, in July 1562, no less than 22 bandits were drowned at Hawick; Kokkonen, Rajaseutu liikkeessä, Loc. Cit. (Note 5), 150; Isabel de Madariaga, Ivan the Terrible. First Tsar of Russia, New Haven/London 2006 [paperback], 246–247, 365–366.

8 See, for example, a letter with enclosures from the Governor of the province of Ostrobothnia, Didrik Wrangel, in Korsholm to His Royal Majesty on 19.5.1681. Vol. 2. Skrivelser till Kungliga Majestät, Landshövdingarnas skrivelser Finland, Österbottens län. Swedish National Archives, Stockholm; Sotkamo district court 4.2.1688. rr 25, 96–98. Finnish National Archives, Helsinki.

9 Karl Bergman uses the Swedish term *nationalisera* when speaking of conflicts on the Swedish-Danish border in the 17th century and refers to the description by Peter Sahlins how the peasant farmers of Cerdanya in the Franco-Hispanic border area of the Pyrenees would similarly "nationalize" their everyday differences of opinion in the 18th and 19th centuries in particular, so that disputes over land holdings, for example, could take on a nationalist character. See Karl Bergman, Makt, möten, gränser. Skånska kommissionen i Blekinge 1669–70. Studia historica Lundensia 7. Lund 2002, 346–348.

10 Janrik Bromé, Jämtlands och Härjedalens historia. Andra delen: 1537–1645, Stockholm 1945, 1, 7; Göran Rystad, Gränskrig och bondefred, in: Ale. Historisk tidskrift för Skåneland (1965) 2, 39; Larsson, Historia om Småland, Loc. Cit. (Note 3), 103, 108 (figure captions); MacDonald, The Steel Bonnets, Loc. Cit. (Note 7), 151; Bergman, Makt, möten, gränser, Loc. Cit. (Note 9), 123–124; Larsson, Gränsfred i krigstid, Loc. Cit. (Note 2), 50–51.

11 Trading that took place outside the official channels (applied to the chartered towns and the official fairs), a forming of trading that was in fact regarded as illegal in Sweden from the Late Middle Ages onwards.

12 Provinces of Denmark located beyond The Sound.

13 Bromé, Jämtlands och Härjedalens historia, Loc. Cit. (Note 10), 50–59; Lars-Olof Larsson, Det medeltida Värend. Studier i det småländska gränslandets historia fram till 1500-talets mitt. Bibliotheca historica Lundensis 12, Lund 1964, 229–237; Larsson, Historia om Småland, Loc. Cit. (Note 3), 103–104; Henry Summerson, Response to war. Carlisle and the West March in the later fourteenth century, in: Anthony Goodman/Anthony Tuck (eds.), War and Border Societies in the Middle Ages, London/New York 1992, 170–172; Jarmo T. Kotilaine, When the Twain Did Meet. Foreign Merchants and Russia's Economic Expansion in the Seventeenth Century. Dissertation: Cambridge [Massachusetts], Harvard University, Graduate School of Arts and Sciences, August 2000, Ann Arbor, Michigan 2002, 679–766; Kokkonen, Rajaseutu liikkeessä, Loc. Cit. (Note 5), 189–212.

14 Antti Lahelma/Joonas Sipilä, Sodankäynti Suomessa kivi- ja pronssikaudella, in: Hannele Klemettilä (ed.), Suomalainen sotilas. [3]. Muinaisurhosta nihtiin, Hämeenlinna 2010, 33.

15 Jukka Korpela, Viipurin läänin historia II. Viipurin linnaläänin synty, Lappeenranta 2004, 144.

16 José Enrique López de Coca Castañer, Institutions on the Castilian–Granadan Frontier 1369–1482, in: Robert Bartlett/Angus MacKay (eds.), Medieval Frontier Societies, Oxford 1989, 134–135.

17 Lindberg, Bondefreder under svensk medeltid, Loc. Cit. (Note 6), 3; Cederholm, De värjde sin rätt, Loc. Cit. (Note 1), 114.

18 Kokkonen, Rajaseutu liikkeessä, Loc. Cit. (Note 5), 87–88.

19 Bromé, Jämtlands och Härjedalens historia, Loc. Cit. (Note 10), 55.

20 Steven G. Ellis, Tudor state formation and the shaping of the British Isles, in: Steven G. Ellis/Sarah Barber (eds.), Conquest and Union: Fashioning a British State, 1485–1725, London/New York, 45.

21 Ellis, Tudor state formation and the shaping of the British Isles, Loc. Cit. (Note 20), 49, 61–62.

22 MacDonald, The Steel Bonnets, Loc. Cit. (Note 7), 3 (include note 2), 362, 364–365, 378; Keith Durham, The Border Reivers, Oxford 2000, 38–41; Steven G. Ellis, Frontiers and Identities in the Historiography of the British Isles, in: Lud'a Klusáková/Steven G. Ellis (eds.), Frontiers and Identities. Exploring the Research Area. Thematic Work Groups 5; Frontier and Identities 1, Pisa 2006, 70.

23 Göinge was the north-eastern part of Skåne.

24 Möre, Värend and Finnveden were the southern parts of Småland, the parts known to the Swedes as *folkland*.

25 Larsson, Det medeltida Värend, Loc. Cit. (Note 13), 199–200; Rystad, Gränskrig och bondefred, Loc. Cit. (Note 10), 34–35; Larsson, Historia om Småland, Loc. Cit. (Note 3), 104–106; Larsson, Gränsfred i krigstid, Loc. Cit. (Note 2), 47–48; Cederholm, De värjde sin rätt, Loc. Cit. (Note 1), 112, 300.

26 For details, see Koht, Norsk bondereising, Loc. Cit. (Note 1), 135–136; Eva Österberg, Gränsbygd under krig. Ekonomiska, demografiska och administrativa förhållanden i sydvästra Sverige under och efter nordiska sjuårskriget. Bibliotheca historica Lundensis 26, Lund 1971, 106, 117–121; Larsson, Historia om Småland, Loc. Cit. (Note 3), 102–103, 106, 110; Mikael Venge, Bondefred og Græensefred, in: Historisk Tidskrift [Denmark] 80 (1980), 43–54, 59–60; Lars-Olof Larsson, Småländsk historia. Stormaktstiden, Stockholm 1982, 56; Larsson, Gränsfred i krigstid, Loc. Cit. (Note 2), 48–51; Göran Rystad, Karl XI. En biografi. (Svenska regenter), Lund 2003, 309; Larsson, Arvet efter Gustav Vasa, Loc. Cit. (Note 2), 181–182; Cederholm, De värjde sin rätt, Loc. Cit. (Note 1), 140, 409; Stefan Persson, Gränsbygd och svenskkrig. Studier i Blekinges, Skånes och Hallands östdanska historia. Lund 2007, especially 111, 133–134.

27 Larsson, Gränsfred i krigstid, Loc. Cit. (Note 2), 51; Larsson, Arvet efter Gustav Vasa, Loc. Cit. (Note 2), 181.

28 See, for example, letters from the Governor of the Ostrobothnia, Gustaf Creutz to His Royal Majesty 02.10.1741, 30.10.1741. Vol. 12. Skrivelser till Kunliga Majestät, Landshövdingarnas skrivelser Finland, Österbottens län. Swedish National Archives, Stockholm.

29 Ilkka Savijärvi/Muusa Savijärvi, Rajaton raja, in: Tapio Hämynen (ed.), Kahden Karjalan välillä, Kahden Riikin riitamaalla. Studia Carelica Humanistica 5, Joensuu 1994, 9–11; Luďa Klusáková/Steven G. Ellis, Terms and Concepts. "Frontier" and "Identity" in Academic and Popular Usage, in: Luďa Klusáková/Steven G. Ellis (eds.), Frontiers and Identities. Exploring the Research Area. Thematic Work Groups 5; Frontier and Identities 1, Pisa 2006, 10.

30 Kalevala 32: 315–324. Kullervo was forced by Seppo Ilmari's wife to become a herder of cattle, and when releasing the cattle into the pastures she utters an incantation over them proposing a "border peace" with the bear in order to protect her animals from it.

31 Finlands medeltida urkunder samlade och i tryckt utgifna af Finlands statsarkiv genom Reinhold Hausen, V, 1481–1495, Helsingfors 1928, Nr 4286; Einar W. Juvelius, Suomen kansan aikakirjat. Suomalaisen historiallisen kirjallisuuden ja Carl Grimbergin suurteoksen pohjalta. I osa. Esihistoria ja keskiaika, Helsinki [4]1930, 469. "[...] ok fara Törnbona vpp i Lappamarken ok köpslaga ok bindha frijdh met Ryssana ok akta oss fatighe män inthe. Then tidh wij fatige män hawa gjorth fridh, tha hawa wij giorth fridh öwer alth Norrabothn."

32 Luukko, Pohjois-Pohjanmaan ja Lapin keskiaika sekä 1500-luku, Loc. Cit. (Note 1), 196, 202–204; Marko Lamberg, Kun Tornion rahvas kirjoitti tsaarille. Ruotsin valtakuntaan kuulumisen tunne Peräpohjolassa 1500-luvun alussa, in: Mirator kesäkuu/juni/june/(2000), 2. http://www.cc.jyu.fi/mirator/Lamberg.pdf. Accessed 10.04.2012.

33 Finnish folklore contains a wealth of tales concerned with the frequently recurring wars and skirmishes typical themes in which are the "dog-faces" (Finn. *koirankuonolaiset*, referring to the Kalmucks, a people of the Central Asian steppes who served in the cavalry of the Russian Army) and how the "persecutors" would torture people to death and plunder, burn and destroy their property. One separate subgroup of tales consists of those telling how people resisted the persecutors, and there are also tales associated with particular people – leaders, guerrillas, warlords, soldiers, peasant chiefs – and with historical events and individual battles during the wars. Urpo Vento (ed.), Kertomusperinteen opas. Tietolipas 67. Helsinki 1971, 132–133, 138–143.

34 Harald Trolle, Solovetskij-klostret och dess betydelse i kampen mellan Sverige och Nord-Ryssland, in: Svensk Tidskrift 38 (1951), 427–428.

35 Fontell, En blick på Österbottens tillstånd år 1571 samt gränsfejden 1573–1585, Loc. Cit. (Note 1), 43–46 (including note 3); Tawaststjerna, Pohjoismaiden viisikolmattavuotinen sota, Loc. Cit. (Note 1), 113–115, 197, 452, 483 (including note 2); Luukko, Pohjois-Pohjanmaan ja Lapin keskiaika sekä 1500-luku, Loc. Cit. (Note 1), 732–736; Aslak Outakoski, Rovaniemen historia I, Rovaniemi 1965, 171; Kauko Pirinen, Savon historia 2:1. Rajamaakunta asutusliikkeen aikakautena 1534–1617, Kuopio 1982, 629–630; Katajala, Viipurin Karjala rajamaakuntana, Loc. Cit. (Note 2), 171. The Governor-General of Tallinn and Estonia reached a truce with the Russian on behalf of Estonia in autumn 1571, but when knowledge of the truce reached King John III, he called it a "chicken peace" (Sw. *hönefred*), perhaps better translated as "scatterbrain peace", and would not accept it. Tawaststjerna, Pohjoismaiden viisikolmattavuotinen sota, Loc. Cit. (Note 1), 23, 29. In connection with the Dacke War in Småland King Gustaf of Sweden wrote to the peasants and aristocracy that they should not trust in the "chicken peace", since it included the truce signed with the rebels towards the end of 1542. Johansson, "The lords from the peasants or the peasants from the lords", Loc. Cit. (Note 3), 71.

36 K. A. Castrén, Tietoja Oulun läänin sota-asioista Gustaw III:nen sodan aikana, Helsinki 1870 (Ylipainos Kirjallisesta Kuukauslehdestä), 16–24; Aslak Outakoski, Puolustustoimenpiteistä Pohjois-Pohjanmaalla vv. 1788–1790 sodan alussa, in: Pohjois-Pohjanmaan Maakuntaliiton Vuosikirja 1939–1940. Oulu 1941, 20–24.

37 Letter from the Crown Bailiff Daniel Elfving to the Provincial Governor, Sotkamo 21.10.1808. Transcripts of letters 1778–1822 (EI:1). Kajaanin kihlakunnan kruununvouti. Provincial Archives in Oulu, Finland; A. H. Virkkunen, Kajaanin läänin oloista 1808 vuoden sodan aikana, in: Historiallinen Aikakauskirja 21 (1923), 228.

38 For details, see Kyösti Julku, Kuusamo valtakunnan rajahistoriassa. Oulun yliopisto, historian laitos, Eripainossarja N:o 231, Oulu 1990.

39 Försök til beskrifning öfwer Kusamo-Sokn uti Kemi=Lappmark. Framgifvit af Elias Lagus Adj. Past., År 1770 = Kuvausyritys Kemin Lapin Kuusamon pitäjästä. Julkaissut Elias Lagus apulaispastori v. 1770. Acta Univ. Oul. B 5. 1975. Hist. 3, Kuusamo [2]1987, 12 (note d), 63; Aimo Halila, Pohjois-Pohjanmaa ja Lappi 1721–1775. Pohjois-Pohjanmaan ja Lapin historia V, Oulu 1954, 361–365, 403.

40 Bromé, Jämtlands och Härjedalens historia, Loc. Cit. (Note 10), 94–95; Richard W. Slatta, Comparing Cowboys & Frontiers, Norman 1997, 67–69. "buying Frontier Peace"; Paul Stephenson, The Byzantine Frontier at the Lower Danube in the Late Tenth and Eleventh Centuries, in: Daniel Power/Naomi Standen (eds.), Frontiers in Question. Eurasian Borderlands, 700–1700, (Themes in Focus), Basingstoke 1999, 93–96.

41 Försök til beskrifning öfwer Kusamo-Sokn uti Kemi=Lappmark, Loc. Cit. (Note 39), 66–67.

42 Larsson, Det medeltida Värend, Loc. Cit. (Note 13), 200; Österberg, Gränsbygd under krig, Loc. Cit. (Note 26), 106; Larsson, Historia om Småland, Loc. Cit. (Note 3), 102, 110; Venge, Bondefred og Grænsefred, Loc. Cit. (Note 26), 41; Larsson, Gränsfred i krigstid, Loc. Cit. (Note 2), 50; Larsson, Arvet efter Gustav Vasa, Loc. Cit. (Note 2), 182.

43 Larsson, Historia om Småland, Loc. Cit. (Note 3), 111–112; Larsson, Småländsk historia, Loc. Cit. (Note 26), 56; Larsson, Gränsfred i krigstid, Loc. Cit. (Note 2), 50–51.

44 Larsson, Det medeltida Värend, Loc. Cit. (Note 13), 202, 205–206; Larsson, Historia om Småland, Loc. Cit. (Note 3), 105; Larsson, Gränsfred i krigstid, Loc. Cit. (Note 2), 48–49; Cederholm, De värjde sin rätt, Loc. Cit. (Note 1), 112–113.

45 Larsson, Gränsfred i krigstid, Loc. Cit. (Note 2), 50; Larsson, Arvet efter Gustav Vasa, Loc. Cit. (Note 2), 181–182.

46 Ciarán Brady, Comparable histories? Tudor reform in Wales and Ireland, in: Steven G. Ellis/Sarah Barber (eds.), Conquest and Union. Fashioning a British State, 1485–1725, London/New York 1995, 75–76; Ellis, Tudor state formation and the shaping of the British Isles, Loc. Cit. (Note 20), 46; Steven G. Ellis, Tudor frontiers and noble power. The making of the British state, Oxford 1995, xxv (Map 4. Dacre estates in northern Cumberland), 7, 41–42, 81–82; Steven G. Ellis, The English State and its Frontiers in the British Isles, 1300–1600, in: Daniel Power/Naomi Standen (eds.), Frontiers in Question. Eurasian Borderlands, 700–1700. (Themes in Focus), Basingstoke 1999, 160; Ellis, Frontiers and Identities in the Historiography of the British Isles, Loc. Cit. (Note 22), 75–76.

47 Ellis, Tudor state formation and the shaping of the British Isles, Loc. Cit. (Note 20), 53; Ellis, Tudor frontiers and noble power, Loc. Cit. (Note 46), 146, 199–200, 233–234.

48 See, for example, Larsson, Det medeltida Värend, Loc. Cit. (Note 13), 207; Larsson, Historia om Småland, Loc. Cit. (Note 3), 103; Bergman, Makt, möten, gränser, Loc. Cit. (Note 9), 94; Cederholm, De värjde sin rätt, Loc. Cit. (Note 1), 138–141; Persson, Gränsbygd och svenskkrig, Loc. Cit. (Note 26), 111, 133–134. On the other hand, Göran Rystad has continued to prefer the term "peasant peace", which he used in a paper on Swedish-Danish border agreements published in 1965 and continued to use in passing in his biography of King Charles XI in 2003, see Rystad, Gränskrig och bondefred, Loc. Cit. (Note 10); Rystad, Karl XI, Loc. Cit. (Note 26), 308.

49 Persson, Gränsbygd och svenskkrig, Loc. Cit. (Note 26), 133–134.

NORWAY'S HARD AND SOFT BORDERS TOWARDS RUSSIA

Good fences make good neighbours. Robert Frost[1]

State borders are physical, material facts, they are "hard borders" in Klaus Eder's definition.[2] However, hard borders are also infused with "soft borders", i.e. immaterial or mental boundaries that define who we are and who the others are. That explains how state borders can symbolize the internal and external status of the state, its attitude towards its own population, as well as towards the neighbouring countries. Establishment of hard borders, or changes in the territorial demarcation of nation-states, undoubtedly in many countries has affected the collective process of creating soft borders. Hard borders, however, are also reinforced with soft ones that invest them with abstract meaning and justify them, so to say. Soft borders become part of the "hardness" of state borders because "the symbolic power inherent in soft borders helps to "naturalize" hard borders, to produce the effect of taking borders for granted".[3]

The present article deals with borders between Norway and Russia, between the Norwegians and the Russians, in the 19th and early 20th centuries; a case that aptly illustrates how soft borders can influence hard borders, making them "harder" even to such a degree that they change their phenotype or physical appearance. The Norwegian-Russian state border became both "harder" and "colder" and ended up as a strict climatic border with a temperate climate on the western side, and a distinctive Arctic climate to the east. We will try to explain how this could happen, starting with an account of how this state border came into existence in the beginning of the 19th century after a period of more than 500 years with vast common territories in the North. The way this came about is an example of how the establishment of hard borders does not necessarily influence the creation of soft ones; the soft borders that will be our main topic below were not, as it seems, inherent in Norwegian-Russian relations but came from without.

THE BELATED BORDER

The establishment of a state border between Norway and Russia took place as late as in 1826 and completed the national splitting up of the vast territories of Arctic Europe – or *Sapmi*, "the land of the Sami" (Norse *Finnmork).*[4] Today this region is often referred to as northern Fennoscandia or the *Northern Cap*. The exact splitting up of territory in political spaces through boundary lines is, as we know, not a universal feature of all societies at all times. It is above all a characteristic of modern society, the outcome of a gradual, century-long development, in which the meaning of boundaries was altered in step with changing social formations. The long overdue drawing of borders between Russia and Norway was certainly a part of this process, but why did it come so late?

In Europe systematic mapping of natural resources together with extensive usage of maps and statistics became customary in the 18th century and delineation of boundary lines as markers of the state's territory was now made easier on a practical level.[5] As a result of the provincial reforms in Norway in 1660 (*amtsreformen*) and in Russia one hundred years later (*gubernskaya reforma*) more exact maps and statistical material gradually became available also in these countries in the periphery of Europe.[6] In the High North, however, several factors counteracted the trend towards careful delimitation and demarcation of boundary lines. One factor was, conceivably, the vastness of the Sapmi/the Northern Cap. It comprised the coastline from Malangen in North Norway – not far from present-day Tromsø – all the way eastwards to the White Sea, including a vast territory of the interior of northern Fenno-Scandia, as well as the Kola Peninsula.[7] The drawing of borders was all the more difficult because of Sapmi's peripheral position in relation to the centres of each respective state. Both the regional and local administration remained weakly developed.

The single most important factor behind the belatedness of the delimitation was presumably the culture and economic adaptation of the Sami, the area's indigenous population. Their old hunting culture was based on an extensive use of land areas, with the Sami moving from dwelling sites in the interior to the coast, and further on to the river valleys, to exploit the natural resources at the right time of the year. Later reindeer-breeding Sami likewise followed their herds from winter pastures in the interior to summer pastures on the coast – and back again into the interior.

This may have been a unique phenomenon in Europe in the nineteenth century, but is reminiscent for instance of some Mongol nomadic tribes, described by Owen Lattimore as late as the middle of the 20th century, crossing back and forth over China's northern borders. For such nomads, no single pasture had much value in itself for their livestock, because it soon would have become exhausted. More important was the control of routes of migration between the different pastures. The right to move prevailed over the right to camp.[8] Likewise it was crucial for the Sami not to loose their right to move, and border delimitations could deprive them of the control of the routes of migration. Their yearly cycle of resource exploitation no doubt delayed the national division of the Northern Cap and the establishment of permanent state borders. Instead, Norway and Russia for centuries accepted the existence of a huge *common district*, where the two states' right to taxation was connected not primarily with territory, but with Sami ethnicity. This was the substance of the Norwegian-Russian border treaty which was concluded between the Norwegian king and the Grand Prince of Novgorod in 1326.[9]

THE CONTRACTION OF THE COMMON AREA

With the immigration of groups representing majority populations from the south of Fenno-Scandia in the late Middle Ages and early modern period, the Sami region was gradually pressed together. The immigrants established their own economic and socio-cultural spaces, which in time were to become extensions of their national territories. Various national rivalries resulted in heavy tax burdens being put on the Sami population – the guiding principle being that "the greater tax gave the greater right to the people and the land".[10] Later the Swedish king too laid claim to the common district, and in the second half of the 16th century the Sami of the northernmost part of Norway had to pay taxes to three different potentates – the Danish-Norwegian king, the Swedish king and the Russian tsar.[11]

Then the common area started shrinking, commencing with the Treaty of Teusina, when Sweden gave up its claim to the Kola Peninsula in return for Russia's promise to withdraw from the coastal areas of North Norway.[12] Then, as a result of Sweden's defeat in the Kalmar War (1611–1613), which by and large was about Sapmi, the Swedish king himself gave up his claim to the coastal areas of North Norway. When a general border regulation was carried through between Norway and Sweden in 1751, the Swedes had to retreat farther into the Finnmark plateau. Finally, after the Finnish War (1808–1809), Sweden gave up her taxation in the remaining part of the common districts. Now only a small strip of common Norwegian-Russian land remained in the Varanger area, comprising the Neiden (*Njauddâm*), Pasvik (*Paccjokk*) and Pechenga (*Peäccam*) siidas.

Yet in Denmark-Norway, this frontier zone continued to be a source of concern, since it was thought that it could easily drag Denmark-Norway into conflict with the Russian great power. It was all the more urgent for Norway to negotiate a boundary line that once and for all made clear where Russia ended and Norway started. We know that from the 1770s Danish-Norwegian authorities time and again turned to the Russian government with requests to open negotiations about a partition of what was left of the common district in the north. Russia, however, was not in a hurry and for several reasons preferred to wait.[13] Why was she so reluctant?

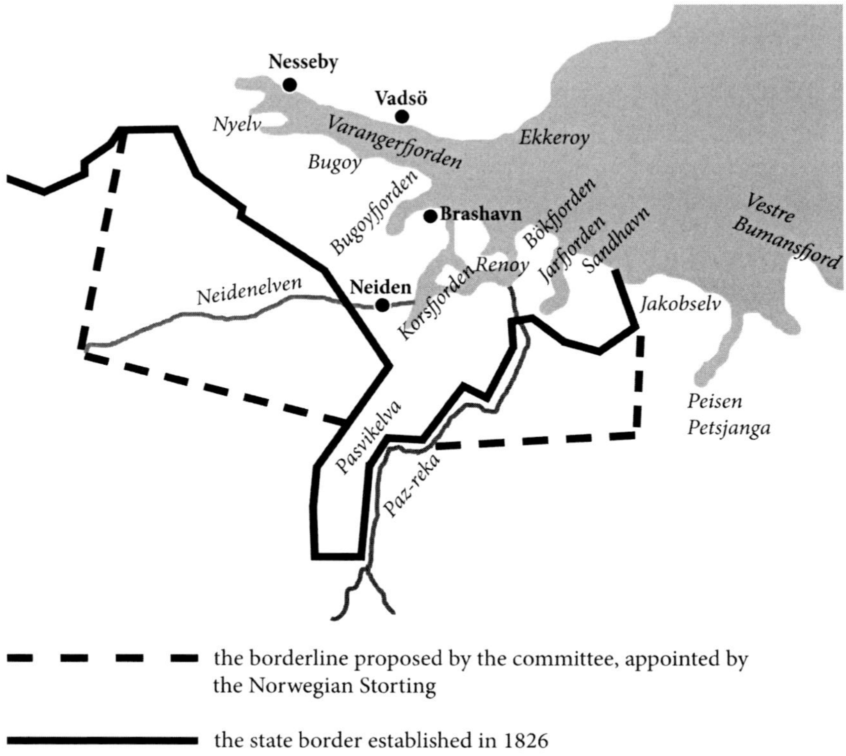

Map 3. *Norwegian-Russian state border established in 1826*

To explain this several factors should be taken into consideration, including national, regional, and local. Like other great empires in the past, Russia was not obsessed with delimiting precise boundaries in every direction. It is significant that by the time of Peter the Great's death in 1725 it was still unknown whether Russia was linked to the American continent or not. And in spite of the subsequent efforts of the great Russian polar expeditions of the eighteenth century exploring the northern coasts of Siberia, a considerable stretch of the northern coasts of the Chukotka Peninsula remained unexplored. It was only through Ferdinand von Wrangel's expedition in the early 1820s to the area east of Cape Shelagskiy that it was possible to establish beyond doubt that Eurasia was not connected with America by a land bridge.[14] It is thought-provoking that chronologically this expedition concurred with the Russian preparations for carrying out the border delimitation with Norway in the north-western corner of the Russian Empire.

RUSSIAN TERRITORIALITY

The vagueness of Russia's territorial extent has been related to an alleged weak sense of distances, borders and places in Russian culture.[15] In one of his odes to the Empress Elizaveta Petrovna, Peter the Great's daughter, poet and playwright Alexander Sumarokov eulogized her because she, through her laws, governed areas which stretched so far that their boundaries were not clearly discernible. Sumarokov was not alone: In the eighteenth century poets speaking in praise of the Russian empresses often mentioned the vastness of Russia's territories as the country's most peculiar feature.[16] Two hundred years later Nikolay Berdyayev developed this idea into a theory about a correspondence between the Russian soul and the Russian landscape, both being distinguished by unlimited space and boundlessness. In the West things are quite the reverse according to Berdyayev: here soul and landscape are more predisposed for orderliness and the development of civilisation.[17]

Generalisations like these doubtless belong to the realm of the unverifiable, and they are superfluous here, since they more or less coincide with the well-known dichotomy of a small budding nation-state, with a strong need for control of its territories and a vast multiethnic dynastically legitimated state with a greater tolerance of porous borders. The very asymmetry between the two countries dictated different attitudes towards the question of delimitation. The Russian great power could count on sheer gravitation to keep her territories together. She could wait, but to the small state the broad frontier zone was a constant source of concern. It was all the more important for Denmark-Norway to negotiate a boundary line that once and for all made clear where Russia ended and Norway started. From the end of the 18th century Danish-Norwegian authorities time and again had turned to Russia with requests to negotiate a partition of the remaining common district. The Russian government declared its readiness to comply, but always had an excuse for postponing the question.[18]

Towards the end of the Napoleonic Wars the signature of the treaty between Alexander I and Crown Prince Karl Johan of Sweden (March/April 1812), created an atmosphere wherein it became easier to find a solution to the Norwegian-Russian border issue. Alexander promised to support Karl Johan's claim that Norway be detached from Denmark and united with Sweden in return for Swedish participation in the struggle against Napoleon. Such a compensation for Sweden's loss of Finland was believed to secure fruitful and peaceful relations between Russia and Sweden in the future. After the formation of the Swedish-Norwegian union in 1814, Stockholm pursued the border question more energetically than Copenhagen had done, and the climate was becoming more favourable for real negotiations about the border in the North.

THE LOCAL LEVEL

Even if the diplomatic process was conducted from the capitals, the regional senior officials played an important part as premise providers. Pressure for border delimitation with Russia was exerted first and foremost from the governors and bailiffs of Finnmark, who contributed significantly to the formation of images of the northern borderland.[19] Given high responsibilities due to the long distances and primitive communications in the North, they were important middlemen between the capitals and local reality. From the middle of the 18th century they frequently warned that Finnmark could easily be overrun by Russia, and that it was of the utmost importance to establish good fences against this great power. Characteristic is the following warning about Russian economic penetration, which Governor Torkel Fieldsted sent to Copenhagen in 1775:

> [...] it has already gone so far that an active and industrious neighbour nation not only uses and possesses indispensable distances of land, that cunningly and high-handedly are as good as teared off from the kingdom of Norway, but even openly force themselves in among his Majesty's subjects, in his own hereditary and incontestable lands, where they with increasing wilfullness from year to year use as property his Majesty's territories, streams and amenities [...][20]

The Russian *chinovniki* (officials) of northwest Russia did not have a similar motivation for initiating a border delimitation with Norway. They rather warned against it. The Governor-General of Arkhangelsk Province in this period reported back to St. Petersburg that a demarcation vis-à-vis Norway was unnecessary, since according to their good judgement the whole common district belonged to Russia.[21] Allegedly, there was already a state border between the two countries, which more or less coincided with the western border of the Neiden siida, the westernmost of the common districts.[22] In 1825 Governor-General S. I. Minitsky succeeded in convincing Count Nesselrode, the Russian minister of foreign affairs, of the fairness of his position.[23] Soon it became clear, however, that the tsar looked differently on this issue.

Usually the central authorities are the part that exert pressure to establish state borders, while for the local communities it is sometimes felt that boundaries are barriers and exist only for the sake of political centres.[24] Boundary lines may ruin the already existing settlement system and disrupt regular social contacts or ethnical and religious ties. However, the Eastern Sami, or Skolts, the indigenous, Russian-Orthodox population of the Norwegian-Russian frontier zone, *did* want a border to be drawn between the two countries, because for a long time they had experienced that an increasing number of Norwegians from northern Varanger were using the natural resources of the common districts. Groups of Lutheran Varanger Sami were tending their reindeer herds on the territories of the common districts, leading their herds as far as Poluostrov Rybachiy. The Eastern Sami wanted to safeguard their old rights to the natural resources and bring an end to the escalating socio-economic integration with Norway.

From a Russian point of view the situation was worrying, since the number of Eastern Sami was decreasing while the number of Lutheran Sami and Norwegians active in the common district rose from year to year.[25] By 1825 in the summer months there were twice as many Norwegians and Lutheran Sami in the common districts as Russian-Orthodox Sami (around 300 as opposed to 150).[26] It was this conflict between the Eastern Sami on the one side and the Norwegians and Varanger Sami on the other that finally unleashed the border delimitation in 1825–1826. The Skolts probably thought they were gaining ground, but in the end Emperor Alexander I decided to disregard the opinion of the regional *chinovniki* concerning the border. He emphasized that what was to be divided was actually a *common* district, which belonged to two countries. Therefore it must be divided between those countries.[27] This was not what the Russian Sami had hoped for and they felt bitterly deceived.[28]

DELIMITATION OF THE COMMON DISTRICT

In the meantime Danish-Norwegian authorities had also lowered their ambitions with regard to what they could obtain. In 1789 the Danish-Norwegian king had declared that he was ready to give up his old claim to the "Northern Mountain", i.e. the Kola Peninsula, if Russia handed over the whole common district to him. In reality, though, the Kola Peninsula and the eastern part of the old common area were lost long ago for Norway and after 1814 the new Swedish-Norwegian position was based on the more realistic premise that the common districts should be divided fairly between Norway and Russia. Once Alexander I too had accepted this view, the two parts were ready for negotiations. In the summer of 1825 border commissaries were sent northwards; Norwegian colonel Johan Henrik Spørck and Russian lieutenant-colonel Valerjan Galyamin with assistants met in Kola town, and in a few weeks time they acquainted themselves with the topography of the border zone and agreed on a line of delimitation.

Different ways of thinking around the territorial questions in the North were reflected in the instructions that the two foreign ministers, Count Gustaf von Wetterstedt and Count Carl Nesselrode furnished their respective commissars with. Colonel Spørck received from Wetterstedt rather precise guidelines. His task was to establish a border and obtain as much as possible from the former common possessions.[29] Nesselrode gave Lieutenant-Colonel Galyamin only a list of general principles, one of them being that he should not abandon territory which was indisputably Russian, another that he should avoid solutions that could provoke new conflicts in the future.[30] He should pay attention to the border dwellers' traditional livelihood. During the negotiations with Spørck, Galyamin was indeed less preoccupied with gaining new territories for Russia than with protecting the traditional way of life of the indigenous Eastern Sami population.

The Pasvik River had in advance been designated as a border river by both contracting parties, but the standpoint of the Norwegian Storting was that from Lake Salmijärvi, which is an extension of the Pasvik River, halfway along the river course, the boundary should turn in a south-easterly direction to the Jakobselv River (Russ. *Vorjema*) and then follow this river until it emptied itself into the Arctic Ocean. The two rivers would then provide a clear-cut boundary line for most of the ca. 200 km of the projected state border. This was the first difficult question the commissars had to decide. Galyamin in the end agreed to the Norwegian desires, even if there were close to no Norwegians living in the area to the east of the Pasvik River. However, Spørck argued that the area was important for people in the Norwegian parishes of northern Varanger , who every summer gathered moss and firewood here. Without wood from the contested area the fortress of Vardøhus would probably have to discontinue its activity.[31]

THE DEVIATION OF THE BORDER AT BORISOGLEBSK

The second major issue was the fact that on the western bank of the Pasvik River, some 25 km north of Salmijärvi, a Russian-Orthodox chapel was situated, devoted to the martyrs Boris and Gleb and consecrated by the Holy Trifon, "the Apostle of the Sami" in the 16th century. Galyamin and the Russian Sami insisted that the chapel and a small area around it were holy to Russian-Orthodox believers and must therefore be ceded to Russia.[32] Spørck was sceptical of providing the Russians with such a bridgehead into Norwegian territory, but in the end he yielded in order to attain an agreement. Since the border would now deviate from the Pasvik River not at Salmijärvi but 25 km farther north, a much larger area was also lost to Russia on the eastern side of the river.

The population of the old common district, altogether 29 Eastern Sami families and 35 permanently residing Norwegian and Sea Sami Lutheran families could choose on which side of the border they wanted to live.[33] The Neiden siida, which had an Eastern Sami population and a tiny Russian-

Orthodox chapel, became Norwegian land. The population consisted of no more than a handful of Eastern Sami families. However, when in the summer of 1826 the new border was staked out on the ground, it was mistakenly drawn much too far to the north, due to which the southern half of the Neiden siida became Finnish territory. This mistake was discovered only many years later.[34]

Later the delineation suggested by Galyamin and Spørck was approved by both countries and ratified in May–July 1826. In the meantime Alexander I had quite unexpectedly died, and the new tsar, his younger brother Nicholas I, was dissatisfied with Galyamin and Spørck's report. He made it clear that the commissars should not have deviated from the course of the Pasvik River. However, he changed his mind after a while and decided to use this opportunity to assure King Karl Johan of his intention to continue his brother's conciliatory policy towards Sweden-Norway and give him "*un noveau gage de son amitié*" (a new pledge of his friendship).[35]

REACTIONS TO THE TREATY IN RUSSIA

Neither Alexander I nor Nicholas I were exactly obsessed with securing as much territory as possible from the Norwegian-Russian common area in the north and dissatisfaction with the border treaty was widespread in Russia; the Skolts were disappointed, as were Finnish authorities, since they had not been a part of the negotiations, even if the border undoubtedly affected Finland. Russian newpapers opened their columns to authors that set themselves on the task of making clear who was to blame for indulging the Norwegians in 1826. Galyamin was an obvious scapegoat.

Allegedly Galyamin was no different from other Russian public servants; he accepted bribes from his Norwegian colleagues. These rumours were based on the fact that after the border delimitations were carried out, he had received a beautiful box, set with diamonds, from the Norwegian state.[36] One version would have it that Galyamin in return for his cooperative attitude had received a whole sack of silver coins. When he opened the sack, however, he discovered that under a thin layer of silver coins there were only copper coins. He then realised that he had betrayed his fatherland and he stole away and hanged himself.[37]

The Galyamin myth fits neatly into a well-known pattern for Russian popular monarchism, which always excused and justified the behaviour of the tsar, but let the public servant or landowner take the blame.[38] The decision to oblige the Swedish-Norwegian desires was in fact taken in St. Petersburg and must be understood on the background of the Russian-Swedish cordiality established through the treaty of 1812. There is no reason to believe that

Galyamin did not follow his instructions, or that he deceived his principals. The criticism should rather be directed towards the two monarchs, Alexander I and later Nicholas I, who let themselves be persuaded to give up a considerable area east of the Pasvik River to Norway. North-Russian, and not the least Eastern Sami interests were apparently sacrificed to consolidate the Swedish-Russian friendship and thereby safeguard the new arrangements in Finland. However, in the Russian newspapers it could be convenient to camouflage disapproval of the tsar as a criticism of Galyamin's person. The conservative newspaper *Moskovskie Vedomosti* in 1892 in connection with mentioning the Norwegian-Russian border stated that Galyamin did not care for what was favourable for Russia, but only thought of "what Europe says".[39]

Here *Moskovskie Vedomosti* ascribed Galyamin statesmanlike reflections and responsibilities that a lieutenant-colonel and topographer would hardly have been in possession of. Of course, in this case, it was the tsar or the Russian government that cared about what "Europe said" and let themselves be dictated by overarching diplomatic considerations. The border treaty of 1826 was certainly a good treaty for Norway, so good, in fact, that during most of the 19th century there was considerable concern that Russia might claim back certain parts of the old common districts – or even more. Russia's restraint in 1826 was not appreciated at its true value, instead it became a prelude to misconceptions about Russian expansionism in the North: From the 1830s the idea became more and more widespread, that Russia needed ice-free harbours in North Norway in order to develop its own naval fleet. This became the geopolitical foundation for the idea about "a Russian menace" towards Norway.

SOFT BORDERS

Russophobia in the 19th century originated from European ideas about Asiatic or "non-European" otherness, connected with the need to create a picture of "the other", the non-European, so that the positive picture of the European could come forward all the more clearly. This was a part played by the Ottoman Empire for centuries in the European imagination. Now, after the Napoleonic Wars it was taken over by Russia. Russia became Europe's "second other".[40]

We can see that many Eastern European countries today are occupied with marking boundaries with Russia, as if they were emphasizing that they belong to Europe.[41] The same phenomenon was in evidence in Norway in the period that concerns us here. Claiming a European identity is and was a mode of defining a boundary between "us" and "them", i.e. those who are European and those who do not have the right to be European.[42]

Norway was the northernmost periphery of Europe and at the same time an advanced outpost towards Russia. And for the Norwegian elite Russian "barbarism" became a necessary back drop for the efforts to build the nation and raise Norway to a place between Europe's civilized nations.[43]

Thus the soft borders established vis-à-vis Russia by the Norwegian elite in the 19th century did not primarily spring from the Norwegians' encounter with Russia and the Russians in a northern landscape or from the establishment of the state border in 1826. The contacts that did take place in the North was between common people from both sides of the border – within the context of the so-called Pomor trade. The Pomor trade was a summer trade, basically Russian flour against Norwegian fish, and it was enormously popular in North-Norway. These relations between Norwegians and Russians in the north were indeed mostly friendly and un-political.[44]

Russophobia was rather one of the ideological impulses that washed over Norway from the south and west. It emanated from Britain and France[45] and found fertile soil in Norway. However, the particular form Russophobia obtained among the Norwegian elite was still geographically related to the northern scene. When talking about "the Russian menace" in connection with Norway in the 19th century, what we usually have in mind is the idea that Russia badly needed *an ice-free harbour* in North Norway, because Russia itself lacked ice-free harbours that gave access to the open sea. This meant that Russia's ability to develop as a naval nation in actual fact depended on a successful acquisition of one or several ice-free harbours on Norwegian territory.[46]

Due to the Gulf Stream there are ice-free waters along the coast of North Norway all the way to the Norwegian-Russian border, despite the high latitudes. On the Russian side, however, the Gulf Stream gradually looses its beneficial impact, and this was the oceanographical-meteorological frame of the idea that Russia wanted an ice-free harbour in North Norway, be it the Varanger Fjord, Hammerfest, Alta or later Narvik, further south in the county of Nordland.

Ever since the Norwegian-American historian Paul Knaplund in 1925 published his article on the diplomatic prelude to the so-called November Treaty of 1855, based on sources in Public Record Office, it has been customary to trace this idea back to the British environment in Norway in the 1830s.[47] Knaplund paid special attention to John Rice Crowe (1790–1874), a British merchant, mining entrepreneur and consul in Finnmark – from 1844 British consul-general in Christiania/Oslo – whom he proclaimed the "real father of the November Treaty". Crowe's reports to the Foreign Office between 1836–1855 about Russian plans to conquer ice-free ports in Finnmark made a real impression both in Stockholm and London. There is a direct line from them to British Prime Minister Henry Palmerston's decision to start negotiations about a great power guarantee to the United

Kingdoms of Sweden and Norway. Towards the end of the Crimean War, in November 1855, England and France signed a treaty with Sweden-Norway, where Swedish-Norwegian authorities undertook not to relinquish any part of their territories or any right to fishery or reindeer herding to Russia. No land was to be exchanged. In return the two great powers guaranteed Sweden-Norway's integrity.[48]

The idea of "the ice-free harbour", on which the November treaty rested, neatly mirrored what was at that time looked upon as the leitmotif of Russian history, the virtually instinctive drive of this inland power towards the oceans. Against this backdrop it was natural to interpret Russia's expansion in Central Asia as directed towards the Indian Ocean, and the advance in the Far East as an offensive to get a foothold on the Pacific. In the same way the conquest of Finland in 1808–1809 was seen as a step towards a firm grip of the Baltic Sea. However, the conquest of Finland could also be interpreted in a different direction, viz. as a step towards the Barents Sea.[49] When the Russians had proceeded as far as Torne River, a quick thrust against the coast of North Norway would give Russia free access to the Atlantic in one stroke. Or, as the Scottish traveller Samuel Laing put it, it would place Russia "at once at the head of the naval powers of Europe. It would give her innumerable harbours and fjords, open to the navigations of the Atlantic at all seasons".[50]

The "ice-free port" can also be understood symbolically. As a metaphor it has been connected with Russia's Europeanization since Peter the Great, reflecting Russia's old wish to "stand Firm-footed by the sea", as it goes in Pushkin's famous poem *The Bronze Horseman.* Without a port at the open sea Peter the Great could not fulfil his ambition: namely to turn Russia into a sea power and strengthen her ties with the west. To the early Slavophiles, however, Pushkin's contemporaries, the ice was not necessarily an obstacle, but an asset. Russia's harsh northern climate was an insurmountable barrier to invaders and influence from the West. It was as if the ice to the Slavophiles appeared as Russia's main safeguard against foreigners: ships did not even dare to approach her shores during half of the year. One of the Slavophiles wrote that Russia's borders were guarded by two *bogatyry* or Old-Russian heroes: The frost and the ice, who made sure that it was possible for the Russians to enjoy their harmonious social and spiritual life in peace.[51]

Finnmark was the only geographical area where Russia in the 19th century met Western Europe directly, without a buffer of Eastern or Central European borderlands in between. And it seems to us that the Russian symbolism around snow and ice also must have played a part in the construction of "the Russian menace" against North Norway – that the bend towards stylization of the Norwegian-Russian border that took place around the middle of the 19th century is somehow connected to this. On reading John Rice Crowe's reports to the Foreign Office, or European newspapers from the period around the Crimean War, one easily gets the impression that the border between Norway and Russia in the North was not only a state border, but a severe climatic border as well, with open waters and ice-free harbours on the Norwegian side and perpetual ice and snow on the eastern side.

The Swedish publisher and politician Gustaf Lallerstedt argues for this misconception in his book *Skandinavien, dess farhågor och förhoppningar* (Scandinavia – its fears and hopes) from the year 1856.[52] If it was hard to understand why the Russians were seeking to conquer territories in North Norway, wrote Lallerstedt, one needed only to compare the fjords in Finnmark with the Russian harbours on the eastern part of the Arctic Sea: "The latter are inaccessible due to the ice until the month of May which thereby makes any development of industries and navigation impossible". This was a widespread view in Norway as well. "It is rather strange", writes the Norwegian jurist and political writer Bernhard Dunker in a letter in January 1855, "that all Russian harbours on the Arctic Sea are covered by ice for as long as seven or eight months a year, whereas the coast of Norway is never covered by ice and abounds in excellent harbours".[53]

Dunker had even discussed the matter with the Russian consul-general in Christiania, Mr Alexander Chevkin, who, apparently, was equally amazed at the climatic conditions in the border area. He remarked that if the border marks were to be moved no more than 10 kilometres or so westwards, Russia would have an excellent harbour free of ice at all seasons. He laconically added, however, that if the Varanger Fjord really were to become Russian sometime in the future, the ice would follow suit and move westwards too.

In this way we can see that the contemporary discourse on the ice-free harbour led to a veritable glaciation of the Norwegian-Russian border. It became part of a politically constructed geography that sprang from the Russophobian delusions of the epoch. For it is a fact that the Russians did have access to ice-free harbours along their own territory in the North. The Norwegian linguist and ethnographer J. A. Friis, who in 1867 made an extensive journey on the Kola Peninsula and in Karelia, made the Norwegian public aware of this on his return. In a lengthy article in the newspaper *Morgenbladet* he pointed out that the Murman coast was in fact ice-free at all seasons, like the coasts of Finnmark.[54]

In other words, if the tsar wanted an ice-free harbour in the North, it was unnecessary to go to the expenses of conquering foreign territory. And it is a fact that until this day not a single historical document has been presented that can verify that Russian authorities actually had any plans of obtaining ice-free harbours on Norwegian territory. Plans for a naval base on the Murman coast, however, were put on the agenda in the 1890s by Russia's powerful minister of finance, Sergey Witte. But the first steps in this direction were first realised during the First World War with the construction of a railway from Central Russia to the Kola Bay (the Murmanstroyka) and the foundation of Romanov-na Murmane (Murmansk) in 1916. With this event most of the basis for the peculiar Norwegian fear of Russia evaporated. Paradoxically, it was only now, with the completion of the Murmanstroyka, and the stationing of a small Russian flotilla in the North that the "Russian menace" to Norway became embodied with a certain amount of realism since Russia would now for the first time be physically capable of undertaking an occupation of Norwegian territory in the North, if she really desired to do so.

However, typically enough, the news of the completion of the Murman railway was first and foremost received with relief in Norway, and many Norwegian observers interpreted it as the final proof that Russia did not plan to take possession of ice-free ports in Norway. With this harbour construction, Russia had shown that she had no intents in respect to Norway. When the decision to build the Murmanstroyka was taken the Norwegian military attaché in St. Petersburg wrote back to Christiania that this "seems to represent a solution which is exceptionally reassuring for Norwegian interests, of the question of an extension of the railway network in Northern Russia that provides a direct link to an ice-free port".[55]

The last tsarist envoy in Christiania, K. N. Gulkevich, did not spare any efforts to get this point across: The building of the Murman railway showed once and for all that Russia had no need for ice-free ports in North Norway. This view also won the day in the Norwegian newspapers. "The building of the Murman Railway", *Tidens Tegn* wrote on 31 January 1917, "has obviously occasioned maximum interest in Norway, where it should, quite correctly, be looked upon as a guarantee for Russia not entertaining any plans whatsoever of [acquiring] an ice-free port in our country".[56]

CONCLUSION

The idea that Russia planned to acquire an ice-free port in North Norway was born in the 1830s and can hardly in any way be connected causally to the border delimitation between Russia and Norway in 1826. During the negotiations in 1825–1826 Russian authorities exercised considerable restraint, and this was not a case of hard borders creating or boosting soft ones. "The ice-free harbour" came from without and seems too have originated from a British naval line of thought and the general European Russophobia of the epoch. On the other hand there can be no doubt that these "soft facts" influenced the perception of the state border, making it "harder" – even to such a degree that their geopolitical justification was reshaped; the Norwegian-Russian state border became a strict climatic border with open waters to the west and ice-covered coasts to the east.

Only very slowly did it dawn upon the Norwegian political elite that this was fallacious geography, that the border did not constitute a "natural" demarcation line topographically and climatically. Finnmark and Murman were of a piece. Like the fjords of Finnmark the bays in West Murman went deep into the country. They had "the character of the Norwegian fjords", as one Russian travel guide stated at the turn of the century, and they were indeed for the most part ice-free.[57] But even if the Murman coast was ice-free, there was still some uncertainty as to whether it was navigable in the winter due to fog and darkness. Only the completion of the Murman railway line in 1916, just a few months before tsarist Russia crumbled, seems to have convinced the Norwegian audience that Russia did not really need an ice-free port in Norway.[58]

REFERENCES

1 Frost (1874–1963) was an American poet.

2 Klaus Eder, Europe's Borders. The Narrative Construction of the Boundaries of Europe, European Journal of Social Theory 9/2 (2006), 255–271.

3 Eder, Europe's Borders, Loc. Cit. (Note 1), 256.

4 Not to be mistaken for present-day *Finnmark*, the northernmost county or 'fylke' of Norway.

5 Jouni Häkli, Borders in the political geography of knowledge, in: Lars-Folke Landgren/M. Häyrynen (eds.), The Dividing line: borders and national peripheries, Helsinki 1997, 12–13.

6 See Oscar Albert Johnsen, Finmarkens politiske historie, aktmæssing fremstillet, Skrifter utgitt av Det norske videnskapsakademi i Oslo, II, Hist. fil. klasse, Kristiania 1922.

7 Lars Ivar Hansen, Interaction between Northern European Sub-Arctic Societies during the Middle Ages. Indigenous Peoples, Peasants and State Builders, in: M. Rindal (ed.) Two Studies on the Middle Ages. KULTs Skriftserie, No. 66, Oslo 1996, 31–95.

8 Owen Lattimore, Studies in Frontier History. Collected Papers 1928–1958, London 1962, 534–535.

9 New research points in the direction that in 1326 also a single political border was established in the Varanger area, which was later forgotten. See Carsten Pape, "Three forgotten Border Treaties: Implications for Our Understanding of the Medieval Russian-Norwegian Frontier", in: Tatjana N. Jackson/Jens Petter Nielsen (eds.), Physical and Symbolic Borders, Languages of Slavonic Culture, Moscow 2005, 29–39.

10 Johnsen, Finmarkens politiske historie, Loc. Cit. (Note 5), 104.

11 See Lars Ivar Hansen, "Norwegian, Swedish and Russian 'tax lands' in the North", in press. Courtesy of the author.

12 Johnsen, Finmarkens politiske historie, Loc. Cit. (Note 5), 74.

13 Johnsen, Loc. Cit. (Note 5), 218–219; The Archive of the Foreign Policy of the Russian Empire (AVPRI) F.53/3. D.661, D.662.

14 M. I. Belov, Istoriya otkrytiya i osvoeniya Severnogo Morskogo Puti, Vol. 1, Moscow 1956, 504–509.

15 S. Medvedev, A General Theory of Russian Space: A Gay Science and a Rigorous Science, in: J. Smith (ed.) Beyond the Limits: The Concept of Space in Russian History and Culture. Suomen Historiallinen Seura, Helsinki 1999, 18.

16 See Vera Tolz, Russia. Inventing the Nation Series, London 2001, 159.

17 Nicholas Berdyayev, The Origin of Russian Communism, London 1937.

18 AVPRI F.53/3.D530, D661, D662.

19 Mari Ishizuka, Norwegian–Russian Borderland in Transition: Spatial Perception among Norwegian Elites in 1826–1852", in: Jackson/ Nielsen, Physical and Symbolic Borders, Loc. Cit. (Note 8), 95–96.

20 Promemoria from Governor Torkel Fieldsted of 06.05.1775 to The Danish Chancellery. Prebensen's collection of transcripts. The Norwegian National Archives (RA), UD box 5405.

21 The State Archive of Arkhangelsk Province (GAAO), F.4, Op.4, D.3.

22 GAAO F. 1367. Op.1, D.87.

23 AVPRI F.1 Adm.Dela II–6, Chast I.

24 See E. Berg/O. Saima, Writing post-Soviet Estonia on to the world map, in: Political Geography 19 (2000), 611.

25 GAAO F.1367 Op.1, D.87.

26 55 families versus 29. Prebensen's collection of transcripts, RA/UD 3C/18 box 5213; AVPRI, F.1, Adm. Dela II–6, Chast I; GAAO F.4, Op.3, D.642.

27 AVPRI: F.1, Adm. Dela II–6, Chast I.

28 In July 1829 the Norwegian tax collector J. H. Cappelen inspected the former common districts. Some Eastern Sami told him that they refused to believe that a state border had been drawn through their territories. They were convinced that the work of the commissars in 1825–1826 was a private deal between these commissars and the Norwegian tradesman Esbensen in Vadsø. They assure Cappelen that the Russian tsar had already learned about this deal and soon would give the Skolts their territories back. J. H. Cappelen to the Governor of Finnmark 27.11.1829. RA/UD 13/18, box 5214.

29 Johnsen, Loc. Cit. (Note 5), 242–243; Prebensen's collection of transcripts, RA/UD 3C/18, box 5213.

30 AVPRI: F.1, Adm. Dela II–6, Chast I; C. F. Palmstierne, Sverige, Ryssland och England 1833–1855. Kring Novembertraktatens förutsättningar, P. Norstedt & Søner, Stockholm 1932, 232.

31 RA/UD, P10, Pakke 2/5212.

32 The Russian State Military Historical Archive (RGVIA): F.442, Op.1, D.26; AVPRI: F.1, Adm. Dela II–6, Chast I; Johnsen, Loc. Cit. (Note 5), 244; Palmstierne, Loc. Cit. (Note 29), 232.

33 Johnsen, Finmarkens politiske historie, Loc. Cit. (Note 5), 242–243.

34 Steinar Wikan, Grensebygda Neiden: møte mellom folkegrupper og kampen om ressursene, Kirkenes 1995, 58–65; The explanation for this mistake could be that on the old Norwegian and Swedish maps used by the commissars the border of Neiden siida was situated too far to the north, See AVPRI:F.1, Adm. Dela II-6, Chast I.

35 See Palmstierna, Sverige, Ryssland och England, Loc. Cit. (Note 29), 234–235.

36 RGVIA F38, Op.1, D62.

37 Johnsen, Finmarkens politiske historie, Loc. Cit. (Note 5), 252: See also J. A. Friis, En Sommer i Finmarken, Russisk Lapland og Nordkarelen, Kristiania 1871, 109–110.

38 Perrie, Maureen, "Popular monarchism: the myth of the ruler from Ivan the Terrible to Stalin", in: G. Hosking/R. Service (eds.), Reinterpreting Russia, Arnold, London – Sidney – Auckland 1999, 156–169.

39 *Moskovskie vedomosti* 24.11.1892.

40 See Iver B. Neumann, Uses of the Other. "The East" in European Identity Formation, Minneapolis 1999.

41 See Berg/Saima, Writing Post-Soviet Estonia, Loc. Cit. (Note 23), 615.

42 Eder, Europe's borders, Loc. Cit. (Note 1), 255–271.

43 See Jens Petter Nielsen, Norwegian Images of Russia and the Russians, in: Rossija I Zapad: Istoricheskiy opyt XIX–XX vekov, Russian Academy of Sciences, Institute of universal history, Moskva 2008, 241–246.

44 Idem, The Barents Euro-Arctic Region – the Return of history? in: Maria Lähteenmäki (ed.), The Flexible Frontier: Change and Continuity in Finnish-Russian Relations, Aleksanteri Series 5, Helsinki 2007, 231–244.

45 See Bruno Naarden, Socialist Europe and Revolutionary Russia: Perception and Prejudice, Cambridge 1992; Dieter Groh, Russland und das Selbstverständnis Europas: Ein Beitrag zur europäischen Geistesgeschichte, Neuwied 1973.

46 Jens Petter Nielsen, The Russia of the Tsar and North Norway. "The Russian Danger' Revisited", Acta Borealia 2 (2002), 75–94.

47 Paul Knaplund, Nye Oplysninger om Novembertraktatens Forhistorie, Historisk Tidsskrift, Oslo (1925).

48 Jens Petter Nielsen, "Novembertraktaten (1855–1907) – Norges første stormaktsgaranti", in: R. Berg (ed.), Selvstendig og beskyttet. Det stormaktsgaranterte Norge fra Krimkrigen til NATO, Fagbokforlaget, Bergen 2008, 19–32: idem, "Russkaya ugroza" na severe Evropy i Noyabrskij dogovor 1855 goda, Rossiyskaya istoriya 3 (2009), 84–89.

49 Sven Eriksson, Svensk diplomati och tidningspress under Krimkriget, Stockholm 1939.

50 S. Laing, Journal of a residence in Norway, during the Years 1834, 1835 and 1836, Longman, London 1937.

51 Otto Boele, The North in Russian romantic Literature, Studies in Slavic literature and poetics, Vol. 26, Rodop, Amsterdam 1996, 4.

52 G. Lallerstedt, Skandinavien, dess farhågor och förhoppningar, Stockholm 1856.

53 Lallerstedt, Skandinavien, Loc. Cit. (Note 51), 6–7.

54 J. A. Friis elaborates on this question in En sommer i Finmarken, Loc. Cit. (Note 36), 226–233; it is indeed here that the Russian northern fleet today has its bases.

55 Military attaché Carl Rustad to the Norwegian Ministry of Foreign Affairs 26.02.1915, RA/UD P5, B1/11.

56 Tidens Tegn 31.01.1917.

57 D. N. Ostrovskiy, Putevoditel po Severu Rossii, St. Petersburg 1899, 93.

58 The idea lived on in the Western world for quite some time, however. During a conversation with the Norwegian foreign minister Trygve Lie in the White House in March 1943, President Roosevelt told him that Russia needed ice-free harbours in North Norway, and that Norway should offer Stalin one or two such harbours, which could be organized as free ports under the United Nations. See Olav Riste, An Idea and a Myth. Roosevelt's Free Ports Scheme for North Norway, Americana Norvegica, Oslo 1973, 379–397.

On the Borderland of East and West – the Karelia-case

KIMMO KATAJALA

FROM CONFLICT TO COOPERATION: PARADIGM CHANGES IN FINNISH RESEARCH INTO THE HISTORY OF KARELIA AND THE EASTERN BORDER

It is a cliché to say that every era writes its own history, but seldom do we stop and think what it really means. Why is history interpreted and written differently at different times? What makes the paradigms and chosen topics in historical research change? Is it an autonomous development in science or are the changes a result of developments in society or politics? Are the changes a result of intentional choices made by researchers, or is the change of paradigm somehow a self-directed process? The main aim of this article is to consider what lies behind changes in topics and paradigms in the field of historical research and writing.

About twenty years ago, two young Finnish historians, Pekka Ahtiainen and Jukka Tervonen, published an article on how historical research mirrors its own time. At one point they wrote "Historical research is, as is often said, a dialogue between the past and present, partly even with a supposed future. It is also a dialogue between historians and the society around them."[1] The focus in that article was on how the Finnish national awakening, the Civil War of 1918 and the result of World War II had affected the political, social, cultural and economic approaches to Finnish historical research in general. Although the main idea of this paper is the same, my approach is a somewhat more concrete one, the materials studied are classified differently and the analysis is limited to Finnish historical research concerned with Karelia and the eastern border of Finland during the 20th century.

Karelia is a territory which was a borderland between the medieval and early modern realms of Russia and Sweden and then between the modern states of the Soviet Union/Russia and Finland. The material collected for this paper, i.e. bibliographical data concerning the literature on the history of Karelia and the eastern border, was organized first according to the periods showing the most visible changes in the nature of this material.[2] Then the source material was organized inside these periods according to the main topics and groups of publications. The changes found in the topics are described and explained in their historical context.

The main source of data on published research and writings on Karelia is the Finnish Historical Bibliography, published in eight volumes since 1940 and covering the years 1554–1990. Source material was collected from this bibliography systematically from the year 1901 up to 1990, after which the bibliography was no longer published in book form but was combined with the Finnish National Library's electronic ARTO database. The last ten years were therefore covered by the searching the ARTO database and the corresponding LINDA database covering all the Finnish university libraries with the keywords "Karelia" and "border" (in Finnish *Karjala* and *raja*). Although the result of such a data search cannot be exactly equivalent to data collected from printed bibliographies, it is the best available. As the source material will not be studied quantitatively, the change in the nature of the primary sources will not substantially affect the reliability of the analysis. The total number of the titles analysed is about 1400.

The material consists not only works by professional historians, but also of writings by archaeologists, linguists, ethnologists, theologians and others who have been interested in Karelian history, in addition to which Karelia and Karelian history have been beloved topics of many amateur historians whose works cannot be distinguished from the others in the material. Short popular writings in magazines have been left out as have histories of local schools, societies etc. On the other hand, there are a very large number of writings on Karelian history that have been published in small journals devoted to the "Karelian issue".

Because of the great mass of titles analysed, only the most important and influential research papers, books and publications can be mentioned by name even in the footnotes. Thus this article should by no means be understood as a sublime bibliographical presentation of the historical literature on Karelia. Before going into the analysis, it is necessary, however, to give the reader a brief outline of the history of Karelia and the eastern border of Finland, as this constitutes the basis for the classification of the primary material.

THE HISTORY OF KARELIA IN A NUTSHELL

The story of Karelia is usually begun from the 14th century, when the powers of Sweden and Novgorod were competing over the region and Karelia was for the first time divided between the eastern and western powers in an agreement reached in 1323.[3] People had lived in the area before this first eastern border of Finland – as the list of border markers in the act is often called – came into being, of course, from about 5000 BC at least, and a rich culture flourished on the shores of Lake Ladoga and on the Karelian Isthmus during the Iron Age and the Viking Age ca. 800–1000 AD. In the 13th century the Swedes had founded a small castle on an island in a bay of the Gulf of Finland, and in time the merchant town of Vyborg grew up around this castle. Almost simultaneously, Novgorod had founded the castle of Nöteborg on an island at the mouth of the River Neva in Lake Ladoga.

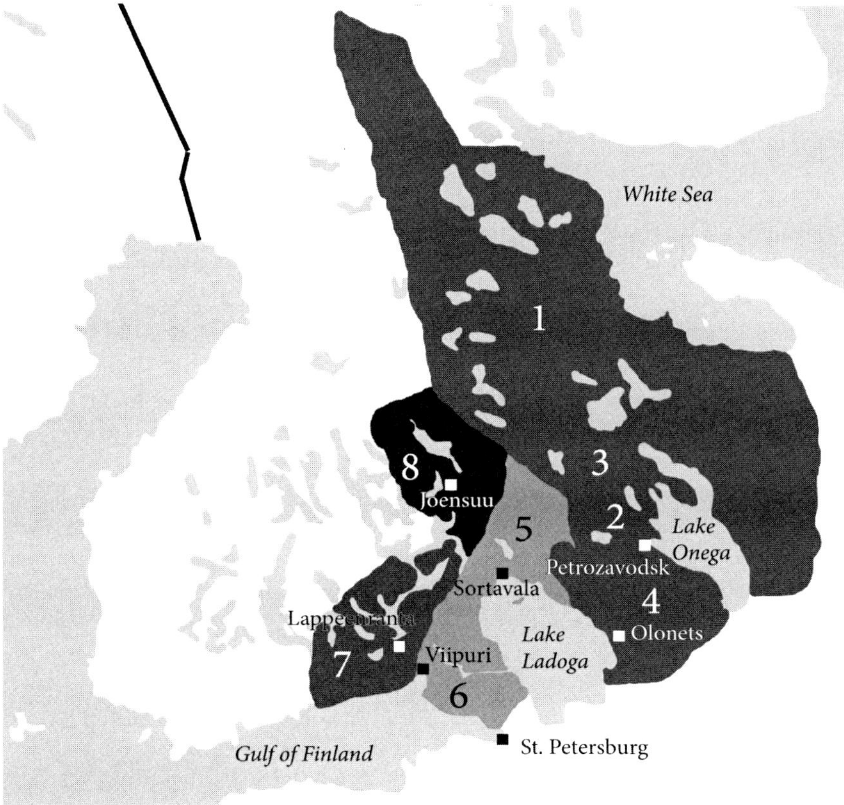

1. White Sea Karelia
2. Onega Karelia
3. "East Karelia"
4. Olonets Karelia
5. Ceded Karelia
6. Karelian Isthmus
7. South Karelia
8. North Karelia

Map 4. *Main regions and towns of Karelia*

After the first division of Karelia, the region became a battlefield on which continuous border disputes took place in the 16th century. Eventually, as a result of the 25-Year War of 1570–1595, a new border between Sweden and Russia was marked out in the terrain. Peace did not last long, however, and after some warfare and bitter resistance from the local people, the Karelians, even more land was ceded to Sweden in a new peace pact in 1617. Now Sweden gained control over the core lands of Karelia, province of Kexholm. When the town of Kexholm (Finn. Käkisalmi, presentday name is Russ. Priozersk) became the governmental centre of the Karelian region the Russians built a new citadel and town of Olonets to be the new centre of Russian Karelia.

Following the Great Northern War, which began in 1700, yet another new border was agreed upon. This time the Swedes had to cede the whole the Karelian Isthmus and the Ladoga area to Russia under the Treaty of Uusikaupunki (*Nystad*) in 1721. The part of Karelia left to Sweden was approximately the territory that forms the present day county of North Karelia in Finland. The Russians begun to call the part of Karelia annexed to their Empire "Old Finland". In a further peace treaty signed in Turku in 1743, after the War of the Hats the border was moved westwards again, and the territories up to the Kymi River and around the town and castle of Savonlinna were ceded to the Russian Empire and became a part of Old Finland. The Russian nobility were given many fiefs in the area of Old Finland, and this caused countless skirmishes between the Finnish and Karelian peasants of the region and their new landlords.

As a result of the Napoleonic Wars, Finland was ceded to the Russian Empire as an autonomous Grand Duchy in 1809, whereupon the territories of Old Finland that had been lost to Russia in the 18th century were united with the Grand Duchy in 1812. This meant that Finland's eastern border was now the same as in 1617 and a large part of Karelia again lay in Finnish territory. The national Finnish awakening held the language in high regard as the main element uniting the kindred nations within a single "family", and new kindred nations were found in the form of the Estonians, Hungarians and certain indigenous peoples living in the area of the Ural Mountains.

The nearest kindred nation speaking a Finnic language, of course, was the Karelians, although they professed the Orthodox faith and had a culture of their own that owed much to that of northern Russia. Karelia first aroused interest among linguists and collectors of folklore, and then artists – painters, poets and men of letters – became inspired by the region and its culture. A large proportion of the poems belonging to the Finnish national epic, the *Kalevala*, were collected from Karelia, and this led to the region being looked on as the original home of the Finnish culture, or some kind of refugium where it had remained almost untouched. This interest in, and even enthusiasm for, Karelian culture from the middle of the 19th century onwards is often referred to as Karelianism. Later, at the end of the century, Karelianism was transformed into a political programme, an idea that the Karelian people, as the nearest kindred nation to the Finns, and the territory where they lived – Karelia – should be united with Finland. This "Greater Finland" ideology was widespread among Finnish intellectuals and civil servants during the first half of the 20th century.

Finland gained its independence in 1917, largely as a result of the Bolshevik Revolution in Russia, but after a bloody Finnish Civil War in 1918 many those who had been on the side of the defeated party, the socialist

"Reds", escaped to Russian Karelia. The first years of independence were therefore marked by a series of Kinship Wars (1918–1922) in which voluntary troops from Finland made forays into the adjacent areas of Russian Karelia and tried to annex them to Finland. Eventually, however, thanks to the Treaty of Tartu, signed in 1920, the border of 1617 and 1812 with slight revisions was accepted as that between Finland and Soviet Russia. For the next two decades the Finns tried to unify the parts of Karelia closest to the border on the Finnish side culturally, linguistically, religiously and economically with the core territory of Finland. On the other hand, Karelia and a Karelian identity were presented and evaluated as something exotic and very special. Similarly, the Soviet Republic of Karelia was founded on the Russian side, and soon the Finnish Reds who had escaped to Russia gained leading positions in the politics of that republic, possession status that they maintained up until Stalin's purges in the 1930s, when they were replaced by Russians.

Finnish participation in World War II was almost totally enacted in Karelia, in the course of the Winter War (1939–1940) and the Continuation War (1941–1944). During the latter the Finns conquered large parts of Russian Karelia as far east as the Lake Onega region. The occupation lasted until 1944, when the Finns were forced to make a rapid retreat. The truce concluded in Moscow 1944 defined a new border that gave most of the Karelian territory to Russia, leaving only the counties of North Karelia and South Karelia on the Finnish side.

The agreement on the new border resulted in 420.000 Finns and Karelians being evacuated to various towns and villages all over Finland from the Karelian territories annexed to Russia. Since that time a powerful movement to restore the lost part of Karelia to Finland has existed among the evacuated Finns and Karelians. Meanwhile, the deserted ceded areas were occupied by people coming from very different and often distant places in the Soviet Union. The northern parts of these territories were incorporated into the Soviet Karelian Republic, and the southern parts (the Karelian Isthmus and the town of Vyborg) came under the Leningrad Oblast. After the collapse of the Soviet Union it has become easier for people and goods to cross the border between Russia and Finland. Nowadays the Karelian Isthmus is almost a suburb of the metropolis of St. Petersburg, but the areas ceded to the Karelian Republic have remained rather poor and development has been very slow, especially in the countryside. Consequently, the border between Finnish North Karelia and the Russian Karelian Republic is marked by one of the greatest differences in living standards between its two sides to be found anywhere in the world.

PROJECTION OF AN EXOTIC KARELIA (1901–1917)

Although political Karelianism was an inseparable part of Finnish nationalism, Karelia was not a very well known region in Finland, and there was a great need for information about it. Roughly speaking, there were three books published in the 1910s that provided a basic knowledge of Karelia. Iivo Härkönen, a journalist and enthusiastic Karelianist, published a large anthology entitled "The Book of Karelia" in two volumes in 1910.[4] This contained over 30 articles on the terrain, people and culture of Karelia, including linguistic questions, mostly written by trained university teachers, professors or other specialists. Despite its Finnish nationalistic undertones, the Book of Karelia served as the best possible contemporary survey of Karelia and its history for a wide audience and it became very popular. When a new, enlarged and totally revised edition in one volume of over a thousand pages was published in 1932, the book had already become a classic work in the field of Karelian studies.

If Iivo Härkönen with his Book of Karelia gave the Finns an outline of Karelian history and culture, the photographer I. K. Inha presented its exotic aspects in his photographs and writings based on his journeys around Karelia in the book "From the Singing Land of the Kalevala" in 1911.[5] This book connected Karelia directly with the Finnish national epic, the *Kalevala*, and represented Karelia and the Karelian people as bearers of the original Finnish culture. Perhaps the most influential book of the early 20th century for historians, however, was Väinö Voionmaa's[6] "History of the Finnish Karelian Tribe" (1915).[7] This represented real research, being based on analyses of original sources, mostly without any nationalistic tones. Posterity will remember this book for its analysis of the Karelian extended families, which has been adopted even by some present-day scholars.[8] Yrjö Blomstedt[9] and Victor Suckdorff had already published a book on Karelian architecture and decoration in 1901, which was published also in German language in 1902. Together with this now largely forgotten work, the three aforementioned books provided people with a basic knowledge of Karelian history, culture and life.

One more publication from the beginning of the 20th century which has greatly influenced the later research into Karelian history must also be mentioned. Around the year 1500, scribers from the Principality of Novgorod who had travelled around Karelia compiled a "Tax book of the Votian Fifth", which survived and was published as a historical document by J. V. Ronimus in 1906. In the same year Ronimus also published his doctoral dissertation on this tax book and settlement in Karelia around the year 1500.[10] The work of Ronimus has been widely discussed among historians[11], and is usually used as a basis for the research into early settlement in the Karelian region.

The original idea had been that the tax book of the Votian Fifth should be published by the Historical Society of North Karelia, founded in 1905 in the town of Joensuu, where Ronimus worked as a college lecturer in history, but Ronimus himself chose to take his book to a more authoritative publisher, the Finnish Historical Society (founded 1875). The active approach of the young local historical society can nevertheless be seen in the great number of historical articles published about North Karelia, accounting, in fact, for the majority of publications about Karelian history during the period 1901–1917. The topics were often concerned with older periods in history, especially the 17th[12] and 18th[13] centuries, and they display a clear trend towards the established use of North Karelia as a regional concept.

Another Karelian region which was noted in publications by historians that centred on the town of Vyborg, in effect the whole of the Karelian Isthmus. The articles about the history of this region, referred to earlier as Old Finland, are fairly neutral in their attitudes towards the Karelian question, the border and Russia, as they concentrate on topics such as the history of agriculture, forestry and the church.[14] It is only in one paper about changes in land ownership that some anti-Russian undertones can be detected. The Russians had bought a great deal of land in the parishes nearest to the border during the 19th century in order to build summer residences there, and this development was looked upon rather critically by Erkki Paavolainen.[15] The White Sea area of Karelia (Finn. *Vienan Karjala)* and Olonets (Finn. *Aunus*), often referred to jointly in Finnish literature as East Karelia, did not attract any special attention from Finnish historians until the first decades of Finnish independence, when, in addition to some short articles, the region was spoken about in the Book of Karelia and the book by I. K. Inha.[16] All this was to change suddenly after 1917, however.

HISTORIANS BUILDING BORDERS (1918–1938)

After Finland had gained its independence, borders became a popular topic of research for Finnish historians. The young state had to define its borders physically and also in the minds of the people and the collective memory of the nation. The task of finding justifications and roots for the national borders was clearly something for historians, and especially important in an ideological sense was the work of Professor Jalmari Jaakkola[17] on the oldest "power borders" of Finland (1923), in which he dated the earliest process of defining the eastern border, that with Russia, to the 12th century.[18] Jaakkola also presented his interpretation of the border defined in the Treaty of Nöteborg in 1323, as being a line running across the inland areas of Finland from the end of the Gulf of Finland to the coast of the Gulf of Bothnia. Although even contemporary historians put forward dissenting views,[19] to say nothing of post-war researchers, Jaakkola's view regarding the border of 1323 has been so authoritative that it still dominates the picture presented in school textbooks and held by the general public opinion even today.

All the main changes in Finland's eastern border have been studied separately at some time or other. The two-volume work of Werner Tawaststjerna (1918–1920, 1926) on the 25-Year War of 1570–1595 gave a detailed description of the procedure by which the border between Sweden and Russia was defined according to the Treaty of Teusina (1595),[20] while Erkki K. Osmonsalo[21] specialized in his work in questions concerning the border of the autonomous Grand Duchy of Finland following the Treaty of Hamina (Sw. *Fredrikshamn*) in 1809.[22] Perhaps the most important research on borders for the young independent state of Finland, however, was contained in the book by Arvi Korhonen[23] entitled "The Birth of the Finnish Eastern Border" (1938).[24] This book published just before the Winter War broke out in 1939 made a careful analysis of the process of defining the border that took place after the Treaty of Stolbov in 1617. This border remained stable for 100 years, until the 18th century, when it was changed several times. The autonomous Grand Duchy of Finland in the 19th century nevertheless regained the territory's 17th-century border with Russia, this was also confirmed as the border between the independent state of Finland and Soviet Russia in the Treaty of Tartu (1920).

It was therefore necessary for the Finns to justify the border of 1617 as the rightful boundary of Finland in the 1920s and 1930s. It should be noted that Korhonen's book was not published in a forum regularly used by professional historians but by the Department of Military History at the headquarters of the Finnish Army, where Korhonen was deputy director at that time. Although all these border studies written in the 1920s and 1930s had somewhat nationalistic undertones, they were well documented and based on an extensive body of source material. Arvi Korhonen in particular was able to use Russian documents alongside Swedish material and his work is still unequalled as research into this topic.

Very soon after the Kinship Wars of 1918–1922 papers began to be published about these Finnish military expeditions into Karelia, but again the authors were not historians but mostly military officers. Likewise, the publications cannot be regarded as research but more as memoirs or nationalistic, glamorized accounts related to this topic.[25] East Karelia, the regions of Olonets and White Sea Karelia in the north, and the living conditions of the Karelian people there were discussed in many articles and publications,[26] and when a group of professional and amateur historians published a book "On the History of Karelia" in 1938,[27] all but one of the eleven papers in it dealt with the history of East Karelia.

Articles by amateur historians on the history and culture of East Karelia were published especially in the journal *Toukomies* (the Plougher) published from 1925 onwards by the Karelian Educational Society (*Karjalan Sivistysseura*), an organization founded by Karelian traders who had settled in Finland after the Soviet Revolution of 1917. Between the years 1935–1944 the journal had the dual name *Toukomies* and *Viena-Aunus* at first, but during the war period it was known only as *Viena-Aunus*, referring directly to East Karelia and the idea of Greater Finland, which was conceived of as including East Karelia. Practically none of the authors of these articles about East Karelia were professional historians, but rather they tended to be army officers, civil servants, directors, journalists and student activists. The aforementioned Iivo Härkönen was a particularly industrious contributor to these journals.[28] Some of these publications were produced in German or English to draw international attention to the efforts of the Karelians and Finns in Karelia.

One topic that was particularly visible in publications about Karelian history was the history of Old Finland, the territories of the Karelian Isthmus and the Lake Ladoga region which Sweden lost to Russia during the 18th century and which were annexed to the autonomous Grand Duchy of Finland in 1812. Since the history of Old Finland was not a much discussed topic in historical writings before Finnish independence, one may ask what made it so relevant in the first few years of independence. During the 18th century the Russian Tsar had given his supporters fiefs in Old Finland, as he had in other parts of the Russian Empire. The Finnish peasants in the region and their Russian masters nevertheless had divergent opinions about the rights of landlords over their tenants, lands and the peasants' obligations to perform day labour for the manors. This caused many bitter conflicts and skirmishes, and stories, both true and false, about the cruelty of the Russian landowners spread all over Finland. The uneasy relations in the region continued during the 19th century until the time when serfdom was abolished in Russia in the 1860s, whereupon the autonomous government of Finland bought out the Russian fief holders of Old Finland in the 1870s.

Old Finland thus became a very suitable tool by which nationalistic Finnish historical writers could emphasize the Finns' struggle for freedom, underline the role of the Finnish autonomous state in solving the land ownership problem in Old Finland and describe the cruelty of the Russian nobility and landlords. Old Finland was used as a tool in nationalistic propaganda directed against Soviet Russia and the Russians in general. It must be emphasized that such a propagandistic or "Russophobic" view is not visible in all these writings, but the motivation to carry out research in this region and on this topic was clearly grounded in a nationalistic viewpoint.[29] Old Finland had to be "Finlandized" again after two hundred years of Russian influence.

In 1894, well before Finnish independence, J. R. Danielson-Kalmari[30] published his work on the annexing of Old Finland to the Grand Duchy of Finland in 1811–1812.[31] As an active "Fennoman" participant in politics, Danielson-Kalmari was well aware of the Old Finland issue, and the topic formed an important part of his published work as a historian. In the early 1930s he published a book in four volumes entitled "On the Road to Independence as a State and a Nation", the third volume of which was devoted to the question of Old Finland. The name Danielson-Kalmari chose for this volume, "The Battle between East and West in Karelia"[32] describes well the years that were to come, in terms of both Finnish-Soviet politics and Finnish historiography.

CROSSING THE BORDER WITH AN ARMY (1939–1944)

One would expect the publishing of historical writings and essays to have practically come to a halt during the war, but this was not the case, especially where the history of Karelia and its borders was concerned. Of course many of the wartime publications served a propagandistic purpose and were written by non-professional historians, but even so there seems to have been an almost continuous flow of publications considering the Karelian issue from many angles during the occupation of Karelia, especially in the years of the Continuation War.[33]

During the Finnish occupation, archaeologists, linguists, ethnologists and specialists in architecture had an opportunity to collect material from the occupied areas for their studies. After a two decades isolation, Karelia was again open to Finnish researchers as a location for fieldwork. Karelian place names and family names were a common topic for linguists, and not only during the war but for a long time afterwards.[34] The aim during the war period was to demonstrate the old historical relations between the two kindred peoples, the Karelians and the Finns, whereas after the war this aim was not so prominent in Finnish studies of Karelian toponyms. The outstanding name among the linguists who published studies on Karelian toponyms would without doubt be Viljo Nissilä[35], who worked on this topic from 1937 up to the 1970s, while Lars Pettersson[36], who collected the main material for his scientific work during the occupation period, became famous after the war as an expert on the Karelian material culture, especially architecture.[37]

Another linguist, J. J. Mikkola had published many essays and articles about Karelian history before the war, and these were collected into an anthology, under the title "From the Ages of Darkness and Dawn" in 1939. Then, during the Continuation War, he published another anthology, in 1942: "On the Border Between East and West. Historical essays".[38] Most of the essays in these two collections considered Karelian history or Finnish-Russian relations at some level or other. As a Slavicist, Mikkola was able to read source material in Russian, and where the former book concentrated mostly on interesting details, Karelian personalities and Finnish-Russian relations, many of the topics of the essays in the latter were chosen to show the cruelty and unreliability of the Russians and therefore fitted well with the needs of Finnish wartime propaganda.

Professional historians published only a few articles about Karelian history during the Winter War of 1939–1940,[39] but immediately following the beginning of the Continuation War and the offensive mounted by the Finnish army in Karelia at the end of June 1941 we find that all the best brains were recruited to explain the Karelian issue. The fourth issue of the main historical quarterly in Finland (*Historiallinen Aikakauskirja*) in 1941 was devoted almost entirely to Karelian history, the authors being professors of history or leading researchers who took up professorships soon after the war. The message of these papers was, sometimes openly and at other times somewhat concealed, that Karelia was originally part of the west and that the Karelians are closely related to the Finns. In addition, all the book reviews in that issue are about Karelian history or Finnish military history.[40] The later wartime issues of the journal contained just occasional articles about Karelian issues, and it seems that the most urgent need to propagate Karelian matters passed over very soon. The only notable article was one by Pentti Renvall[41] on the fate of the Finns in Soviet Karelia at the beginning of Stalin's purges in 1935.[42]

The Finnish historians were fairly active writers outside their professional journals as well, however, and immediately after the Winter War Professor Jalmari Jaakkola wrote a short essay on the "outlines of the history of Finland"[43] in which he underlined the interpretation of Finland as an outpost of western civilization. This was perhaps not a new idea, but it now came to be the main doctrine for Finnish historical research into borders and Karelian issue for the war period and long after that. Soon after his "Outlines" and just before the outbreak of the Continuation War, Jaakkola finished his book on "The Finnish eastern question".[44] These two books, translated into several European languages, were intended to inform the Germans of the Finnish territorial goals in Karelia and to explain the Finnish aggression in Russia to the western Allies.[45] A rather similar message was conveyed by the book by Professor Einar W. Juva[46] on Finland's fight against the east.[47]

If Finland was presented as an outpost of the western culture, then the small book by the anthropologist Yrjö von Grönhagen, published in Germany in Dresden, depicted Karelia as a Finnish palisade against the east.[48] There seems to have been some kind of division of labour with regard to publishing in foreign languages, in that the Finnish-speaking historians – amateurs and professionals – seem to have published their wartime works first in German and a little later in English and French while the Swedish-speaking Finnish scholars published in Swedish and aimed to convince the Scandinavian countries about the Finns' mission to protect the western civilization against the Bolshevik and Russian threat and about Karelia as an essential part of the Finnish territory.[49]

The wartime publication that is usually remembered best – perhaps because of its name – is the book put together very quickly on the orders of the Finnish government by the historian Eino Jutikkala[50], the geographer Väinö Auer[51] and the ethnologist Kustaa Vilkuna[52] during the first months of the Continuation War in 1941. Its purpose was to prove that Karelia was historically, geographically and culturally an organic and natural part of Finland. The text of the book was reworked by Yrjö von Grönhagen, who was then serving as the representative of the Finnish army information office in Berlin, to suit the tastes of the German Nazi government better, and the original title *Das Geographische und Geschichtliche Finnland* was changed at the request of the German publisher to the rather Nazi-sounding *Finnlands lebensraum*. The main author of the book, Eino Jutikkala, asked the Finnish censorship authorities to forbid its publication in Finland, and this was done.[53]

It seems that the enthusiasm to publish research and propagandistic works on the Finnish eastern border issues and Karelian history was at its height at the beginning of the Continuation War. The aim was first to convince the Finns of the necessity for conquering the Karelian territories lost in the Winter War and even the Eastern Karelia, and to explain to the Germans about the "natural rights" of the Finns over the Karelian territory. In the second phase, old and new writings were published in English and French to justify the Finnish acts of occupation in the east in the eyes of the Allies.

KARELIA LOST, BUT REGAINED IN HISTORY (1945–1960)

The result of World War II was a catastrophe for the Finns. They not only lost the war but most of their Karelian territories, both those that they had occupied and also the parts of Karelia that had belonged to Finland in the 17th century and again since 1809 or 1812. The Finns and Karelians were evacuated from the ceded areas into the remaining parts of Finland and Soviet government settled the abandoned territory with people from all over the Soviet Union. After the first shock, there was a steady flow of essays, articles and books published in Finland about the refugees' old home regions in the ceded areas of Karelia, their societies, parishes, churches, schools and everyday lives. It seems that people were trying somehow to preserve the memories of their forfeited homes, lands and ways of life in books and writings about the loss of Karelia.

These writings about the lost home villages and parishes were mainly published from the 1940s up to the 1970s in various small magazines intended for the Karelian refugees and people interested in the Karelian issue. These were *Karjalan Heimo* (The Karelian Tribe, published since 1945), *Nuori Karjala* (Young Karelia, published since 1935), *Karjalan Aamu* (The Karelian Morning, published 1942–1975), *Karjalainen Kansa* (The Karelian People, published 1945–1958), *Puukello* (The Wooden Bell, published since 1947) and *Muistojen Karjala* (The Karelia of our Memories, published 1950–1967). The magazine *Karjalan Heimo* was actually same publication as *Toukomies* which had been published since 1925 and had changed its name to *Viena-Aunus* in 1935. The latter name, referring strongly to the idea of Greater Finland, became impossible in the altered political situation of the post-war period and the name was changed again. *Karjalainen Kansa* was the organ of The Finnish Karelian Association (*Karjalan Liitto*), founded in 1940 to unite the Karelian refugees, while *Karjalan Aamu* and *Nuori Karjala* belonged to local youth associations from Southern Karelia and the Ladoga region and *Puukello* belonged to the association of Karelian students at the University of Helsinki. *Muistojen Karjala* was published by the *Karjalan heimoseura* (Karelian Kinship Association).

The authors contributing to these magazines were from highly heterogeneous backgrounds. Some of them were professors (or later became professors), such as Onni Okkonen[54], Kustaa Vilkuna and Viljo Nissilä, but there were also government ministers, politicians, diplomats, but also teachers and ordinary people from among the Karelian refugees and those interested in the Karelian issue. The quality of the writing thus varied a lot, as did the topics, covering themes ranging from local historical memoirs to the analysis of Karelian toponyms and from biographical writings of notable Karelian citizens to articles about scientists who had carried out research in Karelia.

It should be noted, however, that the writings of professional historians were absent from these journals. Very little historical research on Karelia was published in the journals and monograph series intended for professional historians in the post-war period. Professor Jalmari Jaakkola continued with his work on Karelian toponyms and Erkki Kuujo[55] published his research on the taxation system in Karelia in the 16th and 17th centuries in 1959.[56] The writings of Seppo Suvanto on Swedish–Russian diplomacy at the end of the 15th century only indirectly concerned Karelian history, but the ethnologist Kustaa Vilkuna did continue the discussion on the border laid down in the treaty of 1323 in an article published in *Historiallinen Aikakauskirja* in 1960.[57] And that is all that was said about Karelia in the journals and monograph series intended for professional historians in the post-war years.

After the rather propagandistic writings of war period about Finland and Karelia as outposts of the western culture against the barbaric east, the

Finnish historians seem to have had some kind of "hangover" regarding the publication of anything about border issues. The historians publishing in Swedish, however, seem to have continued in the same tone as before. Jarl Gallén[58] and Eirik Hornborg published articles about medieval east–west divisions. Some general border works cherishing the tradition of "Finland as a western outpost" were also published in Swedish, and there was even a book *Finland, voorpost van het Noorden* published in Dutch.[59]

One part of the process of "preserving the lost Karelia" was the publishing of local histories of the parishes and municipalities of the ceded territories. There has always been a strong tradition of local histories in Finland, but, the local historical research based on the ceded territories of Karelia really blossomed after Second World War. These local histories, mostly published in the 1950s, can be roughly divided into two groups: the memoirs and other local historical writings of amateur historians, and the local histories written by university-trained researchers.[60] Although these two groups were rather different in content and outlook, they both answered the same need to preserve the history and life of people's lost homes in Karelia. These books were ordered, paid for and published by associations founded to preserve the memories and traditions of various parishes and areas in the ceded parts of Karelia.

Unlike the historians, ethnologists and linguists were fairly active in publishing research on Karelia. The material collected during the war period needed to be analysed and published, and a number of writings about Karelian place names, Karelian poems and traditional religion appeared in the yearbooks of the Kalevala Society (*Kalevalaseuran Vuosikirja*) and other publications.[61] The Orthodox Church in Finland cherished the memory of the lost areas of Karelia by publishing articles and books about ecclesiastical issues involving the Karelian Orthodox parishes, especially in their journal *Aamun Koitto* (The Dawn). The authors were not trained historians but held clerical posts in the Orthodox Church, and this influenced the content of their writing.[62]

FROM AN OUTPOST TO A BRIDGE (1961–1980)

If the historians were not publishing much about Karelia and the border region immediately after the war, a change in their activity certainly took place during the next two decades, there was seventeen papers about Karelia and its borders in *Historiallinen Aikakauskirja* and several articles and monographs were published in other forums for professional historians. The topics mostly concerned the medieval and early modern periods, but there were also some papers about 19th and 20th-century Karelian history. By this time historians were ready to study topics which were more delicate in terms of relations with the Soviet Union, as well as being traumatic for the Finns. These included Finnish Karelianism in its artistic and political forms, the Kinship Wars of 1918–1922[63], the flow of Karelian refugees into Finland after 1917[64], the migration of American Finns to Soviet Karelia in the 1930s[65] and resettlement of the Karelian refugees in Finland after World War II.[66] Nothing was yet written about the Finnish occupation of Karelia during the Continuation War 1941–1944, but this difficult and traumatic topic was clearly on the horizon,[67] and it seems that the history of Soviet Karelia in the 1920s and 1930s was similarly not yet a suitable topic for research, although this may have partly been because of the inaccessibility of the necessary sources.

The tone in which historians wrote about borders was different from that adopted in former decades. One important initiative in this field was Jarl Gallén's new theory regarding the nature of the eastern border of Finland in medieval times. Where the discussion had previously concentrated mostly on the exact location of the border of 1323, Gallén now proposed that it was linear only in its southernmost parts while in the sparsely settled north there may have been a common frontier zone between two indefinite borders.[68] This new interpretation challenged the concept of a linear division and separation of territories adopted in the 1920s and 1930s when the young Finnish state was defining its historical borders, and was consequently rejected by the most authoritative historians of the "old school". The discussion was to continue later, however, when Kyösti Julku[69] wrote several papers on the early modern border in the north of Finland[70] and Heikki Kirkinen[71] published a number of lively works on the medieval east–west divisions in Karelia. As if offering a foretaste of what was to come, one of his early articles was entitled "A Battlefield and a Bridge. The Historical Function of Karelia."[72]

The writings of Heikki Kirkinen on Karelian history played a crucial role in altering the paradigm of Finnish research on this topic. His main thesis was that Karelia had not been a dividing border between East and West, nor an outpost of Finland or of the western civilization but a unique territory with an identity, character and culture of its own lying between those of the western and eastern powers. His first monograph on Karelian history (1963) was still concentrated on tracing the contacts of the Karelian culture with Byzantium and Russia, but his second book – which should perhaps be regarded as his major work in terms of research – proclaimed even in its title that Karelia was lay in between east and west (1970), dealing as it did with the history of Russian Karelia in the Renaissance period (15th and 16th centuries). This book was followed by a second volume bearing the sub-title "Karelia as a Battlefield" (1976). For the first time since the works of Arvi Korhonen, Kirkinen based his research into early modern Karelian history on both Russian and Swedish source material.[73]

It is significant that Professor Kirkinen emphasized on many occasions that he had to struggle for almost the whole of the 1960s before his new paradigm for Karelian history was accepted. This serves well to indicate that there must have been much more at stake than the works and writings of a single researcher. The political atmosphere had to change first, and this took place only in the late 1960s, when the left-wing parties gained greater weight in Finnish society and milder attitudes were adopted towards the Soviet Union and Russia. It was at that time, too, that it became possible to take the first steps towards cooperation between Finnish and Soviet scientists, including historians, and what topic could have served these purposes better than the history of Karelia, presented in the light of a mediator between east and west? Thus, when the yearbook of the Kalevala Society, devoted to Karelian history and culture, was published in 1973, it was given the title "Karelia, the Bridge between East and West."[74] Similarly, when a series of five volumes about Karelia was published in 1982–1983 the main title was simply "Karelia", but since each volume had its own sub-title, the first one was called "Karelia. Gateway to the East and to the West".[75] This represented a dramatic change of paradigm relative to former decades.

Hannes Sihvo[76], editor of the aforementioned yearbook of the Kalevala Society, was another important figure in the new rise of Karelian studies in the early 1970s. Sihvo had specialized in the development of Karelianism, and his works "Founders of Karelia" (1969), about the scholars and collectors of poems who wandered around Karelia in the 19th century, and "Image of Karelia" (1973), on Karelianism in Finnish politics and the arts during the 19th century, still form the basis for research into these topics even today.[77] Finally, when the political Karelianism of the 1920s and 1930s was studied by Risto Alapuro[78] in his doctoral thesis on the radical Karelianist student movement known as the Academic Karelia Society,[79] it seemed that a real revitalization of research into Karelia was taking place in the early 1970s.

The changes in political conjunctures do not explain all the growing interest in the Karelian issue, however. There were also some institutional reasons for the revitalization of Karelian studies. In 1969, a new university was founded in Joensuu, the principal centre of the Finnish province of North Karelia, and with Heikki Kirkinen and Hannes Sihvo both becoming professors in this new university, Karelian history and culture naturally established itself as one of its main fields of research expertise. A new research unit, the Karelian Institute, was founded in there in 1971, and the first researcher to be appointed to it was a historian, Veijo Saloheimo[80], who had published a pile of local historical articles and books about North Karelia during the late 1950s and 1960s. His main task at the institute was to write a history of the province. Two volumes of this history, covering the 17th and 18th centuries, were published in 1976 and 1980.[81]

The building of an identity and territorial consciousness in North Karelia had begun in the 19th century, but it was only after the war, when the centre of the Ladoga region, the town of Sortavala, was ceded to Russia and North Karelia was separated from this old Ladoga connection, that Joensuu became the main town. The "project" of creating a common history and identity for the people of the province of North Karelia was intensified in the 1960s, with many of the characteristics of this identity being taken from the easternmost parishes, especially Ilomantsi, which showed the strongest influence from the culture of the ceded core lands of Karelia. This process can be seen in the great number of local historical articles about North Karelia published in the 1960s.[82] This work of identity building was continued in the provincial histories of the 1970s.[83]

A similar process of growth in research into a "new" province took place in South Karelia – i.e. the areas surrounding the town of Lappeenranta beside Lake Saimaa. The border agreed upon in Moscow in 1944 had separated these areas from their old connections with the town of Käkisalmi on the shore of Lake Ladoga and with Vyborg on the Gulf of Finland to the south, so that they had to be given an identity of their own. Lappeenranta had a college of technology but not a university with teaching in the arts, and it was perhaps for this reason that the identity building of the 1970s did not produce the same kind of results as in North Karelia. Anyway, as most of the Karelian territories had been lost in the war, it was clear that new territorial identities had to be produced for the parts of Karelia that remained in Finland, and much of this work was done by the historians.

On the other hand, the movement devoted to the writing of local histories of the parishes of the ceded territories came to an end in the early 1970s, the histories of the town of Sortavala (1970) and the parish of Virolahti (1970) being the last books in this "conservation" process to be written by university-trained historians.[84] The flow of books of memoirs written by amateur historians had already ended in the mid-1960s.[85] The trauma of the loss of homes and parishes in Karelia had received the necessary "first aid" through the local histories of the 1950s and 1960s, but more continuity can be seen in the small-scale magazines about Karelia, most of which continued to publish short articles mostly on local history. Publication of the journal *Muistojen Karjala* ceased in 1967 and that of *Karjalan Aamu* in 1975, but the others mentioned above are still extant even today.

CROSSING THE BORDER AGAIN – PEACEFULLY (1981–2000)

The last period to be discussed here can be divided roughly in two: to the Soviet part and the post-Soviet part. The opening of the largely closed Soviet system and scientific world to cooperation with western and Finnish scientists during the 1980s was clearly visible in the volume of research concerning Karelia. New opportunities to work in Russian archives made it possible for professional historians to take up new topics, and following the collapse of the Soviet Union in 1991, the opening of the Finnish–Russian border to allow people to cross fairly freely had a considerable impact on the work and writings of amateur historians interested in Karelia.

Raimo Ranta published several papers in quick succession in the 1980s about Old Finland and the defining of borders between the Kingdom of Sweden and the Russian Empire in the 18th century,[86] his work on this topic culminating in three books published in 1985–1987, one about the system of government in Old Finland in its early stages and a large two-volume monograph about the economy of Old Finland during the first half of the 18th century. These works were strictly based on archival sources and lacked all the propagandist or Russophobic undertones which had been characteristic of writings on this topic in the 1920s and 1930s in particular.[87] This is all that can be said about research into the question of Old Finland in general in the 1980s.[88] Old Finland was a suitable topic for research again, but the publications were now politically correct. Some Soviet historians also published articles in Finnish journals during the 1980s, and often the topic was Old Finland.[89] Although this cannot perhaps be called real research cooperation, it can be described with a term borrowed from the vocabulary of Finnish-Soviet foreign policy, as "peaceful co-existence" in research concerned with Karelia.

Two main lines of discussion can be perceived in the research into border issues that took place in the 1980s and 1990s. Professor Kyösti Julku published more than ten short articles about the northern part of the Russian-Swedish (Finnish) border, his major work being a monograph published in 1987 on the delineation of the "eastern border" from the medieval times up to the Treaty of Teusina in 1596.[90] This profound analysis of the written sources that remained in Swedish archives was still based largely on the concept of a linear border and the author went to great pains to locate the places where the border of 1323 ran. Another discussion concerning the border was starting at around the same time, however. A Danish historian, John Lind, became interested in the ideas that Jarl Gallén had presented in the 1960s about the possibility of a zonal border in the uninhabited interior of Finland, and together with Gallén, he published the idea anew and challenged the predominating concept of a linear border in medieval times. After the death of Gallén in 1990, Lind continued to defend the new interpretation in discussions with some Finnish historians who were opposed to this new theory.[91] Roughly speaking, Lind's interpretation was based on the lively discussion in the 1980s over medieval and early modern state-building processes in Europe and comparisons of the treaty of 1323 with contemporary treaties concluded by the Principality of Novgorod in particular. One of the most vivid discussions took place between Lind and

Professor Heikki Kirkinen, in which the latter underlined the process of moving local borders which had produced contradictory historical sources with regard to the medieval linear border.[92] It can be said today that the research community has largely adopted the new interpretation of a zonal border dating from 1323, although the linear interpretation still predominates in elementary school and college textbooks.

Professor Heikki Kirkinen was perhaps the most prominent figure in the field of historical research on Karelia during the 1980s and 1990s. Not only the Nöteborg Peace Treaty and its border, but also the date of the foundation of the Monastery of Valaam in Lake Ladoga and the origins of the Kalevala poetry were topics on which Professor Kirkinen entered into heated discussions with other scholars. According to the traditional interpretation based on mostly hagiographic texts, the monastery was founded in the 12th century and may be regarded as the oldest surviving monastery in the whole of Russia. The Danish medievalist John Lind opposed this interpretation as well, although it had been supported by Kirkinen, and maintained on the basis of source criticism that the monastery was founded in the 14th or 15th century, as were most of the Orthodox monasteries in north-west Russia, which led to a lively discussion with Kirkinen in various historical journals.[93] Most of the epic poems that formed the basis of the Finnish national epic, the *Kalevala*, were collected from Karelia and Ingria, although this tradition in a weaker form was known in western Finland, too. Finnish ethnologists quarrelled for about hundred years as to whether the *Kalevala* epic was originally a western or an eastern tradition, and finally a compromise was reached in the 1980s that the tradition was known among all Finnish-speaking people. When Professor Kirkinen published his study on this issue, lending much weight to the eastern, Karelian tradition, his views were strongly rejected by some ethnologists.[94] One of his main topics in the 1980s and 1990s was the Karelian identity, to the extent that the creation and strengthening of this identity seems to have been one of the main goals of his vast publishing activity during those decades.

The opening of the Finnish-Soviet/Russian border in the 1980s and 1990s enabled Finnish researchers to reach places in Karelia which had been closed to the foreigners since the Second World War. Finnish archaeologists were now able to visit Karelia and take part in excavations there in cooperation with their Soviet/Russian colleagues, and this can be seen in reports published about these expeditions, and especially in many articles published about Stone Age petroglyphs (stone carvings) on the shores of Lake Onega and the White Sea.[95] Similar "co-existence" between Finnish and Soviet researchers as in the case of Old Finland can be seen where Iron Age and Medieval topics in Karelian history were concerned during the 1980s.[96] The change in Soviet policies, the opening up of the Soviet scientific world and of the border made it possible to study topics that had previously been unreachable in the Soviet/Russian archives. It now became possible for Finnish historians to study documents related to the role of the Finns in Soviet Karelia in the 1920s and 1930s, and this resulted in many publications that are still basic works on these topics.[97] The Kinship Wars, the idea of Greater Finland and the Finnish occupation period during the Continuation War had been topics on which silence had reigned in the 1950s and 1960s, but by the 1980s they were being studied avidly by Finnish historians.[98]

If the 1980s opened the doors of the Soviet archives to the Finnish professional historians, the collapse of the Soviet Union in 1991 and the subsequent opening of the Finnish-Russian border resulted in a flow of Finnish tourists into Karelia. Many of these were the same people who had left Karelia for Finland at the end of the Second World War, or else descendants of these people. As a result of this movement there was a revitalization of the production of books of memoirs relating to the home villages in Karelia. In 2000 alone, the last year studied here, over 20 books of memories of villages and parishes in Karelia were published.[99] Other novelties to appear in the 1990s were pamphlets discussing the possibilities of annexing the ceded Karelian territories to Finland once more[100] and travel guides for visitors to Russian Karelia[101], each of which made use of history and interpreted it in a way that supported the particular aims of the book.

The new situation in the 1990s made it possible for Finnish and Russian historians to initiate real cooperation in the study of Karelian history, and especially the history of the Russian-Finnish border and borderlands. The border was no longer presented as a dividing line, nor even as a bridge, but as a borderland having a long tradition of mutual economic cooperation and cultural interaction between the people living in the two parts of the Karelian territory.[102] This development was connected not only with the opening of the Russian-Finnish border in the 1990s, but also with the breakthrough in border studies which took place in Western Europe in the course of the formation of the European Union. The former enclosing, separating and dividing borders that existed in Europe were now being seen as diffuse and porous, and these same elements were being emphasized and studied in connection with the history of Karelia as well.[103]

FROM CONFLICT TO COOPERATION – HISTORY AND SOCIETY

It is evident from the above discussion that the paradigms affecting Finnish historical research into the eastern border and the territory of Karelia have altered in the course of time. At first, in the 1920s and 1930s, the young, independent Finnish state was in need of a history of the limits of its territory. The space occupied by the state was justified by recounting the origins of its borders, a task entrusted to historians. The evolution of the borders was presented as a series of wars, conflicts and battles, and the historical borders were precise demarcation that separated territories. At the beginning of the 20th century, Karelia was seen as the exotic land of the *Kalevala* epic poetry and the seat of the original Finnish culture. In this phase the main interest was centred on the White Sea and the Olonets region. After Finland had gained its independence and the idea of Greater Finland had emerged among the political Karelianists, much effort was put into research focused on what were known as East Karelia and the Olonets and Onega regions. Much research was also carried out in the occupied regions of Karelia during the Second World War, mainly with the task of demonstrating that the territory belonged to the sphere of Finnish culture and was therefore an integral part of Finland.

After the Second World War, when Finland was left with its "unhistorical" eastern border, the history of borders was not a topic of research at all, but once the worst of the trauma caused by the loss of the Karelian territories had been dealt with in the 1950s and the political climate had become more tolerant towards the Soviet Union in the 1960s, Karelia and its borders returned to the historical research agenda in a new form. The border was no longer presented as a demarcating barrier but as a bridge between the Finnish and Russian cultures, and Karelia was seen as a mediator between the two. Much emphasis was again placed on the study of those parts of Karelia that Finland had had to cede to the Soviet Union after World War II. Topics such as the history of Old Finland and Karelian medieval history in particular were handled by both Finnish and Soviet historians in the 1970s and 1980s, perhaps not in cooperation but at least side by side.

At the end of the century, especially in the 1990s, a new approach could be seen in the research into borders and the history of Karelia. European integration had led to changes in the European borders. They had become diffuse and porous, and this development had its impact on historical research. Many researchers were now interested in studying the ordinary life of the borderlands and the cross-border cooperation practiced by their inhabitants – and the history of Karelia was no exception. The eastern border of Finland and the associated territory of Karelia had changed from being a dividing line and scene of continuous conflicts to the role of a mediating bridge and eventually to that of a borderland with a long tradition of cross-border cooperation.

A look at the immense causes of the changes referred to above shows, interestingly, how the orientation of historical research can be affected by many kinds of changes and phenomena in society. At the beginning of the 20th century, Karelianism in its artistic and political forms affected the research and the view of Karelia that was presented. By the late1930s political and diplomatic antagonism with the Soviet Union strengthened the divisive interpretation of the border, and by the outbreak of the Continuation War, propagandist research in particular was presenting Karelia as an integral part of the Finnish territory.

After the war, historical studies of the parishes, villages and homes left behind in Karelia were one means of coming to terms with the traumatic outcome of the war. On the other hand, those parts of Karelia left on the Finnish side of the border, the Finnish provinces of South Karelia and North Karelia, needed to create their own regional identity, and historical research into the past of these territories was one part of such a process. Even the founding of a new university in North Karelia affected research into the history of Karelia. During the 1970s and 1980s, which are often labelled as the period of Finlandization, the officially cordial relations with the Soviet Union resulted in works on Karelian history which were politically neutral in approach and in terms of their topics.

The opening up of the Soviet world, especially the "perestroika" of the 1980s, made it possible for researchers to address topics which had been avoided before as being politically incorrect, such as the Karelian refugees who came to Finland after the Bolshevik revolution in Russia, Stalin's purges of the Finns in Soviet Karelia in the 1930s and the Finnish occupation of Karelia during the Continuation War. The collapse of the Soviet Union and the opening of Russia's border and archives to foreign researchers made it possible to use new sources and to investigate new topics, including the nationality policy pursued in Soviet Karelia in the 1920s and 1930s. Finally, when Finland joined the European Union in 1995, interest in the eastern border of Finland increased among researchers and the approaches used were fitted to these new circumstances. On the other hand, the opportunity to visit the ceded areas of Karelia again provoked a flow of small-scale publications on the histories of the parishes and villages Karelia.

In conclusion, we can see that the approaches and topics that prevailed in the history of Karelia and the eastern border of Finland were chosen on ideological, nationalistic, propagandist and institutional grounds at least. In addition, some of the Finns coped with their traumatic experiences after World War II though historical writings and publications. Changes in Finnish foreign relations and the country's position in the international community have also been of importance. Given that domestic and international trends and innovations within the scientific world have affected the methods used in the research and the questions asked, these rather unscientific factors may be seen to have set the outlines for the paradigms observed and topics chosen in historical studies of Karelia and the Finnish eastern border.

REFERENCES

1 Pekka Ahtiainen/Jukka Tervonen, Historiatiede oman aikansa tulkkina. Katsaus suomalaisen historiankirjoituksen vaiheisiin viimeisen sadan vuoden ajalta, in: Pekka Ahtiainen et al., Historia nyt. Näkemyksiä suomalaisesta historiantutkimuksesta. Historiallisen yhdistyksen julkaisuja 5. Porvoo 1990, 11–38, quotation on page 11.

2 The periods were: the last two decades of Russian rule (1900–1917), the first two decades of Finnish independence (1918–1938), the period of World War II in Finland (1939–1944), the first two post-war decades (1945–1960), the period of political and cultural change in Finland (1961–1980) and the period of Soviet "perestroika" politics and the collapse of the Soviet Union (1981–2000).

3 There is no suitable general account of the history of Karelia available in English. In more detail, see the general presentations of the history of Finland in English. One of the latest of these is Jason Lavery, The History of Finland, Greenwood Press 2006. On the evolution of the Swedish/Finnish – Russian/Soviet border (in German) see Kimmo Katajala, Zwischen West und Ost. 800 Jahre an der Ostgrenze Finnlands, in: Kirchliche Zeitgeschichte 23 (2010), 81–110.

4 The names of the publications mentioned in the text are translations, the original names are mentioned in the endnotes. Iivo Härkönen (ed.), Karjalan kirja I–II, Porvoo 1910.

5 I. K. Inha, Kalevalan laulumailta, Helsinki 1911. (^{2}1921).

6 Väinö, Voionmaa, Professor of History at the University of Helsinki 1918–1936. Leena Ellonen (ed.), Suomen Professorit 1640–2007, Jyväskylä 2008, 827.

7 Väinö Voionmaa, Suomen karjalaisen heimon historia, Helsinki 1915 (^{2}1969).

8 See Päiviö Tommila, Suomen historiankirjoitus. Tutkimuksen kuva, Porvoo 1989, 152–153; Pekka Ahtiainen/Jukka Tervonen, Menneisyyden tutkijat ja metodien vartijat. Matka suomalaiseen historiankirjoitukseen, Käsikirjoja 17:1, Helsinki 1996, 151.

9 Yrjö Blomstedt, Professor of Legal History at the University of Helsinki 1963–1974. Suomen Professorit, Loc. Cit. (Note 6), 81.

10 J. V. Ronimus, Novgorodin vatjalaisen viidenneksen henki- ja verokirja v. 1500. Todistuskappaleita Suomen historiaan, Joensuu 1906; J. V. Ronimus, Novgorodin vatjalaisten viidenneksen verokirja v. 1500 ja Karjalan silloinen asutus, in: Historiallinen Arkisto 20:I (1906).

11 See, for example, P. Toikka, Novgorodin Karjalan historiasta, in: Historiallinen Arkisto 25:4 (1915); P. Toikka, Muutamia oikaisuja ja lisiä Vatjan viidenneksen verokirjan suomennokseen, in: Historiallinen Arkisto 26:7 (1916).

12 See L. Pelkonen, Käkisalmen läänin luterilaistuttamisesta, in: Iivo Härkönen (ed.), Karjalan [I], Loc. Cit. (Note 4), 12–30; J. M. Salenius, Kauppa-oloista ja kauppapaikoista Käkisalmen läänissä kuudennentoista sataluvun loppupuolella, in: Historiallinen Aikakauskirja 6 (1908), 119–124; J. M. Salenius, Käkisalmen läänin oloista kuudennentoista sataluvun loppupuolella, in: Historiallinen Arkisto 22:I:4 (1911); Väinö Vesterdahl, Käkisalmen läänin oloja 17:llä vuosisadalla. Historiallinen tutkielma, Käkisalmi 1908; Veikko Piipponen, Talonpoikaiskapinoista Karjalassa vv. 1696–97, in: Historiallinen Aikakauskirja 9 (1911), 127–135; Mandi Nevalainen, Lisiä Pielisen ympäristön kreivinaikuiseen historiaan, in: Historiallinen Arkisto 25:7 (1915).

13 For example A. R. Cederberg, Pohjois-Karjalan kauppaolot vuosina 1721–1775, in: Historiallinen Arkisto 23:I:2 (1911); A. R. Saarenseppä [Cederberg], Kuvauksia Pohjois-Karjalan maataloudellisista oloista. I. Vuoden 1800:n vaiheille, Mikkeli 1912.

14 Yrjö E. Rainio, Piirteitä Viipurin läänin metsäoloista vuosina 1811–1911, in: Kaukomieli 5 (1912), 184–206; Lauri K. Relander, Maanviljelyksen kehityksestä Viipurin läänissä vuosina 1811–1911, in: Kaukomieli 5 (1912), 123–140; Albin Simolin (ed.), Urkunder rörande det äldre Wiborgska stiftet. Suomen Kirkkohistoriallisen Seuran Toimituksia 13, Helsingfors 1916.

15 Erkki Paavolainen, Maiden siirtyminen muukalaisille Karjalan Kannaksella, in: Kaukomieli 5 (1912), 107–122. Erkki Paavolainen was a rector of a folk high school, politician, Member of the Parliament and minister. See Suomen kansanedustajat. Eduskunta. (www.eduskunta.fi).

16 E. Ahtia, Silmäys kansallisuusoloihin Aunuksen ja Vienan lääneissä, in: Virittäjä 7 (1903), 1–11; Uuno Karttunen, Itä-Karjalan vaiheet, Porvoo 1912.

17 Jalmari Jaakkola, Professor of History at the University of Helsinki 1930–1954. Suomen Professorit, Loc. Cit. (Note 6), 226–227.

18 Jalmari Jaakkola, Suomen muinaiset valtarajat vuoteen 1323, Historiallisia Tutkimuksia 7, Helsinki 1926; see Tommila, Suomen, Loc. Cit. (Note 8), 187.

19 See, for example, K. R. Melander, Mitä suuntaa kulki Pähkinäsaaren rauhan rajan pohjoisosa? in: Historiallinen Aikakauskirja 29 (1931), 241–267; P. O. v. Törne, Nöteborgsfredens gränsbestämmelser, in: Historiallinen Arkisto 40:2 (1933).

20 Werner Tawastjerna, Pohjoismainen viisikolmattavuotinen sota. Vuosien 1570–1590 välinen aika. Historiallisia Tutkimuksia 1, Helsinki 1918–1920; Werner Tawastjerna, Pohjoismainen viisikolmattavuotinen sota. Sotavuodet 1590–1595 ja Täyssinän rauha. Historiallisia Tutkimuksia 11, Helsinki 1929.

21 Erkki K. Osmonsalo, Professor of History at the University of Helsinki 1948–1949. Suomen Professorit, Loc. Cit. (Note 6), 514.

22 Erkki K. Osmonsalo, Valtion ja valtakunnan rajankäynnit Suomessa Venäjänvallan ja itsenäisyyden aikana, in: Suomen maanmittauksen historia III:4, Porvoo 1933; about the bordering process against Sweden see Erkki K. Osmonsalo, Suomen rajapolitiikka Venäjän vallan aikana. I. Ruotsin vastaista rajaa koskevat kysymykset 1809–1824. Historiallisia Tutkimuksia 17:1, Helsinki 1933; see Tommila, Suomen, Loc. Cit. (Note 8), 173.

23 Arvi Korhonen, Professor of History at the University of Helsinki 1940–1959. Suomen Professorit, Loc. Cit. (Note 6), 316.

24 Arvi Korhonen, Suomen itärajan syntyhistoriaa. Puolustusvoimain Pääesikunnan Sotahistoriallisen toimiston julkaisuja 3, Porvoo 1938; see Tommila, Suomen, Loc. Cit. (Note 8), 184–185.

25 See Aunuksen vapaustaistelun 20-vuotismuistojulkaisu 1919–1939; O. V. Itkonen, Muurmannin suomalainen legioona, Helsinki 1927; J. Takkinen, Metsäsissipäällikön muistelmat I. Karjalan metsä-sissit nousevat II. Taistelut Karjalan vapauttamiseksi, Porvoo 1927; Aarne Sihvo et al. (eds.), Aunuksen retken muistojulkaisu, Helsinki 1930; Roope Takala/Iivari Ievala (eds.), Karjala. Karjalan vapaussodan 10-vuotismuistojulkaisu 1922–1932, Helsinki 1932; Yrjö Laine, Muistelmia Repolan ja Porajärven Suomeen kuulumisen ajoilta, in: Rajan Turva 4 (1934), 30–31; Aarno Karimo, Karjalan nousu 1918, Porvoo 1937.

26 See W. Keynäs, Itä-Karjalan asia ja pakolaiskysymys vv. 1922–1925, Helsinki 1926; W. Keynäs, Itä-Karjalan olojen kehitys, Oulu 1930; Erkki Räikkönen, Valkoinen upseeripartio Karjalan sodassa, Helsinki 1932 ([2]1938); Esitys Itä-Karjalan maasta ja kansasta, sen vapausliikkeen tähänastisista vaiheista, nykyisistä taloudellisista, sivistyksellisistä ja valtiollisista olosta sekä Karjalan kysymyksestä, Helsinki 1934; Same published in English: East Carelia. A survey of the country and its population, and a review of the Carelian question, Helsinki 1934; An outline of the East Carelia question. Publ. by the Carelian Delegation, Helsinki 1935; Paul Marttina, Miesten syöjiltä sijoilta. Muisteluksia Vienan ja Aunuksen vainovuosilta, Porvoo 1935; Der nationale Kampf der Karelier. Denkschrift, abgefasst von der Karelisch-Ingermanländischen Delegation, Helsinki 1937; Toivo Kaukoranta, Itä-Karjalan kysymys kansainväliseltä kannalta, in: Karjalan historiaa. Jyväskylä 1938, 101–114; Keijo Loimu, Itä-Karjalan viimeisintä historiaa, in: Akateemisen Karjala-Seuran Vuosikirja 2 (1938), 158–167.

27 Karjalan historiaa. Historian Aitta 8, Jyväskylä 1938.

28 See, for example, A. R. Niemi, Heikki Meriläinen. Kansankirjailija ja Karjalan kansantiedon suuri kerääjä, in: Toukomies (1927), 142–146, 172–179; A. R. Niemi, Vienankarjalainen runonkerääjä. I. Marttisen elämänvaiheita ja sivistyshistoriallinen kuvaus Vienan Karjalasta vuosisadan jälkipuoliskolla, in: Toukomies (1928), 78–82; Vallas Homanen, Karjalaisten kansallisten liikkeiden ja ajatustapojen historiaa. Katsausta Karjalan Sivistysseuran aikaisempaan äänenkannattajaan "Karjalaisten Sanomiin", in: Toukomies (1931), 84–88; Valter Päivinen, Kun Karjalaisten Pakinain ensimmäisiä numeroita levitettiin Aunuksen-Karjalaan, in: Toukomies (1931), 129–130; N. Ruotsi, Maanomistusoloista Etelä-Aunuksessa, in: Toukomies (1931), 77–79; N. Ruotsi, Muistelmia Aunuksen vapaustaistelun siviilihallinnosta v. 1919, in: Toukomies (1932), 136–138; 1933, 16–17, 44–45, 89–90, 104, 125; Jussi Sihvo, Liittolaisten Muurmannin retki 1918–1919 ja sen vaikutus Vienan Karjalan itsenäisyyspyrkimyksiin, in: Toukomies (1931), 183–186; 1932, 5–8; Iivo Härkönen, Karjala Suomen kirjallisuudessa. Pääasiassa yleiskuvauksia ja kaunokirjallisuutta koskeva katsaus, in: Toukomies (1933), 88; (1934), 36–38, 88–91, 112–114, 139–140, 160–161; Viena-Aunus (1935), 16–18; Mikko Karvonen, Kantalahden rannoilla vuosina 1915–1918, in: Toukomies (1934), 136–138, 168–169; Viena-Aunus (1935), 54–55; Kaarlo Merikoski, Uhtualainen kansanopettaja [Pekka Lesejaff]. Eräs uranuurtaja rajantakaisen Karjalan kansallisen valistuksen tiellä, in: Viena-Aunus (1936), 6–7, 10; Erkki Reijonen, Muistelmia Karjalan retkeltä lähes 50 vuotta takaisinpäin, in: Viena-Aunus (1936), 12–17.

29 Erkki Paavolainen, Karjalan Kannaksen kysymyksiä, Viipuri 1921; O. Hj. Granfelt, Rättskipningen i Gamla Finland under Ryska tiden (1721–1811), in: Tidskrift utgiven av Jurdiska Föreningen i Finland (1931), 274–314; Ragnar Rosén, Mielialoja Vanhassa Suomessa vuonna 1767. Muutamia tietoja suomalaisten osanotosta Katariina II:n lakikomissioniin, in: Historiallinen Arkisto 40:10 (1933); Eevert Laine, Eräs vaihe Salmin-Suojärven lahjoitusmaiden vapauttamisessa. Historiallinen Arkisto 40:13 (1933); Erkki Paavolainen, Kannaksen pakkorauha. Entisten lahjoitusmaiden yhteismetsäkysymyksen loppuvaihe, Viipuri 1935; Matti Kähäri, Riita Taubilan sopimuksesta Vehmaisten lahjoitusmailta, in: Kaukomieli 7 (1935), 29–37; E. V. Hietalahti, Lahjoitusmaakruununpuistot Viipurin läänissä ja niiden lunastamiskysymys, in: Maanmittaus 11 (1936), 73–83; Matti Kähäri, Läänitys- ja verotusolot Raudussa ennen isoa vihaa, in: Kaukomieli 8 (1937), 12–26; Ragnar Rosén, Vanha Suomi, in: Historiallinen Arkisto 8 (1938), 117–159.

30 Johan Richard Danielson-Kalmari, Professor of History at the University of Helsinki 1880–1913. Suomen Professorit, Loc. Cit. (Note 6), 868.

31 J. R. Danielson-Kalmari, Viipurin läänin palauttaminen muun Suomen yhteyteen, Helsinki 1894 (^{2}1911).

32 J. R. Danielson-Kalmari, Tien varrelta valtiolliseen ja kansalliseen itsenäisyyteen. Kirjoituksia ja puheita. Osa III. Idän ja lännen taistelua Karjalassa, Porvoo 1931; see Tommila, Suomen, Loc. Cit. (Note 8), 168–170, 191; Päiviö Tommila, Historia, in: Päiviö Tommila (ed.), Suomen tieteen historia 2. Humanistiset ja yhteiskuntatieteet, Porvoo 2000, 73.

33 About war period research see Antti Laine, Tiedemiesten Suur-Suomi – Itä-Karjalan tutkimus jatkosodan vuosina, in: Eeva-Liisa Aalto/Rauno Endén, Historiallinen Arkisto 102, Helsinki 1993, 91–202; Ilkka Herlin, Linjoilla ja linjojen takana, in: Pekka Ahtiainen/Jukka Tervonen, Menneisyyden tutkijat ja metodien vartijat. Matka suomalaiseen historiankirjoitukseen, Käsikirjoja 17:1, Helsinki 1996, 84–119; Karl-Erik Michelsen, Tiede sodassa, in: Päiviö Tommila (ed.), Suomen tieteen historia 4. Tieteen ja tutkimuksen historia 1880-luvulta lähtien, Porvoo 2002; Marjatta Hietala, Tutkijat ja Saksan suunta, in: Marjatta Hietala (ed.), Tutkijat ja sota. Suomalaisten tutkijoiden kohtaloita toisen maailmansodan aikana, Historiallinen Arkisto 121, Jyväskylä 2006, 30–141; Mervi Kaarninen, Yliopisto sodassa, in: Marjatta Hietala (ed.), Tutkijat ja sota. Suomalaisten tutkijoiden kohtaloita toisen maailmansodan aikana, Historiallinen Arkisto 121, Jyväskylä 2006, 142–235.

34 See Viljo Nissilä, Ajatuksia Karjalan paikannimien keruukilpailun johdosta, in: Virittäjä 45 (1941), 240–243; Jalo Kalima, Äänisen tienoon paikannimiä, in: Virittäjä 45 (1941), 323–329; Sulo Haltsonen, Suomalaiset tutkijat Tverin karjalaisten mailla, in: Virittäjä 46 (1942), 175–185; Jalo Kalima, Itä-Karjalan paikannimiä, in: Virittäjä 46 (1942), 160–163; Viljo Nissilä, Venäläisperäisiä henkilönnimiä Itä-Karjalan paikannimistössä, in: Virittäjä 47 (1943), 46–78; Veikko Ruoppila,

Ylisen Syvärin suomalaisperäisiä paikannimiä, in: Virittäjä 47 (1943), 78–96; Viljo Nissilä, Itä-Karjalan paikannimien apellatiivisista piirteistä, in: Virittäjä 48 (1944), 399–405.

35 Viljo Nissilä worked first as a college lecturer then as an associate Professor 1962–1966 and after retirement in 1969 was called to hold a personal professorship of toponymy in the University of Helsinki. See Suomen Professorit, Loc. Cit. (Note 6), 489.

36 Lars Pettersson, Professor of Art History at the University of Helsinki 1951–1981. Suomen Professorit, Loc. Cit. (Note 6), 548.

37 See Lars Pettersson, Ikonmålare i Aunus under 1800-talet, in: Finskt Museum 50 (1943), 48–65. The post-war publications of Pettersson were based on material collected during the occupation years, see Lars Pettersson, Ilomantsin kreikkalaiskatolisia kirkkoja ja tsasounia, in: Suomen Museo 52 (1945), 40–74; Lars Pettersson, Uikujoen luostarin ikonitaiteesta, in: Pyhä Pääsiäinen. Ortodoksisten Nuorten Liitto r.y:n Julkaisuja 1, Helsinki 1945, 10–22; Lars Pettersson, Die kirchliche Holzbaukunst auf der Halbinsel Zaonez'e in Russisch-Karelen, Herkunft und Werden. Dissertation, Helsinki 1950; Pettersson, Lars, Äänisniemen kirkollinen puuarkkitehtuuri. Aineiston esittely, in: Suomen Muinaismuistoyhdistyksen Aikakauskirja 50 (1950); Lars Pettersson, Kring några karelska bord i Finlands Nationalmuseum, in: Corolla Archaeologica in honorem C. A. Nordman, Helsinki 1952, 267–275; Lars Pettersson, Kahdet kirkonpiirustukset Suojärven Varpakylästä, in: Suomen Museo 60 (1953), 65–85.

38 J. J. Mikkola, Hämärän ja sarastuksen ajoilta, Porvoo 1939; J. J. Mikkola, Lännen ja idän rajoilta. Historiallisia kirjoitelmia, Porvoo 1942.

39 For example, Historiallinen Aikakauskirja, the main historical journal in Finland, carried only three articles about Karelian history in the years 1939–1940. See Veikko Mattila, Siirtolaisuutta Karjalasta ja Itä-Uudeltamaalta Viroon 1500-luvulla, in: Historiallinen Aikakauskirja 37 (1939), 53–57; R. Rosén, Oikeustaistelua Viipurin läänissä 1700-luvulla, in: Historiallinen Aikakauskirja 38 (1940), 97–109; Martti Ruuth, Kristillinen pohja Savossa ennen Pähkinäsaaren rauhaa, in: Historiallinen Aikakauskirja 38 (1940), 310–317.

40 See Historiallinen Aikakauskirja 39 (1941). The research articles concerned are Jalmari Jaakkola, Muinaisen 'Karialan' – Karjalan – alku, 187–203; Kaarlo Blomstedt, Karjalan ja muun Suomen myöhäiskeskiaikaisista laamanneista, 204–214; Martti Ruutu, Karjalan nousu Suomen sivistyneistön näköpiiriin, 215–231, and as a review article Pentti Renvall, Itä-Karjalan historiantutkimusta neuvostovallan aikana, 232–240.

41 Pentti Renvall, Professor of History in the University of Helsinki 1950–1973. Suomen Professorit, Loc. Cit. (Note 6), 593–594.

42 Pentti Renvall, Neuvosto-Karjalan suomalaisuuden alkuvaiheista, in: Historiallinen Aikakauskirja 42 (1944), 77–106.

43 Jalmari Jaakkola, Suomen historian ääriviivat, Porvoo 1940. (Transl. Finska folkets historia 1941, Précis d'histoire de Finlande 1942, Die Geschichte des finnischen Volkes 1942, A finnek törtenete 1943).

44 Jalmari Jaakkola, Suomen idänkysymys, Porvoo 1941 (Transl. Finlands östproblem 1941, Die Ostfrage Finnlands 1941, The Finnish Eastern Question 1942, Le problem oriental de la Finlande 1942).

45 Keijo K. Kulha, Jutikkala, tinkimätön akateemikko, Helsinki 2006, 168.

46 Einar W. Juva, Professor of History at the University of Turku 1927–1955. Suomen Professorit, Loc. Cit (Note 6), 243.

47 Einar W. Juva, Suomen taistelu itää vastaan, Helsinki 1942.

48 Yrjö von Grönhagen, Karelen, Finnlands Bollwerk gegen den Osten, Dresden 1942.

49 See, for example, Eirik Hornborg, Sverige och Ryssland genom tiderna. Politiska relationer och krigiska konflikter, Stockholm 1941; Kampen om östkarelen, Åbo 1941; Ragnar Hemmer, Lagman i Karelen under medeltiden, in: Tidskrift utgiven av Jurdiska Föreningen i Finland (1941), 239–243, (1942), 130–136; A. W. Rancken, Karelens vapen, in: Finsk Tidskrift 130 (1941), 163–170; Eirik Hornborg, Gränsfästet Viborg från korstågstiden till våra dagar, Helsingfors 1942; R. Rosén, Finland, Karelen, Aunus, in: Finsk Tidskrift 131 (1942), 163–170; Torsten G. Aminoff, Mellan svärdet och korgsabeln. 700 års kamp om karelarnas land, Helsingfors 1943.

50 Eino Jutikkala, Professor of History 1947–1974, Suomen Professorit, Loc. Cit. (Note 6), 241.

51 Väinö Auer, Professor of Geography 1929–1950, Suomen Professorit, Loc. Cit. (Note 6), 71.

52 Kustaa Vilkuna, Professor of Ethnology 1948–1959. Suomen Professorit, Loc. Cit. (Note 6), 817.

53 Väinö Auer/Eino Jutikkala, Finnlands Lebensraum. Das geographische und geschichtliche Finnland. Als Sachkundiger in philologischen und etnographischen Fragen Kustaa Vilkuna, Helsinki 1941. On the backgrounds to these books, see Kulha, Jutikkala, Loc. Cit. (Note 45), 169–171.

54 Onni Okkonen, Professor of Art History at the University of Helsinki 1927–1948. Suomen Professorit, Loc. Cit. (Note 6), 509.

55 Erkki Kuujo, Professor of History at the University of Helsinki 1969–1984. Suomen Professorit, Loc. Cit. (Note 6), 345.

56 Jalmari Jaakkola, Vielä hiukan Karjalan vieraskielisistä nimistä, in: Historiallinen Aikakauskirja 50 (1952), 91–105; Erkki Kuujo, Taka-Karjalan verotus v:een 1710. Historiallisia Tutkimuksia 52, Forssa 1959.

57 Seppo Suvanto, Neuvottelut Ruotsi-Suomen rauhasta Venäjän kanssa vv. 1503–1504, in: Historiallinen Aikakauskirja 53 (1955), 37–45; Seppo Suvanto, Suuren venäläissodan (vv. 1495–97) ideologista ja reaalista taustaa, in: Historiallinen Aikakauskirja 51 (1953), 149–157; Kustaa Vilkuna, Pähkinäsaaren rauhan raja kansatieteellisessä katsannossa, in: Historiallinen Aikakauskirja 58 (1960), 407–431.

58 Jarl Gallén, Professor of History at the University of Helsinki 1964–1975. Suomen Professorit, Loc. Cit. (Note 6), 124.

59 Jarl Gallén, Öst och väst i kamp om Finland, in: Olaf D. Schalin et al. (eds.), Här restes Kristi kors, Borgå 1955, 40–50; Eirik Hornborg, Viborg 1495, in: Nils F. Holm (ed.), Det Svenska svärdet, Stockholm 1948, 34–52; See also Paavo Ravila, Finland mellan öst och väst, in: Svensk Tidskrift (Uppsala), 6 (1960), 355–362; Eric Born, Finlands gränser genom seklerna, in: Finland och vi, 2 (1958), 7–10; Helmer J. Wahlroos, Finland – gränslandet, in: Norden i tusind aar, Odense 1951, 237–240, also in English: Finland – the borderland, in: Jørgen Bukdahl (ed.), Scandinavia past and present. From the Viking Age to absolute monarchy, Odense 1959, 230–234; R. K. Broersma-Luomajoki/Sj. Broersma, Finland voorpost van het Noorden, Meppel 1952.

60 Local histories written by the professional historians were for example Aulikki Ylönen, Jääsken kihlakunnan historia vuoteen 1700, Imatra 1957; Esteri Kähönen, Vanha Äyräpää vuoteen 1700, no place of print 1959; Erkki Kuujo/Eino Puramo/J. Sarkanen, Käkisalmen historia. Käkisalmen kaupungin ja maalaiskunnan vaiheita, Käki-Säätiö 1958; Erkki Kuujo/Toivo Immonen/Eino Puramo, Kurkijoen kihlakunnan historia. Hiitola – Kurkijoki – Lumivaara – Jaakkima, Hiisi-Säätiö 1958. Local history or memoir books written by amateurs were for example Tommi Kilpiö et al. (eds.), Jaakkima, muistoja ja kuvia Laatokan rantamilta, Jaama-Säätiö 1955; Matti Kähäri, Vuoksela, nuoren kannakselaispitäjän vaiheita, Vuokselaisten pitäjäseura 1955; Unto Seppänen (ed.), Valkjärvi: pitäjä kohtaloitten Kannaksella, Lahti 1953; Metsäpirtti, entisen Kaakkoisrajan äärimmäinen kulmakunta, Metsäpirtin historiatoimikunta 1953; Impi Wilska, Vpl. Pyhäjärvi: kappale Kannakselaispitäjän vaiheita, Pyhän säätiö 1950; Väinö Seppä, Säkkijärvi kautta aikojen: muistojulkaisu, Säkkijärvisäätiö 1952. Other fairly large anthologies were: Yrjö-Pekka Mäkinen (ed.), Laatokan Karjalan nousun vuosikymmenet. Laatokan Karjalan henkisen ja taloudellisen kehityksen vaiheita 1880–1940, Pieksämäki 1956; J. Kivi-Koskinen et al. (ed.), Viipurin kirja: muistojulkaisu, Pieksämäki 1958.

61 See, for example, Jyrki Mäntylä, Paikannimisananparret impilahtelaisen aineiston valossa, in: Kalevalaseuran Vuosikirja 39 (1959), 246–256; Viljo Nissilä, Itä-Karjalan matkanimistöä, in: Kalevalaseuran Vuosikirja 35 (1955), 247–261; Viljo Nissilä, Viipuri paikannimien valossa, in: Kalevalaseuran Vuosikirja 37 (1957), 154–180; Alpo Sailo, Karjalan laulajia kuvaamassa 1909, in: Suomi IV:8 – Kalevalaseuran Vuosikirja 36 (1956), 249–254; Martti Haavio, Pyh' Äkräs [Agricolan karjalaisten jumalain luettelossa] in: Virittäjä 38 (1958), 313–330; Julius Mägiste, Suomen Sakkolan murteen Noisniemi ja Viron "nugis" näätä, in: Virittäjä 39 (1959), 323–325; Viljo Nissilä, Kuujärven paikannimistä, in: Virittäjä 51 (1947), 13–19; Martti Haavio, Karelarnas gudar, in: Budkavlen 38 (1959), 96–107; Martti Haavio, Karjalan jumalat. Uskontotieteellinen tutkimus, Porvoo 1959; Väinö Kaukonen, Karjalais-suomalainen kansanrunous Karjalan kansan alkuperäkysymyksen valossa, in: Neuvostoliittoinstituutin vuosikirja 3 (1952), 20–32; Viljo Nissilä, Lisiä venäläisperäisiin henkilönnimiin Itä-Karjalan paikannimistössä, in: Suomi 104 (1947), 1–40; E. A. Tunkelo, Karjala ja karjalaiset -sanain muunkieliset vastineet, in: Societas Scientiarium Fennica, årsbok 29 B:7 (1950–1951), 1–16; Eliel Wartiainen, Kun haltiat elivät... Kuvauksia runon ja taian mailta. Raja-Karjalan Säätiön julkaisuja 4, Jyväskylä 1953.

62 See, for example, Leo Kasanko, Suojärven seurakunnan kirkot, in: Aamun Koitto (1960), 6–8; Leo Kasanko, Tiurulan ja Kurkijoen kirkot. Yhteenveto kertyneestä aineistosta vuosilta 1917–1939, in: Aamun Koitto (1960), 84–86; Leo Kasanko, Tiurulan seurakunnan kirkot [Kurkijoki], in: Aamun Koitto (1960), 64–65; P. Kontkanen, Katsaus ortodoksisuuden vaiheisiin Karjalassa, in: Aamun Koitto (1958), 172–176, 207–212; Ari Surakka, Valamon luostarin kirjasto, in: Aamun Koitto (1959), 241–242; P. Kontkanen, Historiallista taustaa Karjalan ortodoksisen kirkon tämänhetkiseen asemaan, in: Elpis, Pieksämäki 1953. 33–53; Erkki Piiroinen, Karjalan pyhät kilvoittelijat, Kuopio 1947; Dimitri Tarvasaho, Mitä tiedämme Valamon luostarin perustajista, in: ONL:n vuosikirja 1955–56, Pieksämäki 1958, 12–16; Suomen kreikkalaiskatolinen pappisseminaari 1918–1948, Kuopio 1948; Ari Surakka, Karjalan ortodoksisen kirkon historiallinen lähtökohta in: Ortodoksia 11 (1958), 27–34.

63 See for example Mauno Jääskeläinen, Die ostkarelische Frage. Die Entstehung eines nationalen Expansionprogramms und die Versuche zu seiner Verwirklichung in den Aussenpolitik Finnlands in den Jahren 1918–1920, Turku 1965; Jukka Nevakivi, Muurmannin legioona. Suomalaiset ja liittoutuneiden interventio Pohjois-Venäjälle 1918–1919, Helsinki 1970; Jaakko Paavolainen, Itä-Karjalan väliaikainen hallitus 1919, in: Historiallinen Aikakauskirja 60 (1962), 10–12.

64 Toivo Nygård, Itä-Karjalan pakolaiset 1917–1922. Studia historica Jyväskyläensia 19, Tampere 1980; Toivo Nygård, Itä-Karjalasta 1918–1922 Suomeen tulleet pakolaiset, in: Scripta historica 6. (1980), 296–314.

65 Reino Kero, Emigration of Finns from North America to Soviet Karelia in the early 1930's. The Finnish experience in the Western Great Lakes region: new perspective, in: Migration studies C 3, Turku 1975, 212–221; Kaarlo Tuomi, The Karelian "fever" of the early 1930's, in: Finnish Americana 2 (1980), 61–75; William Copeland, Amerikansuomalaiset "pyhiinvaeltajat" Neuvosto-Karjalassa, in: Historiallinen Aikakauskirja 71 (1973), 287–300.

66 Keijo K. Kulha, Karjalaiset Kanta-Suomeen. Karjalaisen siirtoväen asuttamisesta käyty julkinen keskustelu vuosina 1944–1948, Studia historica Jyväskyläensia 7, Jyväskylä 1969; Leena Alanen, Laatokankarjalaiset toisen maailmansodan jälkeen. Sosiologinen tutkimus laatokankarjalaisen siirtoväen alueellisesta ja ammatillisesta uudelleensijoittumisesta sekä väestörakenteesta, Karjalan tutkimuslaitoksen julkaisuja 11, Joensuu 1975.

67 A historian, Veli-Matti Syrjö, published an article about the archival sources left by the occupation administration: Veli-Matti Syrjö, Itä-Karjalan sotilashallinto 1941–1944 ja sen arkistot, in: Historiallinen Aikakauskirja 70 (1972), 308–321. Several writings of amateur historians, mostly memoirs, were also published.

68 Gallén, Jarl, Nöteborgsfreden och Finlands medeltida östgräns, Skrifter utgivna av Svenska litteratursällskap i Finland 427:1, Helsingfors 1968; see also Gallén, Jarl, Nöteborgstraktaten och rikets gräns i öster, in: Gunvor Grenholn (ed.), Den Svenska historien 2, Stockholm 1966, 306–307.

69 Kyösti Julku, Professor of History at the University of Oulu 1966–1994. Suomen Professorit, Loc. Cit, (Note 6), 238–239.

70 Kyösti Julku, Korela Semidetskaya, Oulun yliopisto, historian laitos, Eripainossarja 1, Oulu 1968; Kyösti Julku, Täyssinän rauhan v. 1595 raja Iivaaran pohjoispuolella, Oulun yliopisto, historian laitos, Eripainossarja 8, Oulu 1971.

71 Heikki Kirkinen, Professor of History at the University of Joensuu 1970–1990. Suomen Professorit, Loc. Cit. (Note 6), 296.

72 Heikki Kirkinen, Kiistakenttä ja silta. Karjalan historiallinen funktio, in: Suomalainen Suomi 33 (1965), 327–334.

73 Heikki Kirkinen, Karjala idän kulttuuripiirissä. Bysantin ja Venäjän yhteyksistä keskiajan Karjalaan, Historiallisia Tutkimuksia 67, Rauma 1963; Heikki Kirkinen, Karjala idän ja lännen välissä. I. Venäjän Karjala renessanssiajalla (1478–1617), Historiallisia Tutkimuksia 80, Joensuu 1970; Heikki Kirkinen, Karjala taistelukenttänä. Karjala idän ja lännen välissä II, Historiallisia Tutkimuksia 89, Helsinki 1976.

74 Hannes Sihvo (ed.), Karjala: idän ja lännen silta. Kalevalaseuran Vuosikirja 53 (1973).

75 Markku Haapio et al. (eds.), Karjala 1. Portti itään ja länteen, Hämeenlinna 1982.

76 Hannes Sihvo, Professor of Literature at the University of Joensuu 1981–2001. Suomen Professorit, Loc. Cit. (Note 6), 668–669.

77 Hannes Sihvo, Karjalan löytäjät, Tampere 1969; Hannes Sihvo, Karjalan kuva. Karelianismin taustaa ja vaiheita autonomian aikana, Suomalaisen Kirjallisuuden Seuran Toimituksia 314, Joensuu 1973 ([2] 2003).

78 Risto Alapuro, Professor of Sociology at the University of Jyväskylä 1986–1991 and at the University of Helsinki from 1991 onwards. Suomen Professorit, Loc. Cit. (Note 6), 53.

79 Risto Alapuro, Akateeminen Karjala-seura. Ylioppilasliike 1920–1930-luvulla. Helsinki 1973.

80 Veijo Saloheimo, Senior researcher at the Karelian Institute, University of Joensuu 1971–1989, Professor in honorem causa 1984. Tommila, Suomen, Loc. Cit. (Note 8), 267.

81 Aulis V. Könönen/Heikki Kirkinen, Pohjois-Karjalan historia 1. Keskiajasta Stolbovan rauhaan, Joensuu 1969; Veijo Saloheimo, Pohjois-Karjalan historia 2. 1617–1721, Joensuun korkeakoulun julkaisuja A 6, Joensuu 1976; Veijo Saloheimo, Pohjois-Karjalan historia 3. 1722–1809, Joensuun korkeakoulun julkaisuja A 18, Joensuu 1980.

82 See, for example, Lauri Saloheimo, Ilomantsin seurakunnat 1700-luvulla, in: Rajaseutu (1965), 78–82; Lauri Saloheimo, Megri ja Pahkalampi. Ilomantsin entiset luostarit, in: Rajamme vartijat 2 (1964), 2–3; Lauri Saloheimo, Möhkö, Ilomantsin suurin teollisuuskeskus viime vuosisadalla, in Rajamme vartijat 7 (1968), 14–15, 41, 51; Pentti Laasonen, Pohjois-Karjalan luterilainen kirkollinen kansankulttuuri Ruotsin vallan aikana, Suomen Kirkkohistoriallisen Seuran Toimituksia 72, Kuopio 1967; Erkki Piiroinen, Ortodoksiset pyhäköt ja kalmistot Pohjois-Karjalassa, in: Rajamme vartijat 3 (1963), 4–6.

83 Viljo L. Alanko et al., Pohjois-Karjala sanoin ja kuvin, Kuopio 1975; Erkki Helasvuo et al. (eds.), Pohjoiskarjalainen maisema taiteessa, Joensuu 1980.

84 Those published in the 1960s and in 1970 were: Matti Kähäri, Raudun historia, Pieksämäki 1965; Aarne Kopisto/Toivo J. Paloposki, Viipurin pitäjän historia 1. Vuoteen 1865, Joensuu 1967; Erkki Kuujo/Jorma Tiainen/Eeva Karttunen, Sortavalan kaupungin historia, Jyväskylä 1970; Yrjö Kaukiainen, Virolahden historia 1. 1850–luvulle, Lappeenranta 1970. The following local histories from the 1920s were reprinted in the 1960s: V. Salminen, Jaakkiman pitäjän historia. 1, Hämeenlinna 1967. ([1]1923); M. Vilska, Parikkalan historia 1–2, Lappeenranta 1969 ([1]1926 and 1928).

85 Books of memoirs from Vuoksela, Uukuniemi and Kivennapa, first published in the 1950s, were reprinted in the 1960s, see Loc. Cit. (Note 60). New books were Ikonen, Veli, Jääsken kirja. Vanhan karjalaispitäjän viimeisten vuosikymmenten historiaa, Helsinki 1966, and Lauri Pelkonen, Suojärvi 1–2, Pieksämäki 1965 and 1966.

86 See the basic work on the defining of borders in the 18th century, Raimo Ranta, Kaakkois-Suomi kiistana rauhanneuvotteluissa 1718–21 ja 1743, in: Viipurin suomalaisen kirjallisuusseuran toimitteita 7 (1985), 15–98.

87 Raimo Ranta, Städernas handelsomland och gränsernas inverkan i Gamla Finland, in: Historisk Tidskrift för Finland 66 (1982), 48–77; Raimo Ranta, Venäläinen sotaväki ja majoitusrasitus Vanhassa Suomessa, in: Turun Historiallinen Arkisto 38 (1982), 135–166; Raimo Ranta, Venäläinen kauppiaskunta ja sen kauppa Suomessa, in: Pauli Kurkinen (ed.), Venäläiset Suomessa, Historiallinen Arkisto 83 (1984), 29–66; Raimo Ranta, Verotus Viipurin komendanttikunnassa revisioon (1728) asti, in: THA 39 (1985), 142–171; Raimo Ranta, Lahjoitusmaat Viipurin komendanttikunnassa Uudenkaupungin rauhaan asti, in: Kyösti Kiuasmaa et al. (eds.), Yksilö ja yhteiskunnan muutos. Juhlakirja Viljo Rasilan täyttäessä 60 vuotta 22.1.1986, Acta Universitatis Tamperensis Ser. A: 202, 122–141; Raimo Ranta, Vanhan Suomen "silta"; vanhoja siteitä ja uusia vaikutteita, in: Rauno Endén (ed.), Historian päivät 1985, Historiallinen Arkisto 88 (1988), 73–89, 416–417; Raimo Ranta, Vanhan Suomen talouselämä vuosina 1721–1743 I–II, Historiallisia Tutkimuksia 130, Helsinki 1985, 1986; Raimo Ranta, Viipurin komendanttikunta 1710–1721: valtaus, hallinto ja oikeudenhoito, Historiallisia Tutkimuksia 141, Helsinki 1987.

88 The Swedish-language historical journal in Finland, Historisk Tidskrift för Finland, published a thematic number on the history of Old Finland in 1982, in which the authors were both Swedish and Finnish-speaking historians and some Soviet historians. See Historisk Tidskrift för Finland 66 (1982). Other improtant works were Yrjö Kaukiainen, Bidragen till bondens historia i Gamla Finland, in Historisk Tidskrift för Finland 66 (1982), 4–31; Yrjö Kaukiainen, Vanhan Suomen aikakausi, in: Markku Haapio et al. (ed.), Karjala 4. Karjalan vaiheet. Hämeenlinna 1984, 85–121; Vilho Hämäläinen, Karjalan kannaksen venäläinen kesäasutuskysymys maamme itsenäisyyden kaudella, Tampereen historiatieteen laitoksen julkaisuja 6, Tampere 1983; Vilho Hämäläinen, Vanhan Suomen venäläiset huvila-asukkaat, in: Pauli Kurkinen (ed.), Venäläiset Suomessa 1809–1917, Historiallinen Arkisto 83 (1984), 115–124.

89 See, for example, I. M. Bobovic, Donationsgodsen i Gamla Finland fram till mitten av 1800-talet, in: Historisk Tidskrift för Finland 66 (1982), 32–47; I. P. Saskolski, Keskiaikaisten kaupunkien, Tallinnan, Riian, Viipurin ja Turun syntyminen Itämeren itärannalle, in: Rauno Endén/Vesa Laulumaa (eds.), Suomalaisneuvostoliittolainen historiantutkijoiden symposium: Riika 1.–7.12.1985, Historiallinen Arkisto 87 (1986), 9–29; S. J. Kotskurkina, Laatokan pohjoispuolen ja Kaakkois-Suomen asuttamisesta keskiajalla (400-luvulta 1400-luvulle), in: Eero Kuparinen (ed.), VIII suomalais-neuvostoliittolainen yhteiskuntahistorian symposiumi Turussa 2.–6.9.1984, THA 41 (1986), 41–55; Aleksandr Saksa, Käkisalmen linna 1200-luvulta in: Geologi 90 (1990), 65–68.

90 Kyösti Julku, Suomen itärajan synty. Studia historica septentrionalia 10, Rovaniemi 1987.

91 Jarl Gallén, Om gränsdragningar i Sveriges och Finlands historia. Ur armod och ur ödemark, in: Historicus skriftserie 4 (1982), 2–16; John Lind, Om Nödeborgsfreden og dens graenser, in: Historisk Tidskrift för Finland 69 (1985), 305–336; John Lind, Omkring de svensk-russiske forhandlinger 1537, 1339-traktaten og Nodeborgs-freden, in: Historisk Tidskrift för Finland 69 (1985), 1–22; John Lind, Pähkinäsaaren rauhansopimuksen ruotsinkielinen teksti ja kaksihaarainen raja, in: Historiallinen Aikakauskirja 91 (1993), 155–162; John Lind, Nygammelt om Nødebogsfredens graense, in: Historisk Tidskrift för Finland 74 (1990), 69–84; Jarl Gallén and John Lind, Nöteborgsfreden och Finlands medeltida östgräns. Andra delen, Skrifter utgivna av Svenska Litteratursällskapet i Finland 427, 2, Helsingfors 1991.

92 Heikki Kirkinen, Mikä oli Pähkinäsaaren rauhan raja?, in: Historiallinen Aikakauskirja 90 (1992), 304–317; Heikki Kirkinen, Pohjanlahti vai Vienan meri 1323?, in: Historiallinen Aikakauskirja 91 (1993), 42–47; Heikki Kirkinen, Valtioidenväliset sopimukset ja tuohikirjeet – lähteiden todistusvoimasta rajatulkinnassa, in: Historiallinen Aikakauskirja 93 (1995), 53–55; Heikki Kirkinen, Salainen lisäpöytäkirjako Pähkinäsaaren rauhansopimuksessa? Keskustelua, in: Historiallinen Aikakauskirja 102 (2004), 393–406.

93 John Lind, Hvornår blev Valamo klosteret grundlagt?, in: Historisk Tidskrift för Finland 63 (1979), 234–261; John Lind, Sources and Pseudo-Sources on the Foundation of the Valamo Monastery, in: Scandinavian Journal of History 11 (1986), 115–133; Heikki Kirkinen, The origins of Valamo

monastery, in Byzantium and the North: Acta Byzantina Fennica 3 (1987), 19–32; John Lind, "Fortællingen om Valamoklosteret. En nyfunden kilde til klosterets ældste historie in Historisk Tidskrift för Finland 76 (1992), 1–30; John Lind, Valamon luostarin perustamisen poliittinen tausta, in: Sari Hirvonen et al. (eds.), Te menitte asumaan meren saareen..., Tutkimuksia Valamon luostarista, Heinävesi 1994, 33–40; Heikki Kirkinen, Valamon luostarin perustamiset, in: Sari Hirvonen et al. (eds.), Te menitte asumaan meren saareen... Tutkimuksia Valamon luostarista, Heinävesi 1994, 41–58; Heikki Kirkinen, The Founding of Valamo monastery, when, who and by whom, in: Ortodoksia 44 (1995), 30–55; Heikki Kirkinen, Valamon luostarin synty yhä tuntematon, in: Tapio Hämynen (ed.), Kahden Karjalan välillä, kahden Riikin riitamaalla, Studia Carelica humanistica 5, Joensuu 1994, 211–220. Kati Parppei studied the historiographic problem of foundation of the Valaam monastery in her dissertation Saints, Legends and Forgeries. The Formation of the Historiographical Image of the Valaam Monastery. Dissertations in Social Sciences and Business Studies 5, Joensuu 2010. See also Parppei, Kati, "The Oldest One in Russia" The Formation of the Historiographical Image of Valaam Monastery, Brill 2011.

94 Heikki Kirkinen, Karjalan ja Kalevalan juuria, in: Matti Kuusi et al. (eds.), Kirjokannesta kipinä. Kalevalan juhlavuoden satoa, Kalevalaseuran vuosikirja 66 (1986), 91–95; Heikki Kirkinen, Pohjois-Karjalan kalevalaisen perinteen juuret, Tietolipas 108, Helsinki 1988.

95 Eero Autio, Karjalan kalliopiirrokset. Otava 1981; Eero Autio, Hirvi ja käärme Uikujoen kalliossa, in: Kotiseutu (1984), 80–84; Niilo Valonen, Ancient folk poetry in Eastern Karelian petroglyphs, in: Ethnologica Fennica 12 (1982–83), 9–48; Pirjo Uino, Luovutetun Karjalan esihistorian tutkimuksesta. Kotiseutu (1990), 118–124; Heikki Kirkinen, Äänisen ja Uikujoen kalliopiirrosten tekijät, Eripainossarja, Oulun yliopisto, historian laitos, N:o 295 (1993); Pirjo Uino, Ancient Karelia: archaeological studies – Muinais-Karjala: arkeologisia tutkimuksia, in: Suomen muinaismuistoyhdistyksen aikakauskirja 104. Helsinki 1997.

96 Many of these publications are proceedings of Finnish-Soviet scientific conferences and seminars. See, for example, Rauno Endén/Vesa Laulumaa (eds.), Suomalaisneuvostoliittolainen historiantutkijoiden, Loc. Cit. (Note 89), and Eero Kuparinen (ed.), VIII suomalais-neuvostoliittolainen yhteiskuntahistorian, Loc. Cit. (Note 89).

97 On the Finns who moved from North America to Soviet Karelia, see Reino Kero, Neuvostokarjalaa rakentamassa. Pohjois-Amerikan suomalaiset tekniikan tuojina 1930-luvun Neuvostokarjalassa. Historiallisia Tutkimuksia 122, Helsinki 1983; Reino Kero, The Role of Finnish settlers from North America in the nationality question in Soviet Karelia in the 1930s, in Scandinavian Journal of History 6 (1981), 229–241. On the role of the Finns in Soviet Karelia, see Auvo Kostiainen, Dominating Finnish minority? On the background of the nationality problem in Soviet Karelia in the 1930s, in: Faravid 8 (1984), 341–366, and on Finns moving to Soviet Karelia during the Great Depression of the 1930s, see Auvo Kostiainen, Loikkarit. Suuren lamakauden laiton siirtolaisuus Neuvostoliittoon, Otava 1988. This research was filled out in a sense by the doctoral thesis of Markku Kangaspuro, Neuvosto-Karjalan taistelu itsehallinnosta. Nationalismi ja suomalaiset punaiset Neuvostoliiton vallankäytössä 1920–1939, Bibliotheca Historica 60, Helsinki 2000.

98 Toivo Nygård, Itä-Karjalan pakolaiset 1917–1922, Studia Historica Jyväskyläensia 19, Jyväskylä 1980; Jouko Vahtola, "Suomi suureksi – Viena vapaaksi". Valkoisen Suomen pyrkimykset Itä-Karjalan valtaamiseksi vuonna 1918, Studia Historica Septentrionalia 17, Rovaniemi 1988; Jouko Vahtola, Östkarelen i finländsk politik 1917–1945, in: Faravid 13 (1989), 177–192; Jouko Vahtola, Itäkarjala Suomen politiikassa 1917–1922, in: Terra 105 (1993), 280–290; Antti Laine, Suur-Suomen kahdet kasvot. Itä-Karjalan siviiliväestön asema suomalaisessa miehityshallinnossa 1941–1944, Otava 1982; Jukka Kulomaa, Äänislinna. Petroskoin suomalaismiehityksen vuodet 1941–1944, Historiallisia tutkimuksia 148, Helsinki 1989.

99 This and subsequent conclusions are based on search results obtained with the ARTO and Linda databases using the keywords Karjala/Karelia. See the introductory chapter.

100 See the following pamphlets, for example: Yrjö Pessi/Reino J. Auvinen, Karjala-kysymys. Taloudellisia näkökohtia, Karjala-lehti 1995; Carita Ahlberg, The Karelian Issue, Helsinki 1996; Jukka Seppinen, Kohti Karjalaa. Pakkoluovutettu Karjala tänään ja huomenna, Lappeenranta 1998;

Yrjö Pessi, Karjalamme rajan takana, Espoo 1998; Ilmari Susiluoto, Pieni karjalakirja, Helsinki 1999; Hannu Takala, Kun Karjala palautuu, Vuoksen Vartio 2000. See also the discussion of these books in Outi Fingerroos, Karjala utopiana, Nykykulttuurin tutkimuskeskuksen julkaisuja 100, Jyväskylä 2010, 133–148.

101 For travel guides, see, for example, Markku Nieminen, Vienan runokylät, Kulttuuriopas, Helsinki 1995; Marjaana Hanki/Eeva Nuutinen, Vienan kävijän opas, Helsinki 1999; Petri Neuvonen et al., Viipuri: opas kaupunkiin – Vyborg: town guide, Helsinki 1999; Markus Lehtipuu, Karjala. Luovutettu Karjala, Itä-Karjala, Vienan Karjala, Helsinki 2000.

102 One example is the history of Karelian people: Heikki Kirkinen/Hannes Sihvo/Pekka Nevalainen, Karjalan kansan historia, Porvoo 1994.

103 The analogy drawn between the processes affecting the EU borders and the history of Karelia and its borders can be clearly seen in the name of one book on the subject: Heikki Kirkinen/Leena Westman (eds), On the Border of European Union. From the Gulf of Finland to the Arctic Ocean, Joensuu 1996. See also Tapio Hämynen, Liikkeellä leivän tähden. Raja-Karjalan väestö ja sen toimeentulo 1880–1940, Historiallisia Tutkimuksia 170, Helsinki 1992; Hämynen (ed.), Kahden Karjalan välillä, Loc. Cit. (Note 90); Katajala, Kimmo (ed), Itä-Suomi ja Pietari. Kirjoituksia toimeentulosta suurkaupungin vaikutuspiirissä, Studia Carelica Humanistica 9, Joensuu 1997. This view became visible soon after the studied period especially in the doctoral thesis of Jukka Kokkonen, Rajaseutu liikkeessä. Kainuun ja Pielisen Karjalan asukkaiden kontaktit Venäjän Karjalaan kreivin ajasta sarkasotaan (1650–1712), Bibliotheca Historica 79, Helsinki 2002.

MARIA LÄHTEENMÄKI

COWS, GUNS AND BOLSHEVIKS: SMUGGLING IN THE BORDERLAND BETWEEN SOUTH-EAST FINLAND AND ST. PETERSBURG

Illegal traffic in people and goods has been taking place between Finland and the other countries of the Baltic region for centuries,[1] and that between Finland and Russia assumed an organized, recorded form early in the 19th century, at the time when Finland ceased to be a province of Sweden and became an autonomous Grand Duchy within the Russian Empire, in 1809. This high degree of autonomy, which Finland retained up until the end of the century, meant that normal customs and border formalities applied on its border with Russia, and a branch of the Finnish administration, known as the Customs Directorate, was created in 1812 to supervise these formalities and combat smuggling throughout the country. Considerable attention was paid to this supervision, as it was envisaged that customs duties could become one of the country's main sources of revenue, and this was in fact the case, as they accounted for over 40% of its tax income in 1850 and as much as 70% by the beginning of the 20th century. One indication of both the tightening of border controls and the continued prevalence of smuggling was an imperial decree issued in 1852 concerning the illegal transport of goods into Russia from Finland.[2]

In spite of the fact that the prevention of smuggling continued to be a matter of major economic importance up until the 1930s, it still took place all the time. During the periods of Russification in Finland (1899–1905 and 1908–1917) it was not only alcoholic beverages that were transported over the border but also proscribed literature, clandestine resistance activists and Bolsheviks. V. I. Lenin, for instance, crossed into Finland from St. Petersburg illegally in 1906 and lived for some time in the border municipality of Terijoki (now the Russian community of Zelenogorsk) along with numerous Menshevik leaders.[3]

The real golden age for illegal traffic on Finland's eastern border, however, covered the transitional years of 1917–1932, the main reason for the rapid growth in smuggling being the official closure of the border at the point when the Bolsheviks took control over Russia and Finland gained its independence. This effectively cut off the once lively trade route between St. Petersburg and Finland over the Karelian Isthmus and caused an economic disaster for the border areas that had previously made their living from trade and services. A second factor that stimulated smuggling, of course, was the Prohibition Law that was in force in Finland from 1919 to 1932, which concentrated the production, sale, supply and warehousing of alcoholic beverages entirely in a state-owned monopoly. During World War II and the years of post-war austerity the border area was a scene for the smuggling of alcohol, foodstuffs and luxury goods either from or to Finland,[4] and even in more recent times smuggling has not passed into history, but rather the newspapers remind us at regular intervals of the illegal passage of goods and people between Finland and Russia, mostly in the hands of professional gangs of smugglers, the mafia and private individuals. Within the last few years, for instance, there have been reports of extensive illegal trading in mobile phones, pedigree dogs and drugs over the border and the organized transport of Russian prostitutes to Finland.[5] It has been estimated that the principal forms of smuggling into Finland in the early years of the new millennium were the drug trade, prostitution and the importing of pirate goods, cigarettes, medicines and doping substances for sports use, together constituting a form of illegal trading worth more than 1000 million euro in 2009.[6] Financial profit has indeed been the principal motive for undertaking smuggling over this border throughout history, and this was also the case in the Finnish border communities in the period 1917–1932.

As one aspect of international crime, smuggling has been studied to date mainly by lawyers, sociologists, geographers and historians, and it is largely in the last couple of decades that attention has been drawn to the vast profits to be made by those engaged in one way or another in trafficking in humans and narcotics.[7] The globalization of the world economy, poverty and the widening discrepancies in standards of living, the opening up of Eastern Europe and the preventive activities of organizations such as the International Labour Organization and the International Confederation of Free Labour Unions have led to a concentration of research efforts specifically on these forms of crime.[8] It has been suggested that the rapid political changes that have taken place in the last couple of decades – in the Soviet Union and Yugoslavia, for example – have led to instability, wars, ethnic conflicts, unemployment and increases in crime and migration, creating a situation in which human trafficking and the smuggling of goods can flourish.[9] Similarly unstable social conditions ravaged the borderlands between Finland and Russia on the Karelian Isthmus as a consequence of the revolutions in Russia and Finnish independence in 1917, the Civil War in Finland in 1918 and that in Russia in 1918–1920. In this case, too, the breakdown of society as it had existed and its reconstruction in a new form gave rise to ethnic conflicts, unemployment and crime,[10] and also led to an increase in smuggling.

The present paper will address this crisis of the second decade of the 20th century by tracing the history of smuggling between South-East Finland and St. Petersburg during its peak years of 1917–1932. The area concerned comprises the districts of Terijoki, Kivennapa, Rautu and Metsäpirtti, which belonged to Finland at that time but bordered on Russia (Map 5).

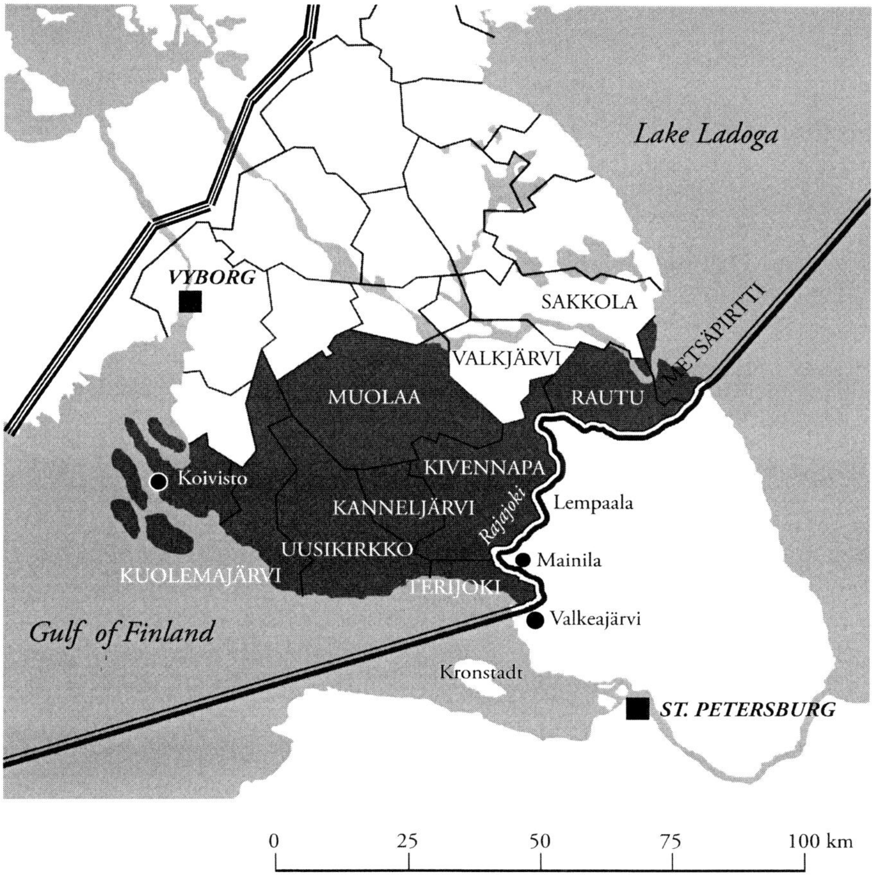

MUNCIPALITIES
- Boundary
- City
- Borough

BOUNDARIES
- State Border after 1944
- State Border before 1939

BORDERLAND
- Oct. 29, 1918* – ca. 1925
- * Sakkola and Valkjärvi added later

Map 5. *The borderland between South-East Finland and St. Petersburg in 1920*

All in all, the border that crossed the Karelian Isthmus from the Gulf of Finland to Lake Ladoga was 120 km in length, running along the narrow river Rajajoki (Russ. *Reka Sestra*) for half of this distance and over marshy and in places forested terrain for the other half. Smuggling and the activities of the smugglers in this area will be described and evaluated from a regional history perspective, employing microhistorical methods.[11] The aim will be to gain an idea of who were engaged in smuggling, what and who they transported over the border and what their motives were in doing so. These variables will then help us to assess the social and political situation in the Finnish borderlands during the period concerned.

In effect we are concerned here not only with smuggling as such but with various associated phenomena as well, so that one could well refer in general to "Illegal economic activity", i.e. economic activity that is totally prohibited by law, such as smuggling itself, procuration (prostitution) and trading in narcotics and also other commercial activities for which no licence has been obtained from the authorities, such as the illicit transportation of goods or persons and black market dealing for the purposes of evading regulations or taxation.[12] During the period from 1917 to 1932 and for some time afterwards this illegal economic activity also had a political dimension, i.e. the illicit conveyance of Bolshevist propaganda and Bolshevik agents into Finland from Russia/Soviet Union. Thus the smugglers were in effect guilty of both economic and political crimes, two elements that were in many cases intimately connected, as we will see below.

ECONOMIC COLLAPSE AS THE STIMULUS FOR SMUGGLING

When the revolutionary events of 1917–1918 cut off the previously lively flow of trade between St. Petersburg and Finland, this completely undermined the basis on which the economy of the borderland communities relied. The resulting crisis is well reflected in a report by an inspector sent to the south-eastern border of Finland in 1919, who wrote that all trade and traffic had been at a standstill for the last year and that there were supplies of firewood worth tens of millions of marks standing on the shores of Lake Ladoga and beside the railway lines waiting to be taken to St. Petersburg. This sudden cessation of all trade and transport and the disappearance of the other employment opportunities offered by the metropolis had given rise to a wave of smuggling. Where this activity had largely been a matter of the bringing of quantities of Russian spirits into Finland in the days before 1914, it now involved a huge selection of products of all kinds. According to the inspector, "a large proportion of the inhabitants of the border districts had given up their other sources of income and had taken to smuggling", or at least to assisting in it. The prices paid for the goods were rising all the time, and were now so high that the business went on even if some of the traffickers were caught in the act and even shot. The profits in any case ran into many millions of roubles.[13]

The Finnish government expended a great deal of resources on preventing illegal crossings of the border, employing an army unit, the Finnish Security Police (Finn. Etsivä keskuspoliisi, EK), the customs authorities and the border guards for this purpose, and even detailing the local police and paramilitary Civil Defence forces to supervise movements in the border zone. But in spite of this the border leaked like a sieve. The authorities were powerless in this situation, as men, women, boys and girls, old people, workers, tradesmen, farmers and officials in dozens of villages close to the border were overcome by the smuggling fever.[14] It was not merely the ensuring of their daily bread that kept everyone who possibly could on the move, but rather the dream of becoming rich overnight. The fact that it provided a source of employment and the hope of making their fortune meant that the local people no longer regarded smuggling as a crime. Admittedly a large proportion of the raids made by the customs officials to confiscate goods were as a result of tip-offs from local people, but these were presumably motivated by jealousy rather than moral rectitude or political revulsion.[15]

"Such huge quantities of goods of so many kinds have never been smuggled into Russia as was the case in 1919 and 1920," it was observed in 1932.[16] An operator on the Karelian Isthmus could cross the Rajajoki border river with a load containing salt, bread, butter, lard, flour, porridge oats, coffee, sugar and matches, medicines, window panes, ironmongery, leather goods and clothes, and many other things. The women would stuff their handbags full of combs, safety pins, babies' dummies, corset ribbons, scarves and buttons, and the men would take seed for the Russians' vegetable gardens and spirits, brandy and liqueurs for thirsty throats. Even animals would be smuggled in, as some of the operators were known to specialize in cows and horses.[17] Impoverished by the revolution, the red city of St. Petersburg (Leningrad from the year 1924) soaked up everything that came its way, from sewing needles, silk stockings and woollen clothes to whole horse-drawn consignments of goods.[18]

Among the most valuable items, however, were firearms and ammunition, and sometimes cars; and there was even some smuggling of people. Altogether this became a highly professional and lucrative form of borderland business, involving a chain of dealers that included people in the St. Petersburg area of Russia and throughout the Karelian Isthmus on the Finnish side: those who ordered the goods (dealers and the heads of various organizations) those who produced them – farmers and their wives, factory workers and managers, smiths, artisans, cobblers and tailors, drivers (women as well as men), dealers, salesmen, organizers – and those who gave assistance.[19]

One Finnish inspector sent to the Russian border said of the smuggling taking place in 1922 that "it was organized like one of the best department stores ... it had a smoothly running supply chain." These well organized groups of operators would usually have between three and ten armed men among their number, so that it was reported that one load being transported by nine men that was confiscated in April 1922 included six rifles, a Browning automatic and a Nagant revolver. Altogether three categories of smugglers may be distinguished: 1) well-armed gangs of hardened professionals who transported large amounts of valuable goods such as firearms and horses, 2) practised non-professionals who indulged in smuggling together with friends or family members when they had the chance, and 3) amateurs who carried small amounts and earned very little from it.[20]

Most of the local inhabitants who took part in the smuggling and crossed the border illegally had become involved for quite practical reasons. One Finnish widow would wade across the river into Russia from time to time because her shoe mender lived there and he charged less than those on the Finnish side of the border,[21] while the career of one local workman called Vilhelm shows that he drifted into smuggling for financial reasons. It was fairly easy to take it up if you wished, since the local people knew the tricks for crossing the border undetected from earlier times, as clandestine trade had been going on there in one form or another since the mid-19th century. The situation had become much more serious since the new boundary had been established after the Finnish Civil War of 1918, but Vilhelm was willing to take the risk as he had no other source of income. He had belonged to the Red Guards in the Civil War and had been captured by the Germans who had come to the aid of the Finnish Whites and been interred in a prisoner-of-war camp. He had been a sick man when he was released in autumn 1918 and had been in hospital for two months, after which he had tried to make a living by speculating in foodstuffs. The following year he had been a lumberjack and had spent some time cutting firewood, but the following spring he had taken up smuggling together with a friend who was in much the same predicament.

Vilhelm had made five trips to Russia altogether. On the very first occasion he had been apprehended while skiing over the sea ice to Kronstadt and had been under arrest for ten days before being released and allowed to return to Finland. Then on the fifth occasion he had been intercepted again and taken to the Russian side village of Mainila, where he was interrogated for five days. From there he was sent to Shpalernaya Prison and sentenced to a year's hard labour for spying. After two months, however, he was transferred to Kresty Prison in St. Petersburg and had continued living in the city after his release. Later he had moved to a place in Ingria close to the Finnish border and from there he had crossed illegally back into Finland.[22]

The case of a Finn by the name of Matti was rather different. He was more of a professional and had mostly been engaged in delivering food to a contact in the Communist Party of Finland, which had been formed in Moscow in 1918. He had made at least six such journeys, and the Finnish Security Police regarded him as a "major operator" who had begun smuggling in the times before Finnish independence, as his first conviction dated back to 1910. Witnesses claimed that he would be armed with a carbine rifle and a Mauser pistol when about his business, and the police agents found among his possessions 12 invoices for goods, a 44-page notebook with details of orders and sales, a paper showing the exchange rates for forged banknotes, some letters and a forged passport.[23]

Many perfectly legal travellers throughout the 1920s also carried smuggled goods. Two Jewish merchants from Finland, for instance, were intercepted carrying large quantities of these and were obliged to forfeit them to the state and pay substantial fines.[24] There were also cases of Finnish sportsmen accused of smuggling alcoholic drinks into Finland, where there was a great demand for these during the prohibition years. One team from the Helsinki Workers' Gymnastics and Sports Club tried to bring 22 bottles of drink home with them, and members of a workers' youth organization in Vyborg were stopped for a similar reason.[25] The Security Police maintained that smuggling was still rife at the crossing point on the border in 1927.[26] Gradually, however, the improvement in living conditions came to be reflected in the goods transported over the border, so that by the 1930s there was an increasing trade in items such as caviar, antique silver, jewellery and icons.

Women were involved in smuggling just as much as men. One lady from Helsinki was stopped by the Russian customs officials when trying to bring cocaine into the country and ended up in Shpalernaya Prison. In fact the Security Police reckoned that almost all travellers to Russia, including those on official business, were trying to smuggle something – some with greater success than others. One Russian lady was discovered wearing several dresses one on top of the other and was obliged to forfeit the superfluous ones to the Finnish state.[27]

SMUGGLING ROUTES BY LAND AND SEA

The routes by which smuggling took place were usually devious ones. One person living in Soviet Russia interrogated on suspicion of involvement in smuggling, Edvard, explained how the goods had been brought over the border to the village of Mainila by Finnish smugglers, after which they had been moved to Valkeasaari near St. Petersburg, and it was only after that that his turn came. He took them by horse-drawn cart to "an old woman" in Postanski Street in St. Petersburg, who gave him a receipt for them. After that they had been delivered to the organization that had ordered them, in this case the Murmansk Fisheries Association, which had a purchasing committee in St. Petersburg run by two Estonians. The smugglers usually had lists of the items intended for the various purchasers, as this whole business was usually done on the basis of orders. On one occasion this same Edvard was asked by one Russian woman to take valuables belonging to some rich Russians to safety in Finland, and he agreed to do so on condition that he could have a new passport. He was supplied with one for a very high fee of 5000 marks.[28]

The smugglers would alter their routes as the customs officials and police discovered them – in addition to which they would use different routes in summer and winter.[29] One of the most popular alternatives in the case of the Karelian Isthmus was through the eastern archipelago in the Gulf of Finland, so that the island of Seiskari was one of the best known places for handing over goods. Detection problems were also made worse by the fact that "the locals are all in league with the smugglers". As the investigation department put it, there was "one huge gang of them" and most of them were "Reds".[30] The people on Seiskari were highly suspicious of all outsiders, and there would always be one of the villagers on the look-out when the mail boat arrived to see who was coming ashore. If there were any strangers, word was passed round to everyone in no time, and this gave the smugglers the chance to move their boats further away. Night crossings were made easier in winter by marking the channels with pine or spruce branches.[31] As elsewhere, smuggling had been forced on the people of Seiskari by the closing of the border, and many of them made a living by specializing in illicit liquor.[32]

Goods were also taken into Russia via Lake Ladoga, over the ice on horse-drawn sledges in winter and by boat in summer, and again the smugglers worked in large groups and were heavily armed.[33] The eight horse-drawn consignments of goods taken via one village by an "export organization" of ten local men, for instance, included a machine-gun and 260 rifles.[34] By the 1920s the whole process had become more professional, the consignments were larger and even the less professional members of the gangs were armed.

BORDER GUARDS IMPLICATED IN SMUGGLING

"It was easy to cross, because the local border guards were in on it with us: they would take people over on foot for 20–30 marks." This, at least, was what the women in one village told police investigators in 1919.[35]

The 120 km of the border between Finland and Soviet Russia was guarded by only 10 Finnish patrols, amounting to about 100 men, in 1918, i.e. it was seriously undermanned. Supervision was intensified in 1919, however, when 40 watchtowers were built and a total of 470 men were stationed at them, and by August 1920, following another reorganization, there were 31 border patrols in the field on the Karelian Isthmus.[36] Nevertheless the smugglers were well informed of the positions of the watchtowers and the movements of the patrols, and the border guards quite simply avoided seeing the people who were crossing illegally, by leaving for the next watchtower at the critical moment or staying in their hut just long enough to let the people and their carts cross over. In one case a border guard had ordered his companions to move to a position several kilometres away from their station in the middle of the night, which they had been reluctant to do and had wondered out aloud why it was so essential to bribe one guard to deceive the others.[37] Sometimes, however, incidents broke out between customs officers and those involved in smuggling. For example, the story went round in the border villages that one customs officer in June 1919 had not shot enemy soldiers dead on the other side of the border but Finnish men. On another occasion a house where customs officers were living was burned down in dubious circumstances and the men lost everything they possessed.[38]

According to a report by a government inspector sent to the border zone it was the customs officers who were in the most difficult position of all. They were “outsiders to everything that was going on in society”. As all the border guards were involved in smuggling while the customs service was trying to prevent it, the local people were hostile towards the customs men. “Not even the soldiers had any sympathy for them”, and certainly not the local Civil Defence forces, as the customs service was a hindrance to them. Even the highest official in the border zone, the commandant assigned there in 1918, had found himself in trouble according to the border inspector, as his “agents” who had conducted operations on the Russian side had often tried to take illicit goods with them without reaching any prior agreement with the customs officers.[39]

POLITICAL LEAFLETS AND BOLSHEVIKS

Large quantities of Communist propaganda magazines, leaflets, books and letters passed through the border parishes on the Karelian Isthmus, i.e. Terijoki, Kivennapa, Rautu and Metsäpirtti, in the hands of Bolshevik agents and smugglers throughout the 1920s and 1930s, and from time to time investigators would find this “inflammatory literature” and expose the carriers. One border guard, for instance, came across a parcel of books on the road between two villages and found that it contained, among other things, copies of the magazine *Vapaus* (Freedom), books on the history of the Russian Communist Party, a book entitled *Oikeudenkäyttö Venäjän neuvostotasavallassa* (The Administration of Justice in Soviet Russia) and leaflets announcing "*Suomen pojat! Lähdettekö suomisyöjiä pelastamaan?*" (Boys of Finland! Will you go to the rescue of those who eat up you country?).[40] Some of the local people protected the couriers who spread this propaganda because it was important for them to find out about relatives who had fled to St. Petersburg and other parts of Russia.[41]

Another common reason for smuggling was to supply the material needs of the Bolsheviks. In order to capture the smugglers and their contacts in the villages the investigators interviewed local informers. In one case their contact was the head of the paramilitary Civil Defence forces at Kivennapa, from whom they received a list of suspicious persons and possible smuggling routes. They were informed that mail and literature for the Reds was conveyed via two villages, and so they set out to visit the "Reds" living in these villages. The first of these was a widow called Ida, whose "late husband was a Red". Pretending to be smugglers themselves, the men met other "Red women" at Ida's home and heard one neighbour praise Ida for being "the cleverest women in the village in these matters" and boast that the border guards were working hand in glove with the smugglers. With their help Ida had skied into Russia almost every day the previous winter and she intended to do so again as soon as the snow came.

When the investigators claimed to be couriers for the Reds, Ida promised to help them to cross the border, but warned them about the houses in the neighbouring village, as the people living there were Whites, so that men couldn't go that way. The men were alarmed that the local Civil Defence forces showed not the slightest interest in searching for those responsible for the smuggling but regarded it as "an ordinary source of livelihood, without which the poorer people in the community couldn't survive". If they were prevented from smuggling the local authorities would have to pay them a subsistence allowance. The investigators ended up with a list of only seven men who were prepared to take part in a campaign against smuggling by the Reds.[42]

One Finnish communist involved in clandestine liaison work, Jaakko Kivi, recalled that there were two routes that the communists used. The first required crossing the Gulf of Finland in a motor boat and the second led from Vyborg to Kivennapa on the border and from there across the river Rajajoki into Russia and on to Lempaala and St. Petersburg:

> They used that route a lot, and when I had to choose my own route in 1925, O. W. Kuusinen himself told me to choose the best way so that I wouldn't get caught, and as I had previously gone across the Isthmus I decided to try it. The guides met us at the river, and brave men they were: three brothers. They fanned out in a snowplough pattern and we struggled along in their wake for about twenty kilometres over a very wet bog until we were safe...[43]

It was said that the most skilful smugglers lived in two villages in Rautu. "They were the Reddest places in the whole district." Here the investigators found a couple of men to act as informers, and one of them boasted that most of the arrests and confiscations of goods had been the result of his tip-offs. He said he could name one "Bolshevik agent" in his own village straight away.[44] Disclosures by neighbours were a political game in the border villages, and offered the simplest means of resolving disagreements. It was not done to inform on your own relatives, however; on the contrary, even on the island of Seiskari smuggling relied on family ties, as they formed the best security network.[45]

The informers took the police to one village where another "Red widow", by the name of Olga, was said to engage in spreading political propaganda among the soldiers. It was also claimed that she and her sister Anna were women of pleasure who offered their services to the soldiers. When the agents, claiming to be Reds returning from Russia, asked the sisters' mother for weapons, she pulled a Russian rifle out from under the bed and asked 100 marks for it, saying that she had found it in the forest a year earlier.[46] She also suggested that the men should go with her to buy cognac from a prison ship. One of the main ways in which the women kept body and soul together was by selling cognac and other spirits to the soldiers.[47] Another person on whom the men's contacts informed was the widow of a householder and was said to be working as a communist agent. This prompted them to inspect her home, where they discovered 23 Finnish and foreign newspapers waiting to be taken to Russia and almost 3000 roubles in cash hidden in clothes.[48] It was common around 1920 to brand socialist women as prostitutes.

The principal organizers of the cross-border smuggling network were reputed to be Eino, Jukka and Jaakko Rahja, Finnish communists working in St. Petersburg. Jukka Rahja was killed in an internal brawl between communists at Kuusinen's club in St. Petersburg on 30th August 1920, and Jaakko was wounded on the same occasion, when altogether eight Finnish communists lost their lives and ten were wounded. The shooters were members of the opposition within the Finnish Communist Party. Eino Rahja, who was fluent in Russian, was appointed as a special commissioner for the border zone, and it was said that one of his main duties was to supervise the undercover trade in goods entering the country from Finland. His chief assistant in this was Jalmari Kotiranta, manager of the "centre for clandestine trade" in Valkeasaari.[49] He was later found guilty of "ordinary smuggling" and sentenced the following year to three years' hard labour for having "contacts with foreign political organizations". The sentence was put into effect and he was sent to the Solovetsk prison camp on the White Sea coast, where he died in 1930. Eino Rahja, on the other hand, remained one of the best-known Finnish communists in St. Petersburg, having been one of Lenin's personal bodyguards during the Russian Revolution, after which he had fought for the Reds on the front at Lempäälä, near Tampere, in the Finnish Civil War of 1918 and had later been an instructor in the Red officers' college in St. Petersburg. He died in 1936 and was buried in St. Petersburg with full honours.[50]

Altogether a total of 119 men, of whom most, 70%, were from Kivennapa, followed by Terijoki and Rautu, were arrested by the Finnish Security Police for expediting communications on the Karelian Isthmus on behalf of the Finnish Communist Party:

Table 1. *Men arrested on the Karelian Isthmus for expediting communications on the Karelian Isthmus on behalf of the Finnish Communist Party in 1932–36*

	1932			1933			1934			1935			1936		
Kivennapa	L	O	T	L	O	T	L	O	T	L	O	T	L	O	T
Terijoki	18	8	26	15	11	26	15	–	15	4	5	9	4	3	7
Rautu	–	–	–	3	–	3	1	1	2	–	–	–	1	–	1
Metsäpirtti	1	1	2	–	2	2	3	–	3	2	–	2	–	2	2
Elsewhere on the Isthmus	–	5	5	–	5	5	1	2	3	–	4	4	–	–	–
Total	19	14	35	18	18	26	20	3	23	6	9	15	5	6	11

L = Locals, O = Others, T = Total

Source: EK:n kiertokirje 24.03.1933, liite. Documents of the Finnish Security Police. Kansan arkisto. Finland.

As may be seen in the table, the numbers of local men involved in this activity were relatively high, altogether 57% of the total, of whom 56 were arrested in Kivennapa, five in Terijoki, six in Rautu and one in Valkjärvi. None were arrested in the areas of the isthmus further away from the border. In other words, this work proved attractive specifically to inhabitants of the border region. The leading role of Kivennapa, on the other hand, may be attributed to the high proportion of Reds among its population and to the occupation structure, although the ease with which the border could be crossed from there was a further consideration. It is interesting to note that one newspaper even in the capital, Helsinki, carried an item in 1923 to the effect that

> "The line marking the border with Russia is entirely overgrown in many places on the Karelian Isthmus. Thus there are points in Kivennapa, Rautu and Metsäpirtti, for instance, where you would not notice the border at all unless you happened to hit upon a marker post. It is quite obvious that such a border is extremely difficult to patrol and that anyone walking in the forest is in great danger of inadvertently straying into Russia, with all the consequences that that might entail."[51]

The fact that the reports of the Security Police frequently confused the terms "Red" and "smuggler" may be attributed to the local informants, who were of the utmost importance to investigators coming from elsewhere but may well have led them to connect the two concepts. It must be noted, however, that the border region's "own Reds" were not deployed in any organized way to assist the work of the Finnish Communist Party. It was this that led the department to observe in 1919 that "the Local Reds do what they do for their own benefit, and they have no more permanent forms of collaboration".[52]

The arresting of smugglers or agents belonging to the Reds generally went off without any serious violence, but a few communists were nevertheless shot. The use of violence usually came out in the interrogation, of course, as was the case with the communist agent Jaakko Lehtoranta, who recalled the time when he was intercepted at the river Rajajoki as he was returning to Finland. Two plain-clothed men approached him and asked him for his identification papers and took him off for questioning. Lehtoranta remained silent, however, whereupon they resorted to harsher methods:

> The men came up to me with their batons raised at the ready… I was covered in blows all over my body, and then I got a blow to the back of my head and I fell on the floor unconscious. I woke up to a battery of heavy blows to my ribs…[53]

FROM A SMUGGLER TO A BOLSHEVIK AGENT

Matti Ilonen, born in 1903 into a family with a small farm in Kivennapa, is a good example of an agent recruited by the Finnish Communist Party. He was arrested for illegal entry into Russia for the first time in February 1920 and interrogated a second time in December of the same year, having been caught by surprise at the border. He is also mentioned in the Security Police's records for February 1924 and again for April 1924, accused of smuggling on both occasions. He had been only 16 years of age at the time of his first smuggling offence. He had not been alone, but was part of a "gang" of men from the border zone who were engaged in smuggling. It was in effect a "family business", as his father and his father's cousin, who was a border guard, were both known in the area as smugglers.

Ilonen had accomplished the journey into Russia that led to his arrest on horseback, whereupon the men had sold the horses there and retraced their steps back to Finland on foot. His father had evidently introduced him to smuggling for financial reasons. The family had five children, of which Matti, at the age of 16, was the oldest, and with jobs hard to come by after the closure of the border, smuggling was just about the only source of income that there was.[54]

Ilonen's smuggling journeys altered greatly in nature during the 1920s, however, when the transport of horses and goods for sale gave way to the communication of communist propaganda. In this capacity he was apprehended for the first time in spring 1928, whereupon the police investigators discovered that he had made a number of visits to "Peltola's shop" (the offices of the Finnish Communist Party), smuggled literature and money over the border and assisted the "shop's" men. He was subsequently sentenced to prison in autumn of the same year for planning acts of treason.[55] At this stage he had clearly moved on to activities that were in a far more dangerous category. This became obvious when he was apprehended, as he was no longer one of a vast number of fairly harmless petty smugglers but part of a wider political circle, which meant that he was placed under special supervision and classified in the documentation as a communist.

The Finnish Security Police's suspicions that he was a communist were borne out by the fact that he spoke Russian tolerably well and that his father had defected over the border in autumn 1924. His mother had also left some time later, and the police knew that they were living in Vologda. His four younger brothers and sisters, aged 17, 16, 13 and 10 years by that time, were living together in the family home in Finland, and Matti Ilonen was also registered as living there, although he spent a lot of time in Vyborg. The police could not find any aggravating circumstances in terms of the political background of his family members, however, as they had not belonged to the Red Guards or the labour movement during the war of 1918 or afterwards.[56]

In spring 1929, following questioning and a trial, Ilonen was sentenced to three years in prison and the forfeiture of his civil rights for five years for the planning of acts of treason. He had been in possession of 5000 copies of May Day posters issued by the Central Committee of the Finnish Communist Party and the communist youth organization at the time of his arrest, and these were confiscated. He served his sentence in the Tammisaari forced labour prison.[57]

Ilonen was released from prison in June 1932, was married shortly afterwards and settled in Vyborg, where he continued his life of smuggling. On one such journey in February 1933 he and four associates were caught in the act and tried to escape from the border guards. In the shooting that ensued one of the border guards was killed. The guards had not been on hand by accident, however, as they were waiting for him, having received a tip-off. News of his return also spread to the railways, and the Terijoki-Vyborg and Valkjärvi-Vyborg lines were placed under surveillance. The preliminary investigations concluded with Ilonen being accused of killing the border guard, as he had been skiing at the head of the party and had been the one who opened fire. Consequently a warrant was issued for his arrest and a reward of 2000 marks offered for information leading to his capture.

Ilonen nevertheless succeeded in returning to Vyborg, where he was concealed by a woman who worked for the labour organization there, but again he was betrayed to the Security Police and the buildings where he was thought to be hiding were encircled by 13 armed men, who were told by the leader of the operation that "Ilonen is a man who will not hesitate to use a gun if the need arises." No sooner had the men taken up their positions than a shot rang out from one house, to which the police and investigators replied with several shots. When the men tried to enter the house they found that the door was locked and set about opening it by shooting the lock out and forcing the door with a crowbar taken from the shed outside. At the same time they called out to Ilonen to give himself up. As the police came into the hallway another shot rang out from the inner room. When they reached the room they found two men covered in blood, still alive but with bullet holes in the head. Both died of their injuries soon afterwards and were recorded as having committed suicide.[58] The co-operation that took place between the Security Police and the local police in the search for Ilonen was one indication that the coordination and division of labour problems between the various law enforcement institutions that had hampered supervision of the border in the 1920s were now over. At the same time it was clear that Matti Ilonen was a key figure in keeping the communists' lines of communication open, since a report on their activities filed in 1938 maintains that action on that front between the Soviet Union and Finland more or less came to an end with his death.[59]

One interesting thing about the Ilonen case is that in the light of the information that has survived he was not an especially enthusiastic supporter of communist ideals in spite of his period in jail in Tammisaari. It would seem, in fact, that smuggling was for the most part simply an occupation for him and that he had been guided into it by the example set by his father and his father's cousin and by the grim everyday realities of life in the border region. That there were tensions within the border communities is evident from the fact that every time Ilonen was arrested it was as a result of either a tip-off or an unguarded remark, the reasons behind which were that he might have been too friendly with someone, or too trusting, or that someone intentionally wanted to do him harm or wanted to settle political differences with him. A smuggler who had been betrayed was felt to be a danger to his partners' existence on one way or another.

If Ilonen and his associates were in the habit of crossing the border on a day-to-day basis, carrying goods or guiding people across, there were also many far more mysterious "secret agents" on the move as well. One internationally celebrated arrest was made in 1925, when the famous English master spy Sidney Reilly, a Russian Jew by birth who was sent into the Soviet Union through the "window on the Isthmus" was intercepted by the Russians on the Finnish border and taken to Moscow for execution. Reilly has since been suggested as the original inspiration for the fictional character of James Bond.

CONCLUSIONS: FACTORS INFLUENCING SMUGGLING

As may be concluded from the above grass-roots stories, the peak observed in smuggling between South-East Finland and St. Petersburg may be attributed to a variety of factors, which may be summed up under ten main headings:

1) The economic crisis that hit households in the border region following the closure of the border in 1917. This event caused a slump in the population base in economic terms and forced people to take up smuggling.
2) The instability of the political situation in the years 1917–1920 on account of the various revolutions and civil wars. The indeterminate political conditions and the brutal, embittered atmosphere left by the civil wars led to a general weakening of morality and encouraged people to turn to crime. The large groups of refugees who were on the move – Reds escaping to Soviet Karelia after the Finnish Civil War, Russians escaping to Finland after the rebellion in Kronstadt, Ingrians of Finnic descent escaping from the St. Petersburg area to Finland, and Finns living in St. Petersburg and elsewhere in Russia returning to Finland[60] – were crossing the same border but in opposite directions, a fact that demonstrates how easy it was to make the crossing.

3) The enormous demand for Finnish goods in Russia. St. Petersburg in the throes of revolution and civil war was suffering from a shortage of everything from farm animals to drawing pins.
4) Disagreements among the Finnish authorities – the Border Guards, the customs authorities, the Security Police, the army, the local police and the local Civil Defence forces – distracted them from the highly important task of supervising the border and made smuggling very much easier.
5) The terrain on the border – a narrow river and sparsely inhabited forest areas – facilitated smuggling.
6) The Border Guards, local police and Civil Defence forces employed largely local people, who also took part in the smuggling, by taking bribes to ignore the transporting of goods over the border.
7) Being local people themselves, the smugglers knew the territory well and also knew the people of the adjacent villages on the Russian side, with whom they had been trading for a long time and had social relations of various kinds, including intermarriages, all of which made it easy to find smuggling routes and trading partners. Some of the Russians involved even lived on the Finnish side of the border, so that people were used to working with them.
8) Some of the local smugglers had Bolshevik sympathies and were prepared to join in the spreading of dissent across the border. Terijoki was especially well known around the turn of the century for its powerful labour movement, and Lenin and many of the Russian communists lived there in 1906–1907 and in 1917.
9) The area already had a reputation as a cross-roads for petty criminals. The main road and railway from St. Petersburg to Vyborg and Helsinki ran through Terijoki and there had always been people passing through on their way to St. Petersburg in search of work and returning to Finland at a later stage, which would have created a disturbance in the area and given it a reputation for an understanding attitude towards petty crime.
10) The smuggling was not a gender-related activity; women were engaged in the illicit transport of goods in the same way as men, which must have increased the number of local smugglers considerably.

Comparison of the present results with other studies of smuggling and attempts at estimating its extent points to numerous common explanatory factors. Vania Ceccato and Robert Haining, for example, found that many of the same factors – such as local knowledge, physical conditions in the terrain, communications, the state of supervision and the local crime situation – promoted smuggling between Sweden and Denmark in the Öresund area, although their list differs from the above in that they quote inequality between the sexes as a factor favouring prostitution and human trafficking. Apart from a few isolated incidents, there were no factors indicative of an organized sex trade in the present material, nor does it in any way explain the increase in smuggling between South-East Finland and St. Petersburg in 1917–1932.

On the contrary, one important finding here is that, in spite of the fact that smuggling is regarded on a global scale as a crime committed typically by men, in this case women played a major role in the operations themselves. Conversely, one significant reason for the rapid growth in smuggling found here over the period 1917–1932 was political motivation, which was entirely absent from the picture presented by Ceccato and Haining.[61]

All in all, it thus emerges that smuggling would seem to involve a most interesting blend of common contributory factors connected with the supply and demand for goods or the geographical situation and others that are independent of historical time and place together with differences linked to the political, economic and cultural features of the time in question. Such factors are also reflected in the present findings, in that, where human traffic from Russia to Finland was a significant and topical problem in the early years of the new millennium, the corresponding problem in the 1920s and 1930s was the carrying of Bolshevik propaganda.

The boom in smuggling between South-East Finland and St. Petersburg and the accompanying flourishing of illegal economic activity declined around the mid-1930s, chiefly because the Soviet authorities moved the Finnish-speaking Ingrians away from the Russian part of the border region and the immediate areas on both sides of the border became militarized zones. Both the Finns and the Russians ceased to have any close connections across the border. At the same time the demand for goods in St. Petersburg declined, so that smuggling was no longer so profitable. Also, the interest in Bolshevist activities waned substantially within the Finnish part of the border region, which reduced the smuggling of political propaganda and agents. In fact the powerful Finnicization policies of the Finnish government and many citizens' organizations within the country and the accompanying vilification of the Russians led to a general change in attitude with regard to Russia both in the border region and throughout the country. In addition, supervision of the border was intensified once the various authorities were able to agree on an efficient division of functions between them.[62] Thus peace prevailed in the Finnish-Russian border area as far as smuggling was concerned for a few years before the outbreak of war in 1939.

REFERENCES

1 See Christopher J. Ulrich/Timo A. Kivimäki, Uncertain security: confronting transnational crime in the Baltic Sea Region and Russia, Lanham MD, Lexington Books, Oxford 2002; Mikko Ylikangas, Unileipää, kuolonvettä, spiidiä: huumeet Suomessa 1800–1950, Atena, Jyväskylä 2009; Aselaiva John Grafton, in: Ase-lehti, Kangasala 1994; Johanna Tuori, Uskonnollisen kirjallisuuden salakuljetus Suomen viranomaisten ja poliitikkojen "pikkusena harmina" 1970–1979, Opinnäyte, Teologinen tiedekunta, Helsingin yliopisto 2004; Martti Lehti/Kauko Aromaa (eds.),Trafficking in human beings, illegal immigration and Finland, European Institute for Crime Prevention and Control, affiliated with the United Nations, HEUNI 38, 2002.

2 Keisarillisen majesteetin armollinen julistus siitä, että mitä täytettäissä joulukuun 12:nä p. 1842 annettua armollista julistusta wastoin luwatonta kauppatawaran kuljetusta Suomesta Wenäjän waltakuntaan, on wississä osissa waarin otettawa. Annettu Helsingin kaupungissa 16 p. tammikuuta 1843, Asetus 1843–01–16, Suomen senaatti, Helsinki 1843; History of the Finnish Customs: http://tulli.fi/suomen_tulli/tulli_tutuksi/historia/index.jsp. Accessed 01.09.2011; Maria Lähteenmäki, Maailmojen rajalla. Kannaksen rajamaa ja poliittiset murtumat 1911–1944, Suomalaisen Kirjallisuuden Seura, Helsinki 2009, 37–41.

3 Lähteenmäki, Maailmojen rajalla, Loc. Cit. (Note 2), 37–41.

4 Raimo Pullat, Itämeren rutto: pirtun salakuljetuksesta vuosina 1919–1939, Pohjoinen, Oulu 1993; Salakuljettaja muistelee, 21.5.2001. Elävä arkisto: http://www.yle.fi/elavaarkisto/?s=s&g=1&ag=3&t=1055&9=10182. Accessed 10.09.2011.

5 See, for example, Koirien salakuljetus Itä-Euroopasta vilkastunut [Smuggling of dogs from the eastern part of Europe has become livelier], in: Helsingin Sanomat 15.05.2010; Savukkeiden salakuljetus itärajan yli kasvaa yhä [Smuggling of cigarettes across the eastern borderline is still expanding], in: Taloussanomat 19.03.2010; Martti Lehti and Kauko Aromaa, Trafficking in Women and Children in Europe, in: Organized crime, trafficking, drugs: selected papers presented at the conference of the European society of criminology. Sami Nevala/Kauko Aromaa (eds.), European Institute for crime prevention and control, affiliated with the United Nations, HEUNI 42, Helsinki 2004, 114–128.

6 Pekka Lith, Laittomat tavara- ja palveluhyödykkeet muuttuvassa maailmassa, in: Markku Hirvonen/Pekka Lith/Risto Walden, Suomen kansainvälistyvä harmaa talous, Eduskunnan tarkastusvaliokunnan julkaisu 1/2010, Liite 8, 4.

7 Georgi Glonti, Human trafficking: concept, classification and questions of legislative regulation, in: Nevala/Aromaa, Organized crime, Loc. Cit. (Note. 5), 70.

8 Dina Siegel/Henk van de Bunt/Damián Zaitch (eds.), Global organized crime: trends and development, Dortrecht, Kluwer Academic Publishers, Boston 2003; Raymond Fisman, Economic gangsters: corruption, violence and the poverty of nations, Princeton University Press, Princeton 2008; Forced labour in the 21th century. Antislavery, International Confederation of Free Labour Unions 2011.

9 Glonti, Human trafficking, Loc. Cit. (Note 7), 70–71.

10 Lähteenmäki, Maailmojen rajalla, Loc. Cit. (Note 2), 221–224.

11 Microhistorical analysis has two fronts. On one side, by moving on a reduced scale, it permits in many cases a reconstruction of "real life" unthinkable in other kinds of historiography. On the other side it proposes to investigate the invisible structures within which that lived experience is articulated. Carlo Ginzburg and Carlo Poni, The name of the game: unequal exchange and the historiographic marketplace, in: Edward Muir/Guido Ruggiero (eds.), Microhistory and the lost people of Europe, The John Hopkins University Press, London and Baltimore 1991, 8.

12 Lith, Laittomat tavara- ja palveluhyödykkeet, Loc. Cit. (Note 6), 4.

13 Kertomus tilanteesta Suomen ja Venäjän rajalla vuonna 1919. Venäjän vastaisen maarajan rajatarkastajan arkisto. Fond 147, opis 1, nro 60. Lenoblogosarchiv. Vyborg. Russia.

14 Kertomus tilanteesta Suomen ja Venäjän rajalla vuonna 1919, Loc. Cit. (Note 13).

15 Kaino Mäkisen kirje Terijoen alaosastolle nro 59/1920. Terijoen alaosaston arkisto. EK-VALPO I. Kansallisarkisto, The National Archives (KA). Finland.

16 Suomalaiset punaemigrantit muonituskomissaareina ja -pyöveleinä. Kirj. Inkeriläinen, in: Ajan Sana 09.07.1932.

17 Matkakertomus komennuksesta nro 16 tiedustelumatkasta Kivennavalle. Etsivät J. Koivuranta ja J. T. Ikonen Terijoelta. Joulukuu 1919. Terijoen alaosaston arkisto. EK-VALPO I. KA. Finland.

18 Terijoen ala-osaston tilannekatsaus 04.09.1925. EK-VALPO I, kansio 373. KA. Finland; Rajajoen, Raasulin ja Terijoen tullivartioiden ilmoitukset 1921. Venäjän vastaisen maarajan rajatarkastajan arkisto. Fond 147, opis 1, nro 95. Lenoblogosarchiv. Vyborg. Russia.

19 Kaino Mäkisen kirje Terijoen alaosastolle nro 59/1920. Terijoen alaosaston arkisto. EK-VALPO I. KA. Finland.

20 Luettelo Rajajoen tullivartion piiristä toimitetuista takavarikoista 16.01.–01.02.1921 ja Ilmoitus takavarikoista 01.01.–30.03.1922. Venäjän vastaisen maarajan rajatarkastajan arkisto. Fond 147, opis 1, nro 95. Lenoblogosarchiv. Vyborg. Russia.

21 Poliisikuulustelupöytäkirja 03.12.1918. Kuokkalan poliisivartioasema. Mikkelin maakunta-arkisto. Finland.

22 Kuulustelupöytäkirja 15.01.1923. EK:n kansliassa Helsingissä; Liite: Terijoen alaosaston pöytäkirja 06.01.1923. Kansio 373. EK-VALPO I. KA. Finland.

23 Kuulustelupöytäkirja 04.03.1921. EK:n kansliassa Helsingissä; Liite: Terijoen alaosaston pöytäkirja 15.02.1921. Kansio 373. EK-VALPO I. KA. Finland.

24 Terijoen alaosaston tilannekatsaus no 1 31.01.1928. Kansio 373. EK-VALPO I. KA. Finland.

25 Suomen Sosialidemokraatti 12.09.1927 and 14.09.1927.

26 EK:n Terijoen alaosaston selostus nro 229, 1927. Kansio 373. EK-VALPO I. KA. Finland.

27 EK:n Terijoen alaosaston selostus nro 229, 1927. Loc. Cit. (Note 26); EK:n Terijoen alaosaston tilannekatsaus nro 18, 29.09.1926. Kansio 373. EK-VALPO I. KA. Finland.

28 Kuulustelupöytäkirja 27.01.1923. EK:n kansliassa Helsingissä. Kansio 373. EK-VALPO I. KA. Finland.

29 Kertomus tilanteesta Suomen ja Venäjän rajalla vuonna 1919. Loc. Cit. (Note 13).

30 Kirje 04.02.1920 Koivistolta. Kirj. G. Jansson. Terijoen alaosasto. EK-VALPO I. KA. Finland.

31 Raportti 03.12.1920. Terijoen alaosaston arkisto. EK-VALPO I. KA; Matkakertomus 15.03.1920. Terijoen alaosaston arkisto. EK-VALPO I. KA. Finland.

32 Petri Rytkölä, Saarelaisyhteisö kriisissä. Seiskarilainen pirtun salakuljetus 1920–32, Opinnäyte, Suomen historia. Helsingin yliopisto 2000, 149–151.

33 Matkakertomus 09.03.–11.03.1920. Terijoen alaosaston arkisto. EK-VALPO I. KA. Finland.

34 Raportti 10.02.1920. Terijoen alaosaston arkisto. EK-VALPO I. KA. Finland.

35 Matkakertomus komennuksesta nro 16 tiedustelumatkasta Kivennavalle. Etsivät J. Koivuranta ja J. T. Ikonen Terijoelta. Joulukuu 1919. Terijoen alaosaston arkisto. EK-VALPO I. KA. Finland.

36 Matti Kosonen and Juha Pohjonen, Isänmaan portinvartijat: Suomen rajojen vartiointi 1918–1994, Otava, Helsinki 1994, 38, 42, 47.

37 Raportti 10.02.1920. Terijoen alaosaston arkisto. EK-VALPO I. KA. Finland.

38 Kertomus tilanteesta Suomen ja Venäjän rajalla vuonna 1919. Loc. Cit. (Note 13).

39 Kertomus tilanteesta Suomen ja Venäjän rajalla vuonna 1919. Loc. Cit. (Note 13).

40 Raportti Kivennavan matkasta 07.11.–10.11.1919. Terijoen alaosaston arkisto. EK-VALPO I. KA. Finland.

41 Poliisikuulustelupöytäkirja 09.12.1918. Kuokkalan poliisivartiokonttori. Mikkelin maakunta-arkisto. Finland.

42 Raportti Kivennavan matkasta. Loc. Cit. (Note 40).

43 Jaakko Kivi's (born in 1892) memoirs, 47–50. Kansan arkisto. Finland; O. W. Kuusinen (1881–1964) was a leading Finnish communist who made his career in the Soviet Union.

44 Raportti 09.02.1920 Raudusta. Kirj. P. Mattonen. Terijoen alaosaston arkisto. EK-VALPO I. KA. Finland.

45 Rytkölä, Saarelaisyhteisö kriisissä, Loc. Cit. (Note 32), 150.

46 Raportti nro 77/1920. Terijoen alaosaston arkisto. EK-VALPO I. KA. Finland.

47 Raportti 3.12.1920. Terijoen alaosaston arkisto. EK-VALPO I. KA. Finland.

48 Raportti 25.3.1920. Terijoen alaosaston arkisto. EK-VALPO I. KA. Finland.

49 Ajan Sana 09.07.1932.

50 Markku Salomaa, Punaupseerit: SKP ja puna-armeijan sotilaallinen yhteistoiminta kansalaissodasta talvisotaan 1918–1940, WSOY, Helsinki 1992, 233–234.

51 Helsingin Sanomat 08.09.1923.

52 Matkakertomus komennuksesta no 16 tiedustelumatkasta Kivennavalle. Etsivät J. Koivuranta ja J. T. Ikonen Terijoelta. Joulukuu 1919. Terijoen alaosaston arkisto. EK-VALPO I. KA. Finland.

53 The incident occurred in 1936. Jaakko Lehtoranta's (born in 1911) memoirs. Kansan arkisto. Finland.

54 Kuulustelupöytäkirja 23.02.1920 Terijoen ala-osaston kuulusteluhuoneessa. Henkilömappi. Matti Ilonen. EK-VALPO I. KA. Finland.

55 Kuulustelupöytäkirja nro 44/1929. Henkilömappi. Matti Ilonen. EK-VALPO I. KA. Finland.

56 Ilmoitus Terijoelta 23.12.1928. Kuulustelija Harry Broms. Henkilömappi. Matti Ilonen; Matti Ilosen henkilökortti. EK-VALPO I. KA. Finland.

57 Tiedonanto Etsivän keskuspoliisin pääosastolle 19. lokakuu 1931. Henkilömappi. Matti Ilonen. EK-VALPO I. KA. Finland.

58 Tiedonanto. KD No 83/1247 33, 04.03.1933. Henkilömappi. Matti Ilonen; Lausunto D 561/33, Helsingissä 27.02.1933. EK-VALPO I. KA. Finland.

59 Ilmoitus No 249/38. Koskee Tauno Aholan kertomaa sotilasvakoilua 30.09.1938. Henkilömappi. Matti Ilonen. EK-VALPO I. KA. Finland.

60 At least 6000 Reds fled to Russia at the end of the Finnish Civil War of 1918, some 8300 Ingrians fled from Russia to Finland in 1920 and about 6300 Russian refugees from Kronstadt came to Finland in 1921. Moreover, thousands of foreigners and Russian emigrants passed through the border zone on the Karelian Isthmus on their way to other parts of Europe in the course of the Civil War in Russia.

61 Vania Ceccato and Robert Haining, Crime in border regions: the Scandinavian case of Öresund 1998–2001, in: Annals of the Association of American Geographers 94 (2004) 4, 809–810, passim.

62 Lähteenmäki, Maailmojen rajalla, Loc. Cit. (Note. 2), 199–204.

OLGA ILYUKHA

FINNS IN RUSSIAN KARELIA: TRANSFORMATION OF THE HISTORY OF A NATIONAL MINORITY

Once the USSR had collapsed, fundamental changes in political, economic, social and cultural life began in the newly formed states. In the transitional society of Russia the processes of consolidation of ethnic groups intensified and national consciousness reached a new level. In the course of the wide public debates on how to set up a legal framework that would ensure a favourable environment for the development of national minority cultures, participants constantly appealed to Soviet history, which had been so painful for many of the peoples of Russia, and thus stimulated research into the subject. As a result, the range of research topics and problems was expanded, new archival sources were opened up, and contacts between researchers in Russia and abroad expanded.

This paper relies on the findings of these historical studies in an attempt to construct a brief overview of the establishment and development of the Finnish diaspora in Karelia in the 20th century in the context of broader socio-demographic processes, and to formulate topical research tasks in the study of the Finns as a national minority in the Republic of Karelia.

POPULATION DIVERSITY IN RUSSIAN KARELIA

According to the Russian National Census of 2002, the population of the Republic of Karelia was 716.281, of whom 12% belong to Finnic peoples (2% Finns, 9% Karelians and 0.7% Vepsians). The biggest group of inhabitants in Karelia was the Russians (77%), and the rest of the population consisted of Byelorussians, Ukrainians, Poles and Tatars. The situation during the 19th century had been somewhat different, and the proportion of Finnic people was still 43% after the revolution.[1]

The population of Karelia was growing at a faster rate than that of neighbouring regions, mainly because of internal migration. During Soviet times the transformations brought about in Karelia had involved the forcible development of industry, primarily logging, and workers and their families had been moved there from various parts of the USSR (chiefly the north-western, western and southern regions, Byelorussia and Ukraine) in the 1920s–1930s and in the 1950s to supply the economy with manpower. Thus the population of Karelia doubled (from 200.755 to 468.898) in the period from 1920 to 1939. This migration peaked in the 1950s, when most of the arrivals were sent to forest villages to work in the logging industry, while some of the migrants were assigned to local collective farms. By the late 1950s the republic's population was 651.000.[2]

The influx of manpower from different parts of the country changed the composition of the population. The Karelian Labour Commune, established on June 8, 1920, was made up of 56% Russians, 43% Karelians and 0.5% Finns, while other nationalities contributed less than 1%, but even during the 1920s the proportion of Russians began growing swiftly, whereas that of Karelians was constantly decreasing, although their absolute numbers were growing. Thus the number of Karelians increased by 22.800 between 1920 and 1939, but their proportion in the population dropped by nearly half, from 43% to 23%. Meanwhile, the number of Russians more than doubled. In the period from 1959 to 1989 the combined number of Karelians, Vepsians and Finns decreased by 17.000 and their proportion dropped from 19% to 13%. At the same time, the percentage of Russians, Byelorussians and Ukrainians increased from 78% to 85%.[3] Thus the trend in the Karelian population in Soviet times was towards a significant enlargement of the "Slavic" component along with a gradual decrease of the proportion of Finnic minorities.

The crucial stage in this process was the first post-war decade, during which migration resulted in the formation of large ethnic groups of Byelorussians and Ukrainians in Karelia. By 1959 there were 72.000 Byelorussians, accounting for 11% of the republic's population, and only slightly lagging behind the titular nation, the Karelians, in numbers. Dozens of communities grew up (mostly in south-western and western Karelia), where Byelorussians outnumbered the other nationalities. By the late 1950s, a Byelorussian stratum had formed in all parts of Karelia, but from the mid-1960s onwards their numbers began decreasing gradually on account of out-migration.

Ukrainian migration was not as massive as that of Byelorussians, and their number in the post-war years remained at a little over 20.000. The last significant wave of Ukrainian immigration, increasing their number to 28.000, occurred in the 1980s, in connection with the building of Kostomuksha, the youngest city of Karelia.[4]

Intermarriage between the nationalities had for a long time been common in Karelia, and the proportion of mixed-nationality families was higher there than anywhere else in Russia. By the 1980s–1990s three out of every four marriages entered into by young Karelians were transnational, while among the Byelorussians, Ukrainians, Finns and Vepsians the figure was 9 out of every 10. The predominant ethnic counterparts in all these instances were Russians.[5] In the 1990s the population of Karelia decreased by 33.000 (from 798.000 to 765.000), chiefly through natural population loss due to a low birth rate and high death rate, the migration balance in the region has also been negative since the mid-1990s, and the tendency is still going on.

Late in the 20th century, new diasporas became visible, ones whose representatives had previously been "obscured" among the rest of the population. Several hundred Armenians (refugees from Nagorno-Karabakh and Baku) and Georgians (refugees from South Ossetia and especially Abkhazia) arrived in Karelia in the early 1990s, and from the middle of the decade onwards there was an increase in the numbers of Azerbaijanis, many of them coming from Georgia, and Chechens escaping the war. Many Russians also arrived in the early 1990s from "hot spots" such as Central Asia, Transcaucasia, the Northern Caucasus and Moldavia.[6] At the same time, quite many Russians, Byelorussians, Ukrainians and Tatars left Karelia. After the collapse of the USSR most of them wished for a reunion with their families and often returned to their homeland. A drastic decline in living standards also affected the demographic situation in Karelia at that time, was and proved to be one of the main reasons for many Finns to move to Finland.

The population of Karelia in general thus underwent substantial changes in both size and ethnic composition in the course of the 20th century. The main factor in that process was internal migration: the government was intentionally attracting people from other parts of the country, including representatives of different nationalities, to the Karelian Republic. Migration in the 1990s, although it added colour to the regional ethnic diversity, caused little change in the overall ethnic composition that had been established by the mid-20th century.

FINNISH DIASPORAS IN RUSSIAN KARELIA

Among the Finnic people of Karelia (Karelians, Vepsians and Finns), the indigenous ones are Karelians and Vepsians. The historical development of these ethnic groups mostly took place in the territory of Karelia, whereas modern Finnish diasporas formed during the 20th century. The first Finnish migrants appeared in the region in the 1830s, seeking refuge from the famine caused by yet another crop failure, and the number continued growing in the second half of the century, so that there were 365 Finnish inhabitants in 1858, 991 in 1865 and 2622 in 1883. By the late 19th century, the population of Finns in the province of Olonets reached 3000 people, remaining at this level (ca. 1% of the total population) until 1917. Owing to the proximity of Finland and constant contacts with the homeland, the immigrants remained virtually unassimilated. For most of the Finns the migration to Olonets was a temporary matter, and they returned to Finland in 1917–1918.[7]

The modern ethnic group of Finns in Karelia formed in Soviet times as a consequence of several migrations of different proportions and taking place at different times. The most noteworthy among the migrant were the Red Finns (political refugees), North American Finns from Canada and USA, and defectors, all of whom arrived in Russian Karelia in the 1920s–1930s, and also the Ingrian Finns who arrived in the 1940s–1950s. These latter had been old-established residents in the territory of the modern Leningrad Region, to which they had moved from Sweden and Finland from the 17th century onwards. About 80% of the modern Finnish population in Russian Karelia consists of Ingrian Finns and their descendants.[8]

The Red Finns, defectors and immigrants from North America arrived in three waves in 1918–1935. After the Finnish Civil War in 1918 had ended in victory for the right-wing Whites, thousands of the left-wing Reds and their families had to leave the country and fled to Karelia to establish an "exemplary socialist republic" capable of promoting a revolution in Finland. By 1926 the political immigrants, who then accounted for less than 1% of the population, held high positions in the party, the government, industries, education and culture.[9]

Between the censuses of 1926 and 1933 the number of Finns in the Republic of Karelia increased to reach 12.088. This was due to immigration from North America, mainly involving white-collar workers recruited in the USA and Canada. A third of the immigrants were women and children. The first half of the 1930s was also a time of immigration from Finland caused by the economic crisis, so that large groups of Finns crossed the Soviet border from 1930 onwards in search of jobs or protection from political persecution. This was in a way promoted by the propagandist campaign launched by the Karelian leadership and the Finnish communists. It is roughly estimated that over 12.000 people left Finland for the Soviet Union in the years 1930–1934. The defectors were sieved through the security service quarantine camps, and were then sent either to work in various parts of the country, or to the GULAG system (Chief Directorate of Correction Camps, Labour Settlements and Prisons). These Finns lived in specialized settlements which they were not free to leave and were forced to work at construction, logging and mining sites.[10]

The result was that the Finnish inhabitants came to be concentrated in certain areas. Nearly a half lived in the Onega District (a third of them in Petrozavodsk), 10% in Kondopoga, 8% in Ukhti, and 5% in Olonets, and by the 1930s large communities had grown up in which the Finns were in the majority. They had a strong ethnic identity, establishing a Finnish theatre in Petrozavodsk, for instance, and publishing newspapers and books in Finnish. Moreover, there was hardly any mixing between the Finns and the local Russian people. During the 1920s and early 1930s Finns occupied a very strong political and cultural position in the Republic of Karelia, and the Finnish language was the second official language after Russian up to the year 1937.

Alongside this Finnish immigration there was some return migration, the biggest group being the North American Finns, some 3000 of whom left Russian Karelia in 1932–1935, either legally or illegally. The attitude of the authorities towards the Finns changed dramatically in the second half of the decade, however, so that the Finnish leaders of the Karelian Autonomous Soviet Socialist Republic (KASSR), starting with the Regional Communist Party Committee Secretary, Kustaa Rovio, and the Head of the Government, Edvard Gylling, were displaced in 1935, and a campaign against "Finnish bourgeois nationalism" was announced in the republic. Many Finnish immigrants were charged with anti-Soviet activities in the late 1930s, and in 1937–1938 several thousand people were arrested and convicted. As the result, a large proportion of the Finnish people was either liquidated or scattered among camps and specialized settlements throughout the country. These repressions reduced the number of Finns by nearly a third, to 8322 in 1939. The events of World War II then completed the eradication of the diaspora, so that hardly any Finns were left in Karelia by 1945.[11] They were regarded as traitors and spies.

The Finnish diaspora in Karelia after World War II consisted predominantly of Ingrians. After the Leningrad Region had been liberated, the Ingrians were prevented from returning to their native land. From 1949 onwards, however, they were actively recruited as loggers, and some 8000 families, or more than 21.000 people, arrived in Karelia by this means alone in that year, most of them from Estonia (41%), the Pskov Region (32%) and Siberia (16%). In 1950 the organized resettlement of Ingrians came to an end, but spontaneous migration to Karelia continued for several years. As the result, the number of Finns in the republic increased notably, reaching 27.800 people (4% of the population) in 1959. In the following prolonged period of the 1960s–1990s, the number of Finns in Russian Karelia decreased steadily. Soviet persecution of the Evangelical Lutheran Church led to bans on the use of the Finnish language, coercive displacement from their traditional places of living and disruption of their ethno-cultural and ethno-linguistic identity.[12]

THE POST-SOVIET PERIOD IN THE HISTORY OF THE FINNS

According to the 2002 Census, there were a little over 34.000 Finns living in the Russian Federation. They were concentrated in seven federal districts, with the biggest group (14.156 people) living in the Republic of Karelia.[13] The turning point in the development of the national identity of the Finns in Russia came in 1989–1990, with the emergence of "ethnic mobilization", a public movement to support national languages and cultures and the proper integration of national minorities into society. The "Ingrian Union of Finns in Karelia", which unites the active part of the diaspora, has operated since 1989 to support the national interests of all Finns living in Karelia. Initially its activities were focused on cultural work and the promotion of a general awareness. One central issue for the national movement in the early 1990s was the exculpation of Finns as a nationality that had been ejected from their land during Soviet time. Slow progress on this issue became another motive for emigration to Finland.

In 1993, the Supreme Council of the Russian Federation passed a decree "On the exculpation of the Russian Finns", in which it was emphasized that "political exculpation of the Russian Finns implies they have the right to free national development, equal opportunities to exercise their political rights and freedoms [...] and are free to return to their traditional places of habitation in the Russian Federation".[14] Once the exculpation issue had been resolved, ethno-cultural and social tasks moved into the foreground.

The modern Finnish diaspora exercises the principles of national and cultural autonomy. The functioning of the Finnish language in the Republic of Karelia is supported at the government level, following the passing of a law "On State Support for the Karelian, Vepsian and Finnish Languages in the Republic of Karelia" on March 17, 2004. The official state language, Russian, has no such special support.

Nowadays there are three Finnish-language newspapers/magazines operate in Russian Karelia (*Karjalan Sanomat*, *Carelia* and *Kipinä*), and there are radio and television broadcasts and theatrical performances. The Finnish language is studied at schools and universities, and a Faculty of Baltic and Finnish Philology and Culture was established at Petrozavodsk State University in 1993.

One important indicator of the deep integration of Finns is the high proportion of inter-marrying. According to an ethno-sociological survey carried out in 1996, over 70% of the Finns interviewed had been or were in a mixed-nationality marriage, although admittedly only 41% of the parents in mixed-nationality families reported their children to be ethnic Finns.[15] On the other hand, emigration of Finns abroad, mainly to Finland, continues. Finland maintained a very liberal attitude towards immigrants from Karelia in the late 1980s and early 1990s, so that many Russian Finns applied for Finnish permanent residence permits and obtained them quite easily. Around the turn of the century the process slowed down considerably as the attitude towards immigration changed in Finland. Since 2001 Finland has required from immigrants to have Finnish language skills in addition to quite a number of other formalities.

SOME RESULTS AND TOPICAL PROBLEMS FOR RESEARCH

A comprehensive scientific study of the situation of national minorities in the USSR had been impossible in Soviet times because of ideological limitations. Some success has been achieved mostly in studies of traditional culture, so that family rites and folk customs were recorded and described in a scientific manner, but although studies of an ethno-sociological and ethno-demographic nature had been growing more common since the 1960s, they were applied to national minorities through the prism of the Soviet doctrine regarding the formation of a new historical community in the USSR called "the Soviet people". The results had to be fitted into a predetermined scheme; otherwise they were doomed to lie on the researchers' desks waiting for "better days".

The gaps in our knowledge of the history and culture of the national minorities in Russian Karelia have now been largely filled. As regards the Finns, researchers have focused since the late 1980s on the political context of the Soviet period, as they have now gained access to the necessary archives. These studies were based on archival sources, statistics and reports of sociological surveys. As a result, a number of papers on the history of the Finns in the USSR and Russian Karelia were published both in Russia and abroad. The period of particular interest for researchers in both Russia and Finland has been the 1920s–1930s, the "Finnish period" in Soviet Karelia, which had long remained a "blank spot" in historical writing. Thanks to studies by Irina Takala, the process by which the Finnish diaspora in Soviet Karelia was established has been reconstructed, the contribution of the Red Finns to the development of the republic has been ascertained and their tragic fates have been demonstrated.[16] Much progress has also been achieved in the study of demographic aspects of the formation of the Finnish diaspora in Karelia, and of the problems of "ethnic mobilization" connected with the revival of the national identity of the Russian Finns that were topical in the 1990s. These studies were greatly advanced by the ethno-sociologists Victor Birin and Evgueni Klementiev. One strength of their papers lies in the extensive background of statistical data and the authors' own sociological surveys carried out in different parts of Karelia.

Recently a joint Russian-Finnish project "Image of Finland in Russia. Image of Russia in Finland" has been carried out by the Karelian Research Centre, the Russian Academy of Science and the Renvall Institute, University of Helsinki, the outcome of which has been the publication of two books on the problems of the perception of one another by Russians and Finns.[17] Several other promising international projects are now under way. One, coordinated by the Petrozavodsk State University, deals with American Finns in Karelia,[18] and another coordinated by the Karelian Research Centre, Russian Academy of Science, with the role of the "Finnish factor" in the 20th century history and culture of Karelia.[19]

In spite of the serious changes in historical writing over the past two decades, some issues and episodes related to the history of Finns in Russian Karelia remain poorly studied. These include the problems of providing general and professional education for the Finns. Despite the repressions, all kinds of restrictions on the use of their language and barriers in educational opportunities, the educational level of the Finns was always higher than the average for the republic. The explanation probably lies in the value orientations of an "average Finn", i.e. in the Finnish mentality, which was largely shaped by the Lutheran religion. Presumably the most persistent ethno-cultural phenomena are rooted in the religious sphere. The grounds for this assumption as applied to the Finns can be found in papers by Svetlana Yalovitsyna.

Many aspects of everyday life, including contacts between representatives of different ethnic groups and different domestic cultures, which could throw light upon the process of the Finns' adaptation to new conditions of life, are still under-studied. It would be important, for instance, to find answers to the following questions. How did people of other cultures perceive the mentality and behaviour of the Finns, and how did the Finns view their "foreign-language surroundings"? What lay at the core of the lack of understanding/misunderstanding? Which traits of the Finnish ethnic culture were irretrievably lost or transformed, and which ones proved to be most persistent and evaded assimilation? Given the situation with written history and the fact that the Finns in Russian Karelia – as in Russia in general – are profoundly integrated into society, it would be expedient to investigate the lessons to be learned from history and the present-day characteristics of routine inter-ethnic contacts, including educational, religious and professional environments.

The sources of information used for this should certainly include archival material both from Russia and from Finland. To fulfil the above tasks one should make abundant use of the "oral history" method, the recording of biographical stories gathered through questionnaires and interviews, with further analysis of the information. The material should be gathered both among Finns living in Karelia and among those who had emigrated to Finland and are now able to present an "outsider's" view of the situation in Russian Karelia.

REFERENCES

1 Nationalny sostav naselenija Respubliki Karelia. Statistitcheskij sbornik, Petrozavodsk 2005, 3–4.

2 Irina Pokrovskaja, Naselenie Karelii, Petrozavodsk 1978, 77–82, 115.

3 Viktor Birin, Naselenie Karelii v XX veke, in: Respublika Karelia: 80 let v sostave Rossijskoj Federatsii (stanovlenie i razvitie gosudarstvennosti), Petrozavodsk 2000, 108.

4 Birin, Naselenie Karelii, Loc.Cit. (Note. 3), 109; Evgenij Klementiev and Aleksandr Kozhanov, Selskaja sreda i naselenie Karelii 1960–1980 gody, Petrozavodsk 1999, 14–24.

5 Viktor Birin, Osnovnye tendencii razvitija braka i sem'i u finnov Karelii vo vtoroj polovine XX veka, in: Olga Ilyukha (ed.), Finskij factor v istorii i culture Karelii XX veka, Petrozavodsk 2009, 401–304.

6 Birin, Naselenie Karelii, Loc. Cit. (Note 3), 116; Evgenij Klementiev et al. (eds.), Ingermanlandskije Finny: modeli etnicheskoj mobilizatsii. Sbornik materialov i dokumentov, Petrozavodsk 2006, 13.

7 Viktor Birin, Finny Olonetskoi Gubernii, Petrozavodsk 1991, 4–9, 31.

8 Viktor Birin, Demografitcheskoje razvitie, in: Evgenij Klementiev/Natalia Shlygina (eds.), Pribaltijsko-finskije narody Rossii, Moscow 2003, 537, 543–544.

9 Irina Takala, Finny v Karelii i v Rossii: istorija vozniknovenija i gibeli diaspory, St. Petersburg 2002, 16–32.

10 Takala, Finny v Karelii i v Rossii, Loc. Cit. (Note 9), 33–61.

11 Paul M. Austin, Soviet Finnish: The End of a Dream, in: East European quarterly 2 (1987), 183–195; Takala, Finny v Karelii i v Rossii, Loc. Cit. (Note 9), 108–123; Birin, Demografitcheskoje razvitie, Loc. Cit. (Note 8), 538–540.

12 Aleksandr Kozhanov/Svetlana Yalovitsyna, Etnosociologitcheskoje obsledovanie finskogo naselenija Karelii, in: Eino Kiuru (ed.), Finny v Rossii: istoriya, kultura, sud'by, Petrozavodsk 1998, 129–153; Sergej Verigin/Leo Suni, Pereseleneje ingermanlandcev v Kareliju v konce 1940 godov, in: Karely. Finny: Problemy etnitsheskoj istorii, Moscow 1992, 200–216.

13 Nationalny sostav naselenija Respubliki Karelia, Loc. Cit. (Note 1), 3–4.

14 Vedomosti Sjezda narodnykh deputatov Rossijskoj Federatsii i Verkhovnogo Soveta Rossijskoj Federatsii, 1993. No 22, 1119: Evgenij Klementiev et al. (eds.), Ingermanlandskije Finny, Loc. Cit. (Note 6), 95–96.

15 Aleksandr Kozhanov/Svetlana Yalovitsyna, Etnosociologitcheskoje obsledovanie, Loc. Cit. (Note 12), 157–160.

16 The other historians who should be mentioned are Markku Kangaspuro, Pekka Nevalainen and Timo Vihavainen from Finland and Leo Suni from Russia.

17 Olga Ilyukha/Aleksei Tsamutali/Gennadii Kovalenko (eds.), Mnogolikaja Finlyandija. Obraz Finljandii i finnov v Rossii, Velikiy Novgorod 2004; Olga Iljuha/Aleksei Tsamutali/Timo Vihavainen (eds.), Monikasvoinen Suomi: venäläisten mielikuvia Suomesta ja suomalaisista, Helsinki 2009.

18 Irina Takala and Ilja Solomeshch (eds.), North American Finns in Soviet Karelia in the 1930s, Petrozavodsk 2008.

19 Ilyukha, Finskij factor v istorii, Loc. Cit. (Note 5).

ANNA LAAKKONEN

RED FINNS BUILDING A PICTURE OF WHITE FINLAND AS THE ENEMY: THE RHETORIC OF A FINNISH-LANGUAGE NEWSPAPER IN SOVIET KARELIA

Thousands of socialist Finns moved to Soviet Karelia after the Finnish Civil War of 1918 aiming to build a socialist society in what was deemed the heartland of their ancestors on the Soviet side of the border.[1] An administrative region known as the Karelian Labour Commune (KLC) was founded in 1920.[2] Despite being a minority nationality in Soviet Karelia[3], the Finns launched a "Finnicization" operation as a part of national Bolshevik policy, with the aim of promoting the status of the Finnish language and culture in schools and other official institutions. They also began publishing a Finnish newspaper in 1920. Initially called *Karjalan Kommuuni* (The Karelian Commune), it was renamed *Punainen Karjala* (Red Karelia) in 1923.[4]

The Tartu peace negotiations in 1920 led to a conflict between Finland and Soviet Russia over the "Karelian issue". The Finns wanted to annex the Karelia area on the basis of the Finno-Ugrian origins of its population, but the Soviet leaders rejected these demands, pointing to the existence of the Karelian Labour Commune with its Finnish leaders. Officially, it seemed that the Finns were making the political decisions in Soviet Karelia, but in fact, the issues were resolved by large-scale definitions of policy issued from Moscow. On the one hand, the foundation of the KLC was related to the important questions of Soviet Russia's foreign policy and political strategy. Promotion of the Bolshevik ideology seemed easier for the Soviet authorities with the help of the Finnish communists, who spoke a rather similar language to that of the local Karelians. On the other hand, the developments in Soviet Karelia were an integral part of Soviet domestic policy and national politics.[5]

RESEARCH QUESTIONS AND SOURCES

This article will concentrate on identity and the image of an enemy in the Soviet Karelian context in the 1920s. Interest will be focused especially on the picture of Finland as an enemy created by the Red Finns, and how this became evident in the newspapers *Karjalan Kommuuni* (The Karelian Commune) and *Punainen Karjala* (Red Karelia). Editorials from 1920 to 1929 will be used as source material. The Red Finns were forming a vicious image of capitalist Finland with their rhetoric, but at the same time they were creating an idealized image of themselves. A further question to be discussed is therefore the identity of the Red Finns, or more specific, what kind of identity they wanted to create for the inhabitants of Soviet Karelia with their newspaper rhetoric.

The newspapers *Karjalan Kommuuni* and *Punainen Karjala* were published three times a week from October 1920 onwards. In September 1927, the size of the paper sheet was increased and *Punainen Karjala* was published six times a week. The source material for this work consisted altogether of 1622 editorials. According to the newspaper itself, *Punainen Karjala* had 2000 subscribers in 1928.[6] One can find clear changes in the content of the editorials during the ten years. Apart from the topics, the picture of Finland as an enemy and the identity of the Red Finns took on different connotations, and were transformed into slightly different forms during the decade.

The main methods used to analyse the material were discourse analysis and qualitative analysis. Words were analysed in their context, whether they signified different nationality groups (Finnish, Karelian, Bolsheviks) positively or negatively, and different political views were taken into account when analysing the descriptions used. When considering the identity building, special attention was paid to expressions such as "we Karelians" or "our Red Army", although in my opinion expressions such as "our Karelia" could not be included in this category, because the White Finns were also distributing propaganda about "Greater Finland" without identifying themselves as Karelians.[7] It was very common to write about "we", or "our" issues in these editorials. According to Benedict Anderson, such a writing style is used to create the image of a homogenous group which also includes the reader.[8]

THE FINNISH CIVIL WAR OF 1918 AS JUSTIFYING THE IMAGE OF AN ENEMY

> Yesterday it was five years since Finland's bloodstained General Mannerheim solemnly marched into Helsinki, where the streets still stank out of the blood of working men and women who had been killed. The White Finnish butchers have always celebrated this day as their special commemoration day.[9]

The Finnish Civil War of 1918 was the most significant single force behind the picture of Finland as the enemy. It was the reason why thousands of Red Finns had fled to Soviet Russia and ended up in Karelia.[10] The Finnish Civil War laid the foundation for the identity of the Soviet Karelian Finns. After the defeat in 1918, the Red Finns lost their civil rights and some of them were forced to flee the country. The new standards of Finnishness excluded the Red Finns from the nation. According to the White Finns, "real Finnishness" included a bourgeois (patriotic) world view and hatred for Soviet Russia.[11]

Karjalan Kommuuni and *Punainen Karjala* actively cherished the memory of the Civil War, and reiterated the cruelties that the White Finns had committed against the Reds in 1918. The editors accused the Whites of murders and persecutions, and also pondered over the reasons for the Red Finns' defeat. In their opinion the focal mistake was the inefficient command skills of the Red leaders. This mistake could have been corrected by founding a Communist Party, which would have been able to resolve the difficult situation. The editors thus reached the conclusion that the Reds lost the Civil War because there was no Communist Party to lead the socialists to the victory.[12]

Although the Finns of Soviet Karelia concentrated their hatred in the early years of the 1920s on bourgeois Finland, the Red Finns who had stayed in Finland were also under severe criticism by the end of the decade. The Social Democrats who had fought on the Red side in 1918 were depicted as being even more evil than the White Finns, as they were now acting on the side of the Whites and representing White Finland. They were depicted as traitors to their class, which made them even more deplorable enemies than the bourgeoisie.[13] The losses of life in 1918 had been heavy, but the Soviet Karelian Finns tried to reasons out the irrational events. The editors pointed out that, although they were not able to create a Red Finland in 1918, the Red Finns were acting for the Soviet state and their battle had created a buffer zone for it against the West. Their heroic struggle had made it possible for the Soviets to strengthen their country while the Finns were securing the western border.[14]

It was not only the Soviet Karelian Finns who were bitter in the 1920s and 1930s, however, for the White Finns also saw the Red Finns as traitors. The trauma of the Finnish Civil War was difficult to deal with, and Bolshevism was seen as one of the reasons for the pointless conflict. It was argued that the Red Finnish leaders had been "infected" and misguided by this foreign danger. Finnish sociologist Risto Alapuro has claimed that the year 1918 defined the Finnish identity.[15] This is an interesting argument, for it seems that the year 1918 defined the Finnish identity on both sides of the front, and later on the both sides of the national border (in Soviet Karelia as well). The Civil War was exploited to create and justify the Finnish identity, and to arouse nationalism, either the White or the Red version. The task was not easy, as the people had been divided into two camps. Those who fought in the Finnish Civil war were influenced by different motives and actions. Their own actions affected their policies and shaped the rhetoric and editorials that were published in the (Finnish-language) Soviet Karelian press.

THE KARELIAN UPRISING AND THE MAINTAINING OF THE PICTURE OF AN ENEMY

> Once again, as so many times before, battalions of bandits hired by Finnish capitalists have invaded Karelia to rob and murder the peaceful inhabitants of the Karelian Labour Commune.[16]

It was a self-evident fact from the Finnish point of view that Soviet Russia was striving to expand westward. The Finnish right-wing literature highlighted the importance of creating a buffer zone between Finland and the aggressive Soviet state, and Karelia was seen as a perfect area for this purpose, so that such groups started to promote the incorporation of Karelia into Finland. This target was mentioned as part of the governmental agenda in 1919, and some right-wing volunteers left for Karelia to put this plan into effect. There were several conflicts between these Finnish volunteers and the Bolsheviks in the border areas in 1918–1922 and some of the local Karelians joined the Finnish or the Bolshevik camp, but most of them were not really interested about the revolts that were going on. The last notable conflict, the Karelian Uprising, took place in 1921–1922, after which the situation in the border regions calmed down.[17]

The Karelian Uprising was the most significant conflict between Finland and Soviet Russia in the early 1920s. The Karelian border municipalities of Repola and Porajärvi announced their interest in being annexed to Finland towards the end of the 1910s, but the Tartu peace negotiations in 1920 put an end to the dispute. Repola and Porajärvi remained subject to the Soviet state and no border changes were made.[18] After the referenda that the local people in Repola and Porajärvi arranged, the White Finns became interested in helping them in their effort to be incorporated into Finland, by founding Finnish schools and a teachers' college in Repola and bringing grain from Finland.[19] This caused the local inhabitants to ally themselves with the White Finns at the end of 1921 and to revolt against the Soviet powers and the results of Tartu Peace Treaty. The Finnish troops and Karelian partisans withdrew in February 1922, and approximately 12.000 Karelian peasants fled with them to Finland.[20] Finland appealed to the League of Nations to resolve the situation, but the international organisation was not interested in interfering in a Finnish-Soviet conflict.[21]

Karjalan Kommuuni followed gleefully the White Finns' wasted pleas to Soviet Russia and the League of Nations. The Red Finnish editors mocked Finland for her efforts to resolve the situation when no other country was paying any attention to these attempts. They rejoiced when Finland failed to gain any support for the "Karelian issue", and the matter was rejected by the League of Nations. Although the Finns were not successful in the Karelian

Uprising, it was the most important single case that was referred to when reminding readers of the White Finns' cruelty.[22] After the uprising some of the Karelians were also seen as enemies of the Red Finns and the Soviets, whereas earlier the Karelians were mentioned only as respectable and harmless kindred people. The Karelians had risen against the Soviets, and the Red Finns had to alter their propaganda in response to this controversy. The editorials explained that the evil Finns had dragged 12.000 Karelians onto the Finnish side of the border by force, and now these poor people were suffering under the White government. The innocent Karelians wanted to come back to their homeland, but they were prevented from doing so by the White Finns. [23]

The Red Finns would have the readers of their newspaper believe that they knew what the Karelians really wanted for their future by convincing them that the actions undertaken by the Red Finns in Soviet Karelia were in line with the will of the Karelians. It was also this rhetoric that the Red Finns used to justify their operations in the area.[24] Instead, when the editors wrote about the White Finns and their shameless intentions in Karelia, they drew attention to the horrifying consequences that would most likely ensue.[25] Karelian Uprising was a very significant case in point when the Red Finns were seeking reasons for looking on the Whites Finns as enemies. The editors wrote more about themes related to Finland at the beginning of the 1920s than at the end of the decade, for as time went by Soviet and international policies became more relevant.

SOVIET KARELIA AS AN EASTERN VANGUARD

> Alongside our everyday work, when we are heading for our fourth year stage, and boosting our area and its population to economic prosperity, let us not forget the incomparable revolutionary mission that the Karelian Labour Commune has in guarding Soviet Russia's north-western border against western capitalism.[26]

The radical right-wing movement depicted Finland as an outpost towards the east in the 1920s. The Finnish mission was to safeguard the western civilization from Bolshevik influence.[27] The Red Finns had rather similar thoughts in Soviet Karelia, and their leader, Edvard Gylling, designated Soviet Karelia as an outpost towards the west. The main task of the Karelian Labour Commune (KLC) was described as that of conveying revolutionary ideas to Finland and Scandinavia. Soviet Karelia was a political asylum for the Red Finns who had escaped persecution from the White Finns after their defeat in the Civil War.[28] The editorials described the important historical mission of the KLC as being to fight against the threat coming from capitalist Finland, and the same arguments were used to justify the very existence of the KLC.[29] Interestingly, exactly the same reasons were given to explain the aims of the anti-Russian movement in Finland: the country had a historical mission to fight against Russianism. The only distinction in this rhetoric was that threat was coming from the east.[30]

It has been stated, that the need to create a picture of an enemy is usually an attempt to unify the nation against the common enemy.[31] It seems natural that the writers working for the newspapers *Karjalan Kommuuni* and *Punainen Karjala* should have seen the importance of creating a picture of White Finland as an enemy, since the unity of the KLC was rather fragile and the organization was mainly held together by the media propaganda. It was for this reason that a high mental border was erected between Finland and Soviet Karelia that would be almost impossible to cross, while the eastern border of the KLC was opened up towards the huge and mighty Soviet state. "Greater Red Finland" seemed not to have any strictly defined eastern border. Soviet Karelia was seen as a significant part of the Soviet state, although the autonomous status of Karelia was mentioned with pride as well.[32]

During the 1920s relations between Finland and the Soviet Union were somewhat frigid. The Soviet Union needed to point out the threat coming from its neighbouring country in order to maintain its propaganda,[33] and the Red Finns promoted this target enthusiastically in their newspapers, which declared that it was an important mission of the KLC to act as a buffer zone against the evil Finns.[34] Finland posed an actual threat to both Karelia and Soviet Russia, and for that reason the Finns and Karelians had to fight together with the Red Army against the country that threatened the existence of the KLC and at the same time represented the whole capitalist world.[35]

The Bolsheviks' national policy was useful for the Red Finns in Soviet Karelia. The *korenizatsia* policies favoured minority nationalities, and the Red Finns were able to rise to the leading posts in Soviet Karelia.[36] *Karjalan Kommuuni* and *Punainen Karjala* wrote about the Finns' duty to help the Karelians in their remote, backward circumstances. It was implied that the Red Finns had come to Karelia not only of their own free will, but also under an obligation to help their kinsmen towards a better future. Besides economic development, political education was mentioned as an asset that would raise the Karelians' quality of life. The Bolsheviks had an important role in this process, as it was their support that made it possible for the Red Finns to operate in Soviet Karelia.[37] During the 1920s the role of Soviet Karelia was transformed from that of being an outpost towards the west more to that of playing a more vital part in the huge family of the Soviet nationalities.

FROM FINNISH NATIONAL IDENTITY TO SOVIET IDENTITY

> Imperialists are threatening our country. [...] We have to make our country's defence stronger. All working troops have to be drawn into this operation. [...] In this way our country's defence will become stronger day by day.[38]

The editorials expressed Finnish identity in two forms. Ethnic and regional identity had their own connotations, while the concept of "Finnishness" seemed difficult to handle among the Red Finns. They had probably lost the idea of a cohesive Finnish national identity at the latest when they lost their civil rights after the Finnish civil war. The concept of Finnishness was mentioned only when writing about the Red Finns. The others were referred to as "White Finns"[39] or the "Finnish butchers"[40]. As a region, Finland was clearly defined as a part of the capitalist bloc.

Since Finnishness seemed to be a difficult concept for the Red Finns, they defined their Finnishness in many cases through "Karelianness". This reference that the White Finns used to justify their interest in the Karelian area was one of the Red Finns' favourite themes as well. The common origin of the Finns and the Karelians was brought to the focus of attention when discussing the ethnic identity of the Red Finns. Here the editors even wrote about the Finnish-Karelian language and nation.[41] This concept might reflect efforts to minimize the differences between the Finns and the Karelians, and it had this effect as a part of the Reds' propaganda. It was important to prove in the annual censuses that the Finns (including the Karelians) were the second largest nationality in Soviet Karelia.

From a regional point of view, the editors considered Karelia mainly a Finnish-controlled area, although they emphasized that it was part of the Soviet family of nations. Regionality was considered on two levels, Karelia being described in the early 1920s as a part of Greater Red Finland, or even of Red Scandinavia. Karelia was to provide a place where a new socialist revolution could be drafted and later brought to Finland. In this sense Karelia was viewed as the mythical birthplace of the Finnish culture. Another view of Karelia was based on its future prospects. Besides the mythical Karelia, the region was seen also as an actual Soviet republic with a present and future defined by the Communist ideology. Although it was described a backward, undeveloped region which the Red Finns were obliged to develop, its rich natural resources were believed to be the key to a great future. However, when the editors were reporting on economic accomplishments, they seemed to identify themselves mainly with the managers or administrators and not with the people who were working in the new factories.[42]

Most of the expressions used in the editorials of *Karjalan Kommuuni* and *Punainen Karjala* described the White Finns as cruel and greedy, while the

Karelians were described as honest, peaceful workers who had been victimized by them. The Bolsheviks, in turn, were the saviours of both of the Karelians and Finns. The idea of a Finn was a somewhat complex one. On the one hand, the Red Finns were destined to assist the Karelians on their way to a wealthier future and were partners in co-operation with the Bolsheviks. On the other hand, the idea of the Finnishness had to be bonded to some concrete object, and the traditional Finnish interpretation was to connect the histories of the Finnish and Karelian peoples, especially now that the Red Finns had adopted Karelia as their new home.

Although Karelia and the Karelians were seen positively, the editors did distinguish some negative features in them as well. The Red Karelians who fought on the Bolshevik side were innocent and pristine,[43] but there were some Karelians who supported the White Finns, and they were described as cruel and bloodstained like the latter. Political views dominated the discussion and ethnic or national arguments were overruled. Yet it was typical that when the Karelians were seen as a part of the White bloc, the editors explained that they had been credulous or unaware of the White Finns' plots, and for this reason had been open to abuse. The underlying reason for the Karelians' resistance to the Bolsheviks had been the agitation and propaganda spread by the White Finns. The people themselves were innocent victims of the White Finns.[44]

The newspapers *Karjalan Kommuuni* and *Punainen Karjala* were published to promote Communist ideology and most of the topics discussed in the 1920s were related to the Soviet Union. Special attention was paid to the minority nationalities. Despite the fact, that most of the editorials were about the Soviet Union, the editors did not write about ethnic "Russianness", or when they did so, they usually referred to tsarist Russia. In those cases, ethnic Russianness took on negative connotations, and monarchist Russia was described as backward-looking. On the contrary, the Bolsheviks had brought salvation not only to the Russians, but also to all other nations.[45]

The integrity of the nationalities within the Soviet Union, and nationality issues as a whole, received a lot of attention in the Red Finnish press. The regional status of Karelia as a part of the Soviet Union was clear to the editors, and they even boasted about this in their writings. The Socialist state was defined as a fatherland, but in the first place it was considered to be a guardian and protector of Finnish activity in the Soviet Union. When the editors wrote about Karelia, they used the Soviet Union as a frame of reference that included Finnish activities in Karelia and in the Soviet Union. As a consequence, Karelia was seen to be developing to reach a new, better level in fulfilling its primary task, which was to safeguard the existence of the Soviet Union and to aid the Finnish workers when the new revolution took place in Finland.[46]

THE RESEARCH TRADITION AMONG THE FINNS IN SOVIET KARELIA

Finnish researchers have traditionally studied Soviet Karelian history in the 1920s from a Finnish point of view: how the Finns were placed within Soviet national policy and what their role was in the government of Soviet Karelia. On the other hand, European research into the early history of Soviet Karelia has mainly been concentrated on economic history and Soviet national policy in general. Often Soviet Karelia has been no more than a case study in research into Soviet minority nationalities. Russian research carried out at the Petrozavodsk State University in Karelia, however, has examined such topics as the relations of the Finns with the local inhabitants, the Karelians and Russians.

A few of the most interesting studies that influenced on this article deserve to be mentioned here. The Finnish point of view is introduced by Markku Kangaspuro, whose dissertation on Finnish nationalism and the Red Finns in the leadership of the Soviet Karelian government[47] attaches considerable significance to the Finns' role in Karelia. He claims that the Red Finns aimed through their actions and Finnization policy to create a Finnish Soviet Karelia. Kangaspuro's dissertation is based mainly on archival sources and as such represents an interesting contrast to the present results, which indicate the Red Finns' eagerness to build a socialist identity and propagate a socialist world-view in public by means of their newspaper editorials.

Taking a British point of view for comparison, we could mention Nick Baron's research[48] on Soviet Karelia, which shows how Karelia was by and large controlled from Moscow. Baron concentrates more on relations between the centre (Moscow) and the periphery (Soviet Karelia and other peripheral Soviet states). Governmental decisions made in Soviet Karelia are looked at from the perspective of Moscow, and Baron draws a larger picture of Soviet politics that includes repercussions in Soviet Karelia. Baron indicates that the centre exercised control over the periphery and questions the significance of the Red Finns' role in Soviet Karelia. Instead of making real political decisions, the Red Finns were seen to act more in the role of a marionette government. Baron's views are interesting when examining the Red Finns' editorials, and suggest that the Finnish topics were left in the shadow of general Bolshevik politics, especially in the late 1920s.

Irina Takala of Petrozavodsk State University, who has studied relations between the Red Finns and the local Karelian people in the 1920s and 1930s from a local perspective,[49] concludes that the picture of the White Finns as an enemy that the Red Finns built up eventually turned against them. Many of the Red Finns worked as foremen and officers of higher rank than the locals, which aroused envy and bitterness among the Karelian and Russian workers. The Bolsheviks' *korenizatsia* policy, which gave privileges to the minority nationalities (such as the Red Finns), created tensions and anger against them at the local level. Relations between the Red Finns and the local people became better only after Stalin's purges in 1936–1937, which were targeted in particular at the minority nationalities.

CONCLUSIONS

The Red Finns' eagerness to lead the socialist construction work in Soviet Karelia with their newspaper rhetoric did not yield the expected results. Tensions arose between the Red Finns and the local people, since the *korenizatsia* policies favoured the Finns. The only Finns that most of the Karelians or Russians had met were the Red Finns, who worked in high positions and enjoyed many privileges. These facts fitted in well with the picture of the bourgeois White Finns as an enemy that the Red Finns were propagating, as they were accused of being greedy masters who exercised wage discrimination and favoured their own people. The Red Finns were eager in their propaganda work against White Finland, but did not realise that their presence in Soviet Karelia was actually considered a threat rather than the existence of the White Finns. [50]

Stalin's purges in the mid-1930s were targeted especially against the minority nationalities, including the Red Finns, who were accused of supporting the Finnish bourgeoisie and spreading Finnish nationalism among the Karelian people.[51] According to Irina Takala, it is still too early to make any final evaluations as to how many people were killed in Stalin's purges, but there are documents to indicate that altogether 3189 Finns had been captured and condemned in Soviet Karelia up to 10.8.1938, accounting for 40% of all those condemned (of whom a further 27% were Karelians and 25% Russians).[52] It is rather ironic that the Red Finns, who had been actively building up a picture of the White Finns as the enemy for 15 years, were accused of assisting the Finnish bourgeoisie and most of them were eventually sentenced to death on these grounds.

REFERENCES

1 Markku Kangaspuro, Neuvosto-Karjalan taistelu itsehallinnosta: Nationalismi ja suomalaiset punaiset Neuvostoliiton vallankäytössä 1920–1939, Hakapaino Oy, Helsinki 2000, 10.

2 Mauno Jääskeläinen, Itä-Karjalan kysymys, Dark Oy, Vantaa 2003 ([1]1961), 291, 296.

3 Timo Vihavainen, VKP(b):n/NKP:n kansallisuuspolitiikka 1920–50-luvuilla ja karjalaisten ja suomalaisten kohtalo, in: Timo Vihavainen/Irina Takala (ed.). Yhtä suurta perhettä. Bolshevikkien kansallisuuspolitiikka Luoteis-Venäjällä 1920–1950 -luvuilla, Gummerus Kirjapaino Oy, Saarijärvi 2000, 27; Markku Kangaspuro, Neuvosto-Karjalan suomalainen kausi, in: Timo Vihavainen/Irina Takala (ed.). Yhtä suurta perhettä: Bolshevikkien kansallisuuspolitiikka Luoteis-Venäjällä 1920–1950-luvuilla, Gummerus Kirjapaino Oy, Saarijärvi 2000, 141; Takala Irina, Kansallisuusoperaatiot Karjalassa, in: Timo Vihavainen/Irina Takala (ed.). Yhtä suurta perhettä. Bolshevikkien kansallisuuspolitiikka Luoteis-Venäjällä 1920–1950-luvuilla, Gummerus Kirjapaino Oy, Saarijärvi 2000, 183.

4 Saarela Tauno, Suomalaisen kommunismin synty 1918–1923, Tammer-Paino, Tampere 1996, 65; Kangaspuro, Neuvosto-Karjalan taistelu itsehallinnosta, Loc. Cit. (Note 1), 37.

5 Kangaspuro, Neuvosto-Karjalan suomalainen kausi, Loc. Cit. (Note 3), 137–139.

6 "Eläköön Karjalan 10-vuotinen lehdistö!" Punainen Karjala (PK) 5.1.1928.

7 Outi Karemaa, Vihollisia, vainoojia, syöpäläisiä. Venäläisviha Suomessa 1917–23, Hakapaino Oy, Helsinki 1998, 97.

8 Benedict Anderson, Imagined Communities: Reflections on the origin and spread of nationalism, Verso, London 1983, 36–37.

9 "Fascistikaappauksen uhka Suomessa". PK 17.05.1924.

10 Saarela, Suomalaisen kommunismin synty, Loc. Cit. (Note 4), 27.

11 Kari Immonen, Ryssästä saa puhua: Neuvostoliitto suomalaisessa julkisuudessa ja kirjat julkisuuden muotona 1918–39, Otava, Keuruu 1987, 439.

12 "Suomen proletaarinen vallankumous ja sen kymmenvuotispäivä". PK 07.01.1928.

13 "Hallitusvaihdos ja tilanne Suomessa". PK 21.12.1927.

14 Kullervo Manner, "Suomen vallankumouksen 11 vuosipäivän johdosta". PK 27.01.1929.

15 Risto Alapuro, Suomen synty paikallisena ilmiönä 1890–1933, WSOY:n graafiset laitokset, Porvoo 1994, 133, 136.

16 "Suksille!" Karjalan Kommuuni (KK) 20.12.1921.

17 Immonen, Ryssästä saa puhua, Loc. Cit. (Note 11), 333.

18 Stacy Churchill, Itä-Karjalan kohtalo 1917–1922: Itä-Karjalan itsehallintokysymys Suomen ja Neuvosto-Venäjän välisissä suhteissa 1917–1922, Werner Söderström Osakeyhtiön kirjapaino, Porvoo 1970, 190; Jääskeläinen, Itä-Karjalan kysymys, Loc. Cit. (Note 2), 319, 321.

19 Mirko Harjula, Venäjän-Karjala ja Muurmanni 1914–1922. Maailmansota, vallankumous, ulkomaiden interventio ja sisällissota. Suomlaisen Kirjallisuuden Seura, Helsinki 2007, 114.

20 Nick Baron, Soviet Karelia. Politics, planning and terror in Stalin's Russia 1920–1939, Routledge, New York 2007, 26.

21 Churchill, Itä-Karjalan kohtalo, Loc. Cit. (Note 11), 190; Jääskeläinen, Itä-Karjalan kysymys, Loc. Cit. (Note 2), 319, 321.

22 "Suomen Karjalapolitiikan viimeinen tappio". KK 28.07.1923.

23 "Kapinaan nousseiden paluu." KK 02.06.1922.

24 "Venäjän tunnustaminen ja Karjalan "kansannousu"". KK 03.01.1922.

25 "Kommuunimme päivänä." KK 07.06.1922.

26 "Neuvosto-Karjalan vuosipäivänä". KK 07.06.1923.

27 Heikki Luostarinen, Perivihollinen. Suomen oikeistolehdistön Neuvostoliittoa koskeva viholliskuva sodassa 1941–44: Tausta ja sisältö, Vastapaino, Tampere 1986, 5; Karemaa, Vihollisia, vainoojia, syöpäläisiä, Loc. Cit. (Note 7), 137, 159.

28 Edvard Gylling, "Suuret rauhan viestit". KK 9.10.1920.

29 "Neuvosto-Karjalan vuosipäivänä". KK 7.6.1923.

30 Karemaa, Vihollisia, vainoojia, syöpäläisiä, Loc. Cit. (Note 7), 166.

31 Sinikka Wunsch, Punainen uhka. Neuvostoliiton kuva johtavassa suomalaisessa sanomalehdistössä maaliskuusta 1938 talvisodan päättymiseen maaliskuussa 1940, Gummerus Kirjapaino Oy, Jyväskylä 2004, 58.

32 "Karjalan Työkansan Kommuuni ja vallankumous". KK 7.11.1922.

33 Timo Vihavainen, Marssi Helsinkiin. Suomen talvisota neuvostolehdistössä, Gummerus Kirjapaino Oy, Jyväskylä 1990, 15.

34 "Karjalan kommuunin muodostaminen." KK 17.2.1921.

35 "Kapinaan nousseiden paluu." KK 2.6.1922.

36 Kangaspuro, Neuvosto-Karjalan suomalainen kausi, Loc. Cit. (Note 3), 141.

37 "Neuvosto-Karjalan vuosipäivänä". KK 7.6.1923.

38 "Työläiset ja talonpojat, lujittakaan Neuvostoliiton puolustusta!" PK 27.08.1927.

39 "Perustuslain ja Karjalan autonomian juhla". PK 01.07.1928.

40 A. Sedjakin, "Karjalan "nousu" ja sen merkitys." KK 10.01.1922.

41 "Karjalamme voimistuu". PK 16.12.1926.

42 A. Nuorteva, "Karjalan hallituksen tervehdys Vienan Karjalalle". PK 1926.

43 See e.g.: O. T., "Karjalan nuoriso luokkatietoiseksi". KK 3.3.1923.

44 See e.g.: "Uhtua vallattu". KK 11.02.1922.

45 "Neuvosto-Karjalan vuosipäivänä". KK 07.06.1923.

46 "Karjalan Työkansan Kommuuni ja vallankumous." KK 07.11.1922.

47 Kangaspuro, Neuvosto-Karjalan taistelu itsehallinnosta, Loc. Cit. (Note 1).

48 Baron, Soviet Karelia, Loc. Cit. (Note 20).

49 Irina Takala 2009, Neuvosto-Karjalan asukkaiden näkemykset suomalaisista 1920–30 -luvuilla, in: Olga Iljuha/Aleksei Tsamutali/Timo Vihavainen (eds.), Monikasvoinen Suomi, Edita Publishing Oy, Helsinki 2009,

50 Takala, Neuvosto-Karjalan asukkaiden näkemykset suomalaisista 1920–30 -luvuilla, Loc. Cit. (Note 49), 290–291, 293.

51 Antero Uitto, Suomea rajan takana 1918–1944, in: Suomea rajan takana. Suomenkielisen neuvostokirjallisuuden historia ja bibliografia, Gummerus Kirjapaino Oy, Jyväskylä 2008, 45–46, 48.

52 Takala, Kansallisuusoperaatiot Karjalassa, Loc. Cit. (Note 3), 224.

‘Us’ and ‘Others’ on Both Sides of the Post-War Borders

HALLVARD TJELMELAND

BORDER AS BARRIER AND BRIDGE: THE NORWEGIAN-SOVIET/ RUSSIAN BORDER AS A POLITICAL AND CULTURAL CONSTRUCTION

The border between Norway and Russia was established in 1826. Up until the First World War this boundary was not very strictly maintained. Since the 18th century there has been transnational contact across the border on the economic level with the so-called Pomor trade. Attempts to restrict this trade in the beginning of the 20th century provoked a strong mobilisation among ordinary people in the northern part of Norway which actually stopped these plans. Russian fishermen also had rights to fish in Eastern Finnmark up until 1913 on the basis of the so-called "Kiberg rights".[1] The border area had low military priority and there was a great deal of transnational contact, both between Norwegians and Russians and between Norwegians and people on the Finnish side. With the Treaty of Tartu in October 1920 independent Finland obtained the Arctic Corridor (Petsamo region), which Finnish nationalists had been working for since the middle of the 19th century, and up to the end of the Second World War, when Finland had to render this border area as a part of the concessions given to the Soviet Union in September 1944. Norway had no common border with its great neighbour to the east.[2] This article discusses what kind of border was established between Norway and the Soviet Union after the Second World War.

BORDERS IN INTERNATIONAL POLITICS

This approach presupposes a border concept that involves more than the physical lines of separation between the states or a line on the map, as in the traditional geographical discourse.[3] Using such a strict concept, border history in the post-war period started with an agreement in 1947 between Norway and the Soviet Union on the reestablishment of the old Norwegian-Russian border from 1826. This was formalised in 1949[4] and ended with a definite agreement on the sea and shelf border between Norway and Russia in 2011. However, how the border was managed differed over time, as did the possibilities for contact and communication across the border. To understand such processes, one has to go beyond the traditional concept of a border and move towards a more fluid concept of what is implied when distinguishing between *border* and *boundary*[5] in border studies. In recent border studies, borders are decomposed and differentiated, in time and in function, as both political and cultural products. By broadening the perspective of the meaning of borders, more actors than just the states become important, such as local and regional authorities and the population of *borderlands*, NGO's etc.[6] Crises in border demarcations and the question of change and continuity becomes relevant with a wider concept of borders.[7]

Border studies are a cross-disciplinary field of research and many approaches from different disciplines are at work.[8] My approach in this article is inspired by the constructivist tendencies, emphasizing cultural and social aspects in borders, but I find it fruitful to include a broader perspective than is dominating this field today, i.e. the character of the international political system. How a border between countries is perceived and functions depends on the image of the neighbouring country as "the other". This has to be understood in the broader context of the position of these particular states in the international system. In the realist approach in the field of international relations, the basis for this system is *international anarchy*, which is structured by power politics from states maximizing their own interests. The character of the international system depends on relative forces between states or groups of states through alliances. But what determines how the states perceive their interests and what determines how the states perceive the interests of rivals in the international system? If, as the realists presume, national security is the most important determinant for the politics of states: what determinates the perception of threats? This is of course of special importance for neighbouring states.

The realist approach has been criticised for simplifying or neglecting such basic questions. One of those critics is the political scientist Alexander Wendt, who attacks the basic idea of international anarchy as an independent variable. The anarchy of states is not one thing, he argues, it is different things in different periods, depending on the norms and ideas which he views as a product of interactions between states. Wendt differentiates between three "cultures of anarchy": a *Hobbesian* ideational structure, where the states are willing to do whatever possible to achieve their goals, without any restraints, and where violence is the basic tool for survival, a *Lockean structure*, where states respect the Westphalian peace and states' right to prevail, but where violence can be used to advance their interests and a *Kantian structure* which is based on a friendly atmosphere, solving disputes through negotiations and not by use of violence. These different cultures of anarchy are based on different representations of state roles: enemy, rival and friend.[9] Now we will begin to see the obvious link to the meaning of border.

The Norwegian-Soviet/Russian case is suitable as a test of the relevance of Wendt's theory for border studies for several reasons. This border is the oldest and most peaceful in Russian history. During the Cold War it was the border between the US-led NATO alliance and the Soviet Union, and therefore the border where the East-West division was sharpest. After the dissolution of the Soviet Empire, the border perceptions and management now reflected the new position of Russia from a fallen superpower in the 1990s to a Russia striving for great power status in the first decade of the 21st century. This also raises a break/continuity problem, connected to aspects in modern border studies, in the studies of international relations, as well as over the last decades, i.e. the relationship between politics and culture, between the central and regional levels, actor and structure explanations. I will concentrate on *periods of transition* and *conflicts of perception* of borders and "the other", and I focus on the relevance of the basic perception of these dimensions in border studies.

THE NORWEGIAN-RUSSIAN BORDER IN THE PROCESS FROM BRIDGE BUILDING TO NATO MEMBERSHIP

The Norwegian bridge building policy was established in the spring of 1944 as a break with the Atlantic policy in the three years before that. The background for this was primarily the turn of the war and the allies' decision to prioritize the continental attack. The Norwegian government was afraid of being isolated in the north with a neighbour that was expected to play a much more important role in international society after the war than in the period of isolation in the interwar period. There was no sign of an alarmism in that connection. The Soviet Union was an ally in the war against Nazi Germany, and the two countries agreed on the procedure for the coming Soviet attack across the border in eastern Finnmark. This policy of balance was the main strategy up to 1947. It was based on an image of the international system as basically based on a Lockean culture.

This apparent harmony was mixed with ambiguity and uncertainty. The Soviet attack on Finland in November 1939 was not forgotten, and the tightening of control in Eastern Europe after 1945 was of course disturbing. So was also a surprising proposal from the Soviet Foreign Minister Molotov to the Norwegian Foreign Minister Trygve Lie at a meeting in Moscow in November 1944 after the Soviet attack on the German forces in Eastern Finnmark. It was a proposal for joint government in Svalbard, implying a break with the Svalbard Treaty of 1925, which gave sovereignty over this archipelago in the Arctic Sea to Norway, with equal rights for utilizing resources for all signature states. In April 1945 the Norwegian exile government responded to this with a proposal for an agreement which was close to the Soviet proposal.[10] In other words: The Norwegian government was forced, or felt itself forced, to go into a bilateral arrangement which was in conflict with an international treaty.

This Norwegian compliance was no doubt based on an image of the Soviet Union as potentially expansionistic, for instance by expanding deeper into Norwegian territory beyond Eastern Finnmark. However, this Hobbesian image was soon replaced by a more relaxed analysis based on a Lockean image. We know that someone at the lower political level and in the military sector in the Soviet Union had some ideas about changing borders in the North, taking back more than what was lost to Finland after the First World War. We also know however that this was never on the agenda on a higher political level.[11] The Soviet Union focused on a much more important question at the time, and the actions in the years to come clearly demonstrated that there were no plans for expansionism in the High North. It should also be easy to conclude that Stalin had no interest in weakening the position of the coming superpower, the USA, with conflicts in such a marginal area. The early Soviet moves in Eastern Europe after the German defeat were at the time considered to be in line with legitimate security interests, based on experiences from two world wars, which also served as the basis for the Yalta agreement in January 1945. In 1946 the Norwegian government came back to its senses and decided to back away from the agreement from April 1945.[12]

What was the background the next step: the break with the bridge building policy, the membership in NATO and the self-imposed restrictions on the membership which were of direct relevance for the future policy in the High North? The assessment of that depends on the analysis of the whole process that divided Europe in the second part of the 1940s. Norway hesitated through the autumn of 1947 before accepting the offer of The Marshall Plan, mostly because it involved a break with the bridge building policy. After that the governing Labour Party was also divided between those who wanted a Scandinavian security solution in a polarized and divided Europe, and those who wanted the Atlantic solution.[13] Those who wanted an alliance on a Scandinavian level were inclined to think in line with the Lockean culture, that the Soviet Union primarily was driven by security motives, and that the danger of a Soviet attack on Norway depended on the global conflict between the new superpowers; an analysis in line with the revisionist or the post-revisionist tradition within Cold War historiography. This position was of course not alarmist, presupposing a Hobbesian enemy. But what about the chosen line, the NATO membership and the policy for self-imposed restrictions?

It is obvious, from my point of view, that there was good reason for feeling insecure as a neighbouring state to the Soviet Union at the end of the 1940s. It is unnecessary to repeat the reasons for that; the suppression of the countries in Eastern Europe with the communist take over in Czechoslovakia in February 1948 as an especially frightening example, not to mention the blackmail policy on the Berlin question and the friendship agreement between the Soviet Union and Finland in the spring of 1948 with the following rumours about a similar offer to Norway. The world had changed. On the other hand, up to this point Stalin had followed a policy in line with the politics of influence, sphere on a more or less Lockean basis – except he considered Eastern Europe, with Finland having an in-between status, as part of their zone of influence.[14] In Norway there were no doubt alarmist attitudes in the military sector and in the military and civil secret services, especially at the regional level.[15] However, the attitudes at the dominant political level cannot be characterised as alarmists. Norway balanced this uncertainty about the character of the Soviet regime by joining the US-led defence organisation on the one hand and with a reassurance policy meant to secure low tension in the High North by implementing self-imposed restrictions to the NATO membership, most importantly the base declaration from 1949 which declared that foreign bases on Norwegian soil should not be established in times of peace.

At the end of the 1940s the northernmost Norwegian border had completely changed character. The border with Russia from 1826 up to the Russian Revolution had been porous, not a fence. This was even more the case after 1920, when this border became a part of the border with independent Finland, even if there was some degree of surveillance and suspicion towards an imagined "Finnish menace".[16] The renewed border towards the Soviet Union from 1944 became something quite different, a border controlled and managed by military forces on both sides, a real barrier for transnational contact. At the base of this new reality were the Cold War and a new international climate of distrust and images of mutual animosity.

WHAT KIND OF INTERNATIONAL ANARCHY AFTER STALIN'S DEATH?

Up to the death of Stalin in 1953 the international anarchy had a Hobbesian structure. Both superpowers considered the other to be expansionistic and an enemy – the international political system had become bipolar and the Cold War global. Today there is wide consensus among historians that the death of Stalin led to a new foreign policy and a new way of thinking.[17] This new way of thinking resulted in a number of initiatives, all based on a more differentiated perspective on international politics. Andrei Zhadanov's "two camps theory", which certainly had a Hobbesian basis, was abandoned and replaced by an attitude closer to a Lockean perspective, with the Nikita Khrushchev's phrase "peaceful co-existence" as the most striking rhetorical symbol. This policy for dialogue and negotiations found several expressions.

One was that the policy towards the decolonized countries changed. They were no longer automatically regarded as pro-western and reactionary. The policy towards the Nordic countries changed too, becoming more positive towards what was later called the Nordic Balance, hoping to strengthen neutralist tendencies.[18] What was between "the two camps" was now an interesting target for Soviet public diplomacy; it was no longer the Jesuitical "those who are not with us, are against us". This signalled a change from perceiving the international anarchy as basic Hobbesian to becoming basic Lockean.

This diplomatic offensive from the new leaders in Moscow got mixed responses from the West, responses which reflected different opinions of the intentions of the new Soviet leaders. At the core of these differences is the question: Did they mean what they said, or was the invitation to perform in line with a Lockean culture just a change of tactics? The first Western statesman willing to follow up on the new signals from the East was the British Prime Minister Winston Churchill.[19] The most consequent representative for the opposite attitude was the American Foreign Minister, Foster Dulles. It is easy to see that the two types of Western strategy, what Stian Bones has characterized as *uncompromised containment* and *critical dialogue*,[20] can be seen as based on two different images of the new Soviet leadership. At the base of the US policy was the opinion that there was no reason for believing that the shift in Soviet diplomacy represented a *real* break. As shown by the political scientist Ole Holsti, who in the beginning of the 1960s analysed Dulles' "belief system and national images", Dulles kept to his firm belief that the Soviet Union was basically expansionistic, "looking at the Soviet Union as a political party rather than a powerful nation".[21] Dulles thought that the USA had to keep to a policy of consequent containment, either the Soviet Union invited them for a dialogue (a sign of weakness, necessary to stick to firm containment) or the Soviet Union did the opposite (a sign of strength, necessary to stick to firm containment).[22] Dulles obviously regarded the international political culture as Hobbesian. It is probably right that President Eisenhower himself moved from a primarily Hobbesian to a primarily Lockean perspective during his period as president. It's a striking fact that the first summit meeting between the leaders of the two superpowers took place in 1959, after the death of Dulles.

This cleavage between regarding the Soviet Union after Stalin's death as an enemy, based on an assumption of a Hobbesian culture, or as a state respecting the Westphalian peace in a Lockean manner, a rival in the international political system, was also represented in Norwegian politics. This was partly a cleavage between the governing Labour Party and the conservatives and partly a cleavage within the Labour Party itself, with the party leader and Prime Minister Einar Gerhardsen on the one side and the profiled party secretary Haakon Lie on the other. Traditionally this schism has been explained in terms of personal conflicts connected to ideology and as a conflict between realist and idealist politics. It is more reasonable to consider this more as two different answers to the question: How should one relate to the Soviet Union after Stalin's death? The formative period for Norwegian security politics after Stalin's death was 1955–1958, a period that ended in a lasting hegemony for a tradition emphasising "critical dialogue".

Three events were in focus for the discussions in this period of restructuring the relationship to the Soviet Union, both at present time and by historians later on: Prime Minister Gerhardsen's trip to the Soviet Union in November 1955, Gerhardsen's speech at the NATO conference in Paris December 1957 and the following Norwegian attempt to arrange a top-level meeting between the leaders of the two superpowers. The relevance of these events for the understanding of the Norwegian-Soviet border is that they demonstrate how actors contribute to making a new international political culture, of relevance for my special case: the construction of the Norwegian-Soviet border. To understand what these initiatives were about, I find it fruitful to put them into a broader international framework concerning the image of the culture in the international system.

Gerhardsen was the first Western state leader to be invited to the Soviet Union. There was no serious disagreement in accepting the invitation. Two aspects were discussed: that the Norwegian base declaration was accepted as a part of the communiqué from the meetings and that Gerhardsen agreed to bring back to the central committee in the Norwegian Labour Party an invitation from the Soviet Communist Party to cooperate on the party level. The idea that this visit was considered problematic is a retrospective construction. The sources also show that there was no important contradiction between the prime minister and the foreign minister in the general view, as some researchers and political actors have assumed. They dealt with the basic idea that it was important to be open to new signals from the new leadership in Moscow. The small conflicts were minor disagreements and can be traced back more to a difference in style than to substance. A number of state leaders and parliament delegations also went to visit the Soviet Union, with the German Chancellor Konrad Adenauer as the first, followed by the Canadian Foreign Minister Lester Pearson, both in the autumn of 1955 – and the Danish and Swedish prime ministers the next year. The central committee of the Norwegian Labour Party did not accept the invitation to cooperate on the party level (but accepted a change of press delegations), but at the same time there were examples of contact on the party level between West European social democratic parties and the Soviet communist parties, for instance the French Socialist Party and the British Labour Party, though not formalised.

Gerhardsen's "stirring speech" at the first NATO meeting at the state leaders' level in Paris November 1957 attracted great attention, both at the meeting and in the world press, and changed the atmosphere and the agenda of the meeting.[23] The background for the Paris conference was the so-called "Sputnik shock" and the American answer: Intermediate nuclear weapons to Western Europe. There was a near consensus among Norwegian politicians, as in other NATO countries such as Denmark and Canada, that a pure military approach to the Soviet sign of technological strength was problematic. The Norwegian delegation actually had consultations with the Danish and Canadian delegations before the meeting. Gerhardsen changed the climate of the meeting, but the Norwegian proposal for postponement of deployment of the intermediate missiles when negotiating was withdrawn. That is probably the reason why Gerhardsen's initiative has been regarded as amateurish, especially since he made his speech more profiled than the modest version he got from the Ministry of Foreign Affairs. However, the difference between Gerhardsen and the foreign minister has been over-exaggerated. There is no doubt that the foreign minister and the prime minister basically had the same attitudes in line with widespread attitudes at the same time: The Cold War had come to a stalemate and fresh diplomatic initiatives were necessary. This thinking was inspired by the lectures George Kennan, the father of containment policy, had on the BBC a short time before the Paris conference, the message in the book *Nuclear Weapons and Foreign Policy* by the new star in political science, Henry Kissinger the same year and political initiatives from the Gaitskell plan (named after the leader of the British Labour Party) and the Rapacki plan (named after the Polish foreign minister) – all of which Gerhardsen and his advisers knew very well and all of which was based on the Lockean premise that serious negotiations with the antagonist in the international political system was possible and necessary.[24]

This retrospective criticism of Gerhardsen as amateurish has also been argued in relation to the third case: The Norwegian initiative for a top-level meeting. The impulse for the Norwegian proposal to host a meeting between the leaders of the two superpowers probably came from the Norwegian ambassador in Paris, Rolf Andvord, who in a meeting with President Eisenhower got the impression that the USA might be interested in such an initiative. Contact was established between Finn Moe, leader of the Committee on Foreign Affairs and the Soviet ambassador, Mikhail Gribanov, at the end of December. In January 1958 this was followed up by meetings between Gerhardsen, Foreign Minister Lange and the Soviet ambassador and through informal contacts in Washington. The American channel was chosen in an attempt to get direct access to the president himself, but without success. This attempt was based on an analysis of a split within the

US administration, between the president and the Secretary of State Foster Dulles. Dulles himself stopped this initiative and it ended in nothing. It was an attempt, though not without prospects as Dulles at the time was under hard pressure both from the media and the democratic opposition, because of his sterile Hobbesian outlook.[25]

SOFTENING THE BORDER

This formative period regarding the Norwegian security policy towards the Soviet Union opened up a process that probably made Norway the West European country that cooperated the most with the Soviet Union.[26] On the political level several members of the government visited the Soviet Union in the years to come. The foreign minister went to Moscow in 1961 and the Soviet Foreign Minister Andrej Gromyko returned the visit in 1963. In 1964 the Soviet leader Khrushchev visited Norway and Gerhardsen returned the visit the year after.[27] In the wake of the agreements in connection with Gerhardsen's travels to the Soviet Union in 1955, a sudden stream of delegations followed, both ways, from parliamentarians to political youth leaders, trade union activists and business people. From 1956 even mutual visits of naval units took place regularly, with Norway being the first NATO country to receive an invitation in 1954.[28] The most important fields of cooperation were research, fisheries and health problems in the High North. Most attention was focused on the cooperation regarding development of water power in the border river Pasvikelva in East Finnmark. The construction work led to easier border passing for the workers involved. As a result of this, a tourist centre was established in the Soviet enclave at Boris Gleb, on the western side of the river Pasvik. This short-term experiment with a border meeting point in a Cold War climate in the middle of the 1960s ended because of the excesses in drinking taking place there and because it was regarded as a security problem.[29]

There were still elements of mistrust and suspicion, which also stopped plans for large-scale industrial and infrastructure cooperation in the High North between Norway, Finland and the Soviet Union which the Minister of Commerce, Trygve Lie put forth in the 1960s. The Ministry of Foreign Affairs was critical to such far-reaching plans, both because of allied scepticism towards Norway's cooperative attitude towards the antagonist to the east, and also due to fear of Soviet dominance and influence. Within the government Lie's idea had some support, but when this plan was presented as a thought in discussions with Soviet representatives, the attitude was lukewarm – probably for the same reasons as in the Norwegian Ministry of Foreign Affairs.[30]

There was still an element of distrust and "securitisation" in policy areas not directly connected to security politics at the top level. At the base of this cautiousness was an image of the border as more of a barrier than a bridge; two rivals in the international system met at the Norwegian-Soviet border. The Soviet Union was not just an asymmetric neighbour to Norway, but also a global rival to the other superpower, the USA. A physical sign of this was that border control on both sides was handled by military units.[31]

However, the main tendency since Stalin's death was to keep low tension in the High North and open up for cooperation on limited fields. In the border region there was pressure towards a more extended cooperation, making the border more porous. In the borderland, on both sides of the border, a lot of contacts were established within tourism, sports and culture. A peculiar example of this regional denying of the strict understanding of the border as a barrier was an event in 1959, when the orchestra Vardø Bymusikk (Vardø City Music) went with a fishing cutter to Murmansk, where they planned to hold a concert with Russian and Norwegian music on the repertoire. This was arranged in cooperation with the Moscow branch of the Norwegian-Soviet Society, but they didn't bother with formalities and just crossed the border without a visa. The concert was very much appreciated on the Soviet side, and this visit was the beginning of a cultural cooperation across the border in the years to come.[32] The first visit of Murmansk athletes to Eastern Finnmark came in the summer of 1959, and through the rest of the Cold War era exchanges of sports visits took place with short interruptions on the bases of agreements between sports associations on both sides, with 60-80 participants involved each time. At the end of the 1960s many delegations travelled across the border, and regular tourist visits to the Soviet Union were arranged by a travel bureau in Kirkenes.[33]

For people in Finnmark these activities were part of a transnational cultural movement, with contacts across the border both in North Sweden and North Finland. Since the 1950s the North Calotte conferences had been a framework for a new transnational cooperation, starting with a cultural conference in Karasjok in Finnmark in 1953, as a dimension within the Nordic cooperation. This cooperation on the North Calotte level was based both on a functional ground, as a cooperation promoting tourism and infrastructure building in these northern regions, and on a political ground, as a cooperation in security policy, first and foremost in fighting communism in a sensitive area with broader support for the communist movement than in the rest of the Nordic countries. The social democratic movement was the driving force behind this dualism of modernisation and Cold War policy in the early North Calotte movement. From 1960 North Calotte conferences were arranged within Foreningen Norden (Nordic Association) on a regular basis in towns in the northernmost parts of Norway, Sweden and Finland, since 1967 organised by the North Calotte Committee (North Calotte Council from 1997). This "official" North Calotte movement was met with a challenge from communists and other parts of the labour movement which wanted to integrate Northwest Russia into the "official" North Calotte cooperation, starting with a meeting in Kemi/Salla in 1964 and then on a regular basis, alternating between the northern peripheries in these four countries.[34]

So the politics of low tension in the High North opened up for contacts across the Norwegian- Soviet border, also at a regional level. The Iron Curtain became perforated. That was the case even after the outbreak of what at the time was called the Second Cold War at the end of the 1970s, after 15 years of detente. Straight up to the end of the Cold War, Norway held on to a policy of low tension in the High North. The High North became even more important in this period, both because of the global dimension and the changes in international law. The increased strategic importance of the High North came to expression through the building up of the military at the Kola Peninsula in the 1960s and 1970s and the new American naval strategy from the beginning of the 1980s. It is a paradox that the contact and bilateral cooperation between Norway and the Soviet Union raised to new heights in this tense period.[35]

The driving force in this intensification of the Norwegian-Soviet relationship at that time was the development of the law of the sea. In the middle of the 1970s there was continuity in the cooperation from the intensified Cold War period in the 1970s up to today's fisheries management in the Barents Sea, in progress, with shifting frequency, in the negotiation of the border line in the so-called Grey Zone (ending in an agreement in 2011, after more than 30 years of negotiations) and in some other fields.[36] This has been a policy based on mutual interest and a minimum of trust concerning the intentions of the other part in a Lockean atmosphere.[37]

This cooperation on a bilateral basis in the Barents Sea during the intensified Cold War climate had its counterpart in continuation in contacts across the border at the regional level. With the new winds in high politics after Mikhail Gorbachev's take over as general secretary in March 1985, this tendency towards cooperation was strengthened, both at the regional and national level. The signal for more and deepened cooperation in the High North came with Gorbachev's famous speech in Murmansk in 1987 in which he launched the idea of the Arctic as a "zone of peace". He wanted a nuclear weapon-free zone in Northern Europe, restrictions on naval activities in Arctic seas and the development of transnational cooperation in areas such as resource development, scientific exploration, indigenous people's affairs, environmental protection and marine transportation.[38]

This anticipated the end of the Cold War in the High North and was the starting shot for building up transnational activity and cooperation well before the end of the bipolarised political system. Norwegian authorities were hesitant before going into deeper bilateral cooperation with the neighbouring superpower. An early start was on the environmental question, which was not regarded as so sensitive and controversial, and the first discussions were on a regional level between the Governor of Finnmark, Anders Aune, and Finnmark County on the one hand and Murmansk Oblast on the other. The first environmental agreement on the state level was signed under Foreign Minister Nikolai Ryzhkov's visit in Norway in 1988, and in 1990 a cooperation regarding pollution from the smelting plant in Nikel was established, connected to a similar agreement between Finland and the Soviet Union the year before.[39]

The invitation for cooperation in Gorbachev's speech in Murmansk was from the beginning picked up on the regional level in Finnmark County. Already in the county plan for 1980–1983 was a pledge for a North Calotte cooperation which was probably also meant to include the Russian side. What was considered to be of special interest at that time was the potential for cooperation in future oil production in the Barents Sea, but also the possibility of strengthening trade between Finnmark, North Finland and Northwest Russia was considered.[40]

Since the end of 1970s, County Governor Aune had met his counterpart in Murmansk, and from 1984 these contacts were intensified. A big push forward came with direct contact between Finnmark and Murmansk in the spring of 1986, well before Gorbachev's speech. The County Governor, Anders Aune, Finnmark County, politicians, municipalities, especially the border municipality Sør-Varanger, and business people were engaged, and some results were obtained, among them a boating route between Kirkenes and Murmansk and the establishment of a shipyard (KIMEK) in Kirkenes in 1987.[41] In 1988 a friendship agreement between Murmansk Oblast and Finnmark County was signed, and later on also between Finnmark and Arkhangelsk. From the end of the 1980s there was a vivid exchange of cultural visits and contacts between Finnmark and Murmansk. That was, as shown, not a new phenomenon, but it expanded greatly from 1989 and became more formalised. The border region was opened up for visits on a daily basis, contacts between schools and teachers were established – from 1990 based on an official exchange program, involving most of the schools in Sør-Varanger – and countless meetings and friendship agreements took place from a wide scale of organisations. In short, a massive number of people to people activities, built up from below, and well before the dissolution of the Soviet Union as a state, brought border people closer to each other.[42] The border between Norway and the Soviet Union in the High North had changed its meaning.

A NEW MEANING OF THE NORWEGIAN-RUSSIAN BORDER AFTER THE COLD WAR PERIOD?

With the Cold War the Norwegian-Soviet border became a strict physical border, supervised by military forces on both sides with just one passing point and a high degree of surveillance of those "unclean" people moving across. It was also a strict political border, making transnational activity difficult as the international political system became bipolarised. In the tense years from the division of Europe in the end of the 1940s and Stalin's death in 1953, the international political system had a Hobbesian ideational structure. Later on we see that the border became more porous after the strategy for critical dialogue became hegemonic in Norwegian security policy from the middle of the 1950s, based on the understanding of the ideational structure as Lockean, though still dominated by rivalry. Regional and local actors utilised this softening of the strict line between East and West in the High North to develop different kinds of transnational contacts on the cultural and political level and, in the second part of the 1980s, also on the economic level. The end of the Cold War around 1990 and the dissolution of the Soviet Union in 1991 opened up for a new political and cultural reconstruction of the border. One important step in that direction was the establishment of a new transnational region in the High North.

Activities both on the national and regional level prepared the ground for Foreign Minister Thorvald Stoltenberg's initiative in 1992 to establish a new transnational region, the Barents Euro-Arctic Region, which was established in January 1993, including from the beginning the counties of Nordland, Troms, Finnmark, Norrbotten, Lapland, Murmansk, Arkhangelsk, Komi, and the Karelian Republic, later extended to also include Västerbotten (Sweden), Oulu, Kainuu (Finland), Nenets (Russia). This new transnational construction was meant to stabilise the High North after the end of the Cold War structure by building networks, transnational activity and trust. However, this new region was not only built from above. As we have seen, there were also strong elements of transnational activity from the building of the North Calotte cooperation in the 1950s to the revitalisation of people to people contact in the last phase of the Cold War.

The Barents Region was initiated by Norway on the basis of Norwegian-Russian talks and negotiations, and no doubt this transnational region had been prioritized higher by these two states than by the two others involved, Finland and Sweden. It is no coincidence that the International Barents Secretariat was co-localised with the Norwegian Barents Secretariat in Kirkenes in Eastern Finnmark when it became permanent in 2008. In the period from 1994–2009, the Barents Secretariat supported around 3000 small and middle-sized, mostly bilateral, projects by Russian and Norwegian partners within target areas such as culture, competence, indigenous peoples' issues, economical development and the environment. In addition youth initiatives and smaller health-related projects have been financed through separate funding programmes.[43] Several student exchange programmes have been implemented and led to contacts across the border, as well as cultural projects and delegations and business activities (in striking contrast to the Cold War situation). The first period of euphoria connected to the new possibilities for cross-border cooperation, especially regarding the environment and business, soon turned out to be overoptimistic. However, with regard to health, people-to-people cooperation and competence much has been done over the last years.[44] The close cooperation regarding the management of the fish resources in the Barents Sea continued after the end of the Cold War, probably making the best fisheries management in the world, and since the turn of the century, much optimism has been aroused concerning cooperation on the oil fields in the Barents Sea, especially the huge Sjtokman field on the Russian side.[45]

All this resulted in much higher frequencies of people-to-people contact. The number of persons crossing the border between Norway and Russia has risen from 8259 in 1990 (before the dissolution of the Soviet Union) to 15.940 in 1992 (one year after the dissolution) to 140.885 in 2010.[46] A sign of these new interests of contacts across the border is also a growing transnational marriage migration, primarily based on migration of Russian women to Norway, married to Norwegian men, and primarily to North Norway. Gender asymmetries, stereotypes involved in the discourse of these transnational marriages, are part of what can be called border gendering.[47] Of course there have also been obstacles to cross for border contact, as there are differences in culture and practical and economical aspects: first and foremost the visa problem.[48] The border between Norway and Russia is a Schengen border, and it is not easy to loosen up the border control on a bilateral basis. A survey in 2009 showed that 26% of the people in Murmansk had visited Norway, but 77% would go to Norway if visa regulations were abolished.[49] An important step towards easier border crossing was the decision in 2012 to make a visa-free zone in a border region stretching 30 kilometres on each side of the border, including the two border towns Kirkenes and Nikel. The inhabitants in this border region have the right to get a "borderer proof". In 2008 these two towns declared themselves "twin cities", demonstrating that they belong to a common borderland. In Kirkenes all streets now have two names, both in Norwegian and in Russian, demonstrating the new narrative and identity of Kirkenes as a border town.[50]

HIGH POLITICS AND THE CONSTRUCTION OF BORDERS

All these processes have changed the meaning of the border between Norway and Russia. It has become a bridge more than a barrier. The tendencies towards softening the dividing line on a regional level before the end of the Cold War accelerated dramatically when new possibilities opened up after the dissolution of the Soviet Union and the establishment of the Barents Region. There has been interplay between regional mobilisation and initiatives and changes on the state level and in the international system, which led to this new construction of the Norwegian-Russian border.

No doubt both these elements, the bottom up and the top down perspective, are necessary in explaining the new border construction over the last two decades. When discussing premises of high politics for changes of the meaning of the border, I have argued that the culture on which the bilateral relationship between the border countries has been based has to be brought into discussion, using Alexander Wendt's concepts, Hobbesian, Lockean and Kantian, as ideal types. Decisive for the turn in the second half of the 1950s towards more cooperation, opening up for more contact across the border between Norway and the Soviet Union, was a break with the assessment of the international political culture as Hobbesian. That was a change on both sides – on the Soviet side as a change from the "two camps theory" under Stalin to "peaceful co-existence" under Khrushchev, and on the Norwegian side as a change from "consequent containment" to "critical dialogue" as the main strategy. This was a change at the political level caused by actors with new perceptions of "the other". This was followed by a policy for low tension in the High North and the opening up for cooperation and contacts, also at a regional level.

The Cold War climate caused uncertainty about the real intentions of the other part, especially of the Norwegian side, as a neighbouring state to a closed superpower with massive military investments at Kola Peninsula as a part of the global rivalry between East and West. The international climate worsened at the end of the 1970s and the beginning of the 1980s, clearly demonstrated by President Reagan's famous phrase referring to the Soviet Union as "an Evil Empire". In this international context, an extensive bilateral cooperation between Norway and the Soviet Union concerning fish resources in the Barents Sea evolved, and also a growing interest and activity on a regional level for making contact across the border. This tendency accelerated after the new leadership in the Soviet Union in 1985. The new "window of opportunity" was gripped both at the regional and national level in Norway, with regional actors as the most active, though with the blessing of the central authorities. There is no doubt that there was a deep feeling of a new international culture underway, making a new understanding of the border possible.[51]

In general the tendency in the period after 1987 has gone towards "desecuritization, rather than (re)securitization", as Kristian Åtland has shown.[52] There are some signs of a Kantian turn, based on mutual respect for the framework of international law and treaties, of looking at "the other" more as "friends" than "rivals", more Lockean than Kantian, to use Wendt's concepts. An expression of this turn towards dialogue and mutual interests is the concept of the disputed border in the Barents Sea as a border of cooperation instead of a border of resources.[53]

Of course there are still elements of pure interest policy and also of alarmism in the discourse on High North policy. The most important expression of that is the idea of a "scramble for the Arctic", which now and then is expressed in the public discussion and from some politicians. The background for this is the prospect for oil and gas production and the climate changes, but as many scholars have pointed out: The Arctic region is thoroughly regulated by a comprehensive international legal framework, which is respected in the international society.[54] Another reason for alarmist attitudes is a tendency to overlook the status of Russia as a Great Power, with multiple interests and conflict lines, with false analogies from politics in Caucasus or looking at a more visible military presence in the High North in a narrow regional framework. Some politicians and analytics also have a tendency to exaggerate the US and EU interests in the area, underlying the ghost of the "scrambling for the Arctic" idea.[55]

To look at the relation between Norway and Russia as a Kantian harmony is of course naïve. It is still "an asymmetric neighbourhood". The relations in the High North are also affected by the general relations between Russia and the West.[56] In Norwegian foreign policy there is also a double standard in argumentation. On the one hand the Ministry of Foreign Affairs in its white papers underline the importance of international law, but on the other hand the most used argument for this is that this is in the national interest of a small country such as Norway. The first is a Kantian argument, the second a Lockean.[57] Here is a vacillation between small state realism and a liberal Kantian outlook. No doubt there is a strong and probably growing underlining of interest politics in Russian foreign policy in general, but the long term tendency is going towards building up a Kantian culture in High North policy; arguments and general interest counts.

These processes on the level of high politics set the frames for cross border activity and contact at the border between Norway and Russia, between Finnmark and Murmansk Counties in the post-Second World War period. This illuminates the general point that the image of a neighbouring country is important for the relations with that country, not following directly from power relations and fixed state interests. Such perceptions are made by actors, and both from the bottom and the top of society. The Norwegian-

Soviet/Russian border was a strict physical and political border during the Cold War, but the border was made porous after a change in the perception of the character of the international political system in the middle of the 1950s and the initiatives taken by the borderland people on both sides of the border. This process towards reconstruction of the border accelerated after Gorbachev became the Soviet leader in 1985. In the last years of the 1980s and the beginning of 1990s the border people themselves changed the realities at the border by changing the character of it through intensive cross border activity, on several levels. The window of opportunity after the break-down of the Cold War system and the dissolution of the Soviet Union was met with the establishment of the Barents Region, which promoted transnationalism in the High North in general and a totally new construction of the meaning of the Norwegian-Russian border in particular.

REFERENCES

1 Einar Niemi, Etnisitet, nasjonalitet og grenseforhold i det nordligste Skandinavia fram til vår egen tid, in: Steinar Imsen (ed.), Grenser og grannelag i Nordens historie, Oslo 2005, 405 f.

2 Maria Lähteenmäki, Dreaming of a Greater Finland. Finnish-Russian Border Demarcations from 1809 to 1944, in: Maria Lähteenmäki (ed.), The Flexible Frontier: Change and Continuity in Finnish-Russian Relations, Aleksanteri Series 5/2007.

3 David Newman, Borders and Bordering: Towards an Interdisciplinary Dialogue, in: European Journal of Social Theory 9 (2006), 174.

4 Svein Erik Larsen, Fra militært tomrom til NATOs vaktpost i nord. Vaktholdet på den norsk-sovjetiske grensen i perioden 1945–59, Master thesis, University of Tromsø 2007, 22, 33.

5 Rob Shields, Boundary – Thinking in Theories of the Present: The Virtuality of Reflexive Modernization, in: European Journal of Social Theory 9 (2006), 224.

6 E.g. Chris Rumford, Theorizing Borders, in: European Journal of Social Theory 9 (2006); Klaus Eder, Europe's Borders: The Narrative Construction of the Boundaries of Europe, in: European Journal of Social Theory 9 (2006).

7 Vladimir Kolossov, Border Studies: Changing Perspectives and Theoretical Approaches, in: Geopolitics 10:4 (2005).

8 Newman, Borders and Bordering, Loc. Cit. (Note 3).

9 Alexander Wendt, Social Theory of International Politics, Cambridge 1999; Wendt himself looks upon the concepts Hobbesian, Lockean and Kantian, which is borrowed from the English School within International Relations, as "metaphors or stylized representations", Alexander Wendt 1999, 247. These concepts relate of course to the three philosophers Thomas Hobbes, John Locke and Immanuel Kant. Wendt's "Social Theory of International Politics" has met some criticism, especially for advancing a linear theory of progress; Stefano Guzzini/Anna Leander (eds.), Constructivism and International Relations. Alexander Wendt and his critics, London 2006 for being too structuralist

and treating the states as if they were persons; cf. Richard Ned Lebow, A Cultural Theory of International Relations, Cambridge 2010, 58, 116; There are good points in these criticisms, but in this article, I use Wendt's concepts as ideal types and his theory as a way of thinking, a perspective, more than a coherent theory.

10 Sven G. Holtsmark, Høyt spill. Svalbard-spørsmålet 1944–47, in: Forsvarsstudier 1 (2004).

11 Holtsmark, Høyt spill, Loc. Cit. (Note 10), chapter 7.

12 Holtsmark, Høyt spill, Loc. Cit. (Note 10), 84 f; Also Olav Njølstad, Jens Chr. Hauge – fullt og helt, Oslo 2008, 310–319; This is also discussed with reference to Wendt's concepts in Hallvard Tjelmeland, Norway and the High North: On political alarmism since the Second World War, in: Stian Bones/Petia Mankova (eds), Norway and Russia in the Arctic, Speculum Boreale, No 12, University of Tromsø 2010.

13 Helge Ø. Pharo, Bridgebuilding and Reconstruction, in: Scandinavian Journal of History, 1 (1976); Jakob Sverdrup, Inn i storpolitikken, in: Norsk utenrikspolitikks historie, vol. 4, Oslo 1996, chapter 5 and 6; Stian Bones, I oppdemmingspolitikkens grenseland. Nord-Norge i den kalde krigen 1947–70, PhD thesis, University of Tromsø 2007, 95 ff.

14 Geir Lundestad, The American non-policy towards Eastern Europe 1943–1947: universalism in an area not of essential interest to the United States, Tromsø 1978.

15 Some examples in Bones, I oppdemmingspolitikkens grenseland, Loc. Cit. (Note 13), 100 ff and in Asbjørn Jaklin, Isfront. Den kalde krigen i nord, Oslo 2009, chapter 4.

16 Knut Einar Eriksen/Einar Niemi, Den finske fare: sikkerhetsproblemer og minoritetspolitikk i nord 1860–1940, Oslo 1981.

17 Vladislav M. Zubok, A failed empire: the Soviet Union in the Cold War from Stalin to Gorbachev, Chapel Hill 2007, 108.

18 Bones, I oppdemmingspolitikkens grenseland, Loc. Cit. (Note 13), chapter 5; Alexey Komarov, Neutralitet i Norden ur ett sovjetiskt perspektiv, in: Lars Elenius (ed.), Fredens konsekvenser. Samhällsföränddringar i norr efter 1909, Studier i norra Europas historia 7, Luleå 2009.

19 Klaus Larres, Churchill's Cold War. The Politics of Personal Diplomacy, London 2002, chapter 11.

20 Stian Bones, Med viten og vilje: Einar Gerhardsens reise til Sovjetunionen i 1955, in: Nytt Norsk Tidsskrift 3 (2006).

21 David J. Finlay, Ole R. Holsti and Richard R. Fagen, Enemies in Politics, Rand McNally Studies in Political Change, Chicago 1967; This chapter is based on Holsti's PhD thesis, The belief system and national images: John Foster Dulles and the Soviet Union, Stanford University 1962.

22 Finlay et al., Enemies in Politics, Loc. Cit. (Note 21), 68 f.

23 Stein Bjørlo, Gerhardsens store tale. Norge og Nato's rådsmøte i Paris 1957, unpublished Master thesis in history, University of Oslo1973; D. F. Fleming, The Cold War and its Origins 1917–1960, vol. 2, London 1961, 897 f.

24 Discussed in Hallvard Tjelmeland, "En utenrikspolitisk amatør?" Einar Gerhardsen som statsmann 1955–58, in: Arbeiderhistorie (2009), 20 f.

25 Tjelmeland, "En utenrikspolitisk amatør?", Loc. Cit. (Note 24), 22f.

26 Knut Einar Eriksen/Helge Pharo, Kald krig og internasjonalisering 1949–1965, in: Norsk utenrikspolitikks historie, Bind 5, Oslo 1997, 198; I go deeper into Gerhardsen's policy in the period 1955 to 1958 in Tjelmeland, "En utenrikspolitisk amatør?", Loc. Cit. (Note 24).

27 Eriksen/Pharo, Kald krig og internasjonalisering, Loc. Cit. (Note 26), 201.

28 Eriksen/Pharo, Kald krig og internasjonalisering, Loc. Cit. (Note 26), 202.

29 Eriksen/Pharo, Kald krig og internasjonalisering, Loc. Cit. (Note 26), 205 ff.

30 Eriksen/Pharo, Kald krig og internasjonalisering, Loc. Cit. (Note 26), 208 f.

31 Larsen, Fra militært tomrom til NATOs vaktpost i nord, Loc. Cit. (Note 4).

32 Willy Wilhelmsen, Til Murmansk med hornmusikk – men uten visum [To Murmansk with brass music – but without visa], in: Varanger årbok, Kirkenes 1988; Niemi, Etnisitet, nasjonalitet og grenseforhold, Loc. Cit. (Note 1), 411 ff.

33 Roger Sivertsen, Idrettssamarbeidet mellom Murmansk og Finnmark, in: Varanger årbok 1988; Steinar Wikan, Kola. Grenselandet i øst, Oslo 2009, 31.

34 Stian Bones, Den ureine fronten. Nordkalotten som sikkerhetspolitisk problem, in: Solveig Halvorsen/Terje Halvorsen/Einar Niemi/Helge Pharo (eds.), I politikkens irrganger. Festskrift til Knut Einar Eriksen, Oslo 2009; Lars Elenius, Förandrade identifikationer på Nordkalotten, in: Lars Elenius (ed.), Fredens konsekvenser. Samhällsföränddringar i norr efter 1909, Studier i norra Europas historia 7, Luleå 2009.

35 Tjelmeland, "En utenrikspolitisk amatør?", Loc. Cit. (Note 24), 149.

36 Rolf Tamnes, Oljealder 1965–1965, in: Norsk utenrikspolitikks historie, vol. 6, Oslo 1997, part 3.

37 Tamnes, Oljealder, Loc. Cit. (Note 36), 298 ff; Pål Christensen and Abraham Hallenstvedt, Kamp om havets verdier. Norges fiskarlags historie, Trondheim 2005, 202–206.

38 Kristian Åtland, The European Arctic in Soviet and Russian Security Policy, 1987–2007, PhD thesis, Political Science, University of Tromsø 2009, 43.

39 Gro Elisabeth Olsen 2005, Moja po tvoja? Vilkår for samarbeid med Russland: en studie av Petsjenganikel-prosjektet 1985–2002, unpulished master thesis University of Bergen 2005; Geir Hønneland and Lars Rowe, Fra svarte skyer til helleristninger. Norsk-russisk miljøvernsamarbeid gjennom 20 år, Trondheim 2008.

40 Lena Elisabeth Ingilæ Landsem, Barentsregionens tilblivelse – en studie av regionale initiativ til opprettelsen av Barentsregionen, unpublished master thesis in history, University of Tromsø 2007, 24 f.

41 Landsem, Barentsregionens tilblivelse, Loc. Cit. (Note 40), chapter 2.

42 Wikan, Kola, Loc. Cit. (Note 33), 50, 76 ff, 294 ff.

43 Margrethe Alnes, Connecting Barents people. The Barents Secretariat's grant programme in steady change, in: Atle Staalesen (ed.), Talking Barents. People, borders and regional cooperation, Kirkenes 2010, 35.

44 Geir Hønneland/Lars Rowe, Nordområdene – hva nå? Trondheim 2010.

45 Peter Arbo/Bjørn Hersoug (eds.), Oljevirksomhetens inntog i nord. Næringsutvikling, politikk og samfunn, Oslo 2010.

46 Thomas Nilsen, Border Crossing Exercises, in: Staalesen, Talking Barents, Loc. Cit. (Note 43), 53.

47 Anne Britt Flemmen/Ann Therese Lotherington (eds.), Transnational Marriage Migration. Russian-Norwegian Encounters, Saarbrücken 2009.

48 The cultural aspect is discussed in Geir Hønneland, Borderland Russians. Identity, Narrative and International Relations 2010.

49 Appendix 1: Opinion poll from Murmansk city and Petchenga rayon 2007, in: Staalesen, Talking Barents, Loc. Cit. (Note 43).

50 Arvid Viken/Torill Nyseth, Kirkenes – A Town for Miners and Ministers, in: Torill Nyseth/Arvid Viken (eds.), Place Reinvention, Northern Perspectives, Farnham 2009, 59 f, 67 f.

51 It is interesting that the expert on Soviet relations to international law, William E. Butler, already in the spring of 1989, saw tendencies in Soviet international law studies towards a more universal acceptance of international law and a shift in the general outlook on diplomacy, as something also striving towards general humanitarian goals, not only state interests. He noted also two important changes before this point of time: A change in the middle of the 1950s, from looking at international law as expressing class interests to considering it an "agreement" between states and the foundation of a new order, and a more explicit recognition of international law in the revision of the constitution in 1977/78. William E. Butler, International Law, Foreign Policy and the Gorbatchev Style, Journal of International Affairs, 42:2 (1989).

52 Åtland, The European Arctic, Loc. Cit. (Note 38), 187.

53 Willy Østreng and Yngvild Prydz, Delelinjen i Barentshavet. Planlagt samarbeid versus uforutsett konflikt? in: Perspektiv 4 (2007), 11 f.

54 Torbjørn Pedersen, Conflict and Order in Svalbard Waters, PhD thesis, University of Tromsø 2008, chapter 8; Alf Håkon Hoel, Jurisdictional issues in the Arctic: An overview, in: Kjetil Skogrand (ed.), Emerging from the Frost. Security in the 21st century Arctic, Oslo files on defence and security, 02/2008.

55 Sven G. Holtsmark, Towards cooperation or confrontation? in: Research Paper no. 45, NATO Defence College 2009: 9; Simen Ramberg, Nordområdene: En blindsone i amerikansk og europeisk energipolitikk? Master thesis in Political Science, NTNU 2007; Atle Staalesen: Introduction. New times for Barents Cooperation, in: Staalesen, Talking Barents, Loc. Cit. (Note 43).

56 Åtland, The European Arctic, Loc. Cit. (Note 38), 181.

57 For instance in the white paper from the Ministry of Foreign Affairs: St.meld. nr. 15 (2008–2009): Interesser, ansvar og muligheter. Hovedlinjer i norsk utenrikspolitikk.

KATARZYNA STOKŁOSA

CONFLICTS AND POTENTIAL ON POLAND'S EASTERN BORDERS: THE EXAMPLE OF THE POLISH-UKRAINIAN AND POLISH-RUSSIAN BORDER REGIONS

Directly after its establishment in the aftermath of the Second World War, the Polish-Soviet border was transformed into a hermetically sealed and exceptionally well-guarded frontier, a state which changed little until 1985.[1] Increased security provisions were taken in the so-called Königsberg district which was transformed into a military base. The Polish border with the Soviet Union was the most impermeable of Poland's borders; indeed, the first crossing point was established only in 1955.[2] For ten years, the populations either side of the Soviet-Polish border were entirely cut off from each other, unable to establish any form of contact. The economic effects of this separation – many wanted to cross the border to reach their former possessions – generated considerable dissent and protest. As in other regions in East Central Europe, the artificial and arbitrary manner in which the border had been drawn also led to the division of towns, villages, estates and forests. However, whereas the Polish borders with Czechoslovakia and even East Germany were open to the passage of goods and people for (predominantly) economic ends, the border with the Soviet Union remained hermetically sealed until 1955.[3]

The advent of de-Stalinization, the Polish October and the Hungarian Uprising of 1956 resulted in the slow relaxation of the strict controls on the Soviet-Polish border. Cross-border cooperation between settlements in the immediate vicinity of the frontier developed exclusively between the two Communist parties; ordinary citizens were unable to cross the frontier. Cross-border travel was also facilitated on the basis of school and university exchanges and between cultural and sporting associations.[4] The 1970s also saw the establishment of regular border crossings within the framework of the so-called "friendship coaches" travelling predominately between the Kaliningrad district and Voivodship Olsztyn. Such official excursions provided Polish citizens with the opportunity to purchase articles which in Poland were either non-existent or over-priced. Such "journeys of friendship" were also often used as a source of additional income; to buy coveted or cheaper Soviet goods to be sold in Poland.[5]

Despite such cross-border contacts, the Soviet-Polish border remained a closed and tightly controlled zone right up into the mid-1980s. The limited contacts that existed were always restricted to a tightly controlled minimum. Indeed, the introduction in the 1970s of a liberalized passport system in Poland produced a situation in which it was easier to travel to the capitalist Western countries than to cross the border to the Soviet "brother state." This situation began to change in the mid-1980s within the framework of Gorbachev's "Perestroika". 1987 saw the conclusion of an agreement between the USSR and Poland establishing a simplified border crossing for the inhabitants of the common border region.[6]

The collapse of the Soviet Union presented Poland with four new Eastern neighbours: Lithuania, Russia, Ukraine and Belorussia. Polish Eastern policy after 1989 concentrated on opening her borders and increasing the level of cross-border cooperation.[7] Since May 2004 the Polish-Russian (Kaliningrad district), Polish-Belarusian, Polish-Lithuanian and Polish-Ukrainian border areas now enjoy direct contact between the newly extended European Union and its neighbours. This article seeks to shed some light on the processes of interaction and coexistence within the Polish-Ukrainian and Polish-Russian border regions.

THE POLISH-UKRAINE BORDER AREA: OFFICIAL POLICY VS. EVERYDAY BORDER LIFE

The 526-km long Polish-Ukrainian border is the longest section of Poland's Eastern border. Its population of over 8 million people is distributed almost equally, with 4.361.700 inhabitants on the Polish side and 3.769.400 on the Ukrainian side.[8] The exemplary nature of official Polish-Ukrainian relations has led some Polish politicians to propose using them as a model for international relations in Eastern Europe. Ukraine was the first of Poland's Eastern neighbours with whom she concluded a mutual cooperation treaty (May 1992), regulating a common approach to political, economic and cultural policies. Both sides recognized the existing Polish-Ukrainian border and recorded that neither side had any territorial claims against the other. Since then, the two countries have developed close and intense political ties, with both Presidents meeting each other regularly.[9] So good are the relations between the two Central European governments that they even speak of a "strategic partnership" in an attempt to apply the model of Polish-German relations to their dealings with Ukraine.[10] In a speech given in the Polish presidential palace in 2004, Tadeusz Mazowiecki, Polish Prime Minister 1989–1990 even claimed that the Polish-Ukrainian rapprochement represented a key contribution to European peace.[11]

This Eastern partnership enjoys almost unanimous support within the Polish population. Surveys by the Polish opinion pollsters CBOS showed that 77% of respondents were of the opinion that Poland should work within the framework of the European Union to intensify relations with the countries of the former Soviet Union.[12] Indeed, the level of support for the Polish-Ukrainian partnership continues to increase. In 2006, two thirds (77%) of Poles questioned supported the Polish-Ukrainian rapprochement.[13] An important factor influencing this nature of public opinion was the "Orange Revolution" of the autumn of 2004.[14] Polish-Ukrainian relations are regarded positively by the great majority of the younger generation;[15] nevertheless, the interesting aspect of opinion polls is the support registered for this partnership amongst the majority of the older generation of over 65s, who remember the Polish-Ukrainian conflicts of the Second World War. 68% of respondents over 65 are optimistic in this question; only 24% do not support moves to establish Polish-Ukrainian friendship.[16]

The positive attitude of the war-time generation can be explained by a widespread resolve to prevent the recurrence of such a conflict. Optimism in this matter also increases with the level of education. Those declaring an interest in politics, regardless of their convictions, are also more optimistic than their apolitical counterparts.[17] Religion also plays a part in shaping attitudes – non-religious respondents judged Polish-Ukrainian relations more positively than those with religious convictions.[18] One very positive finding of the survey was that only 5% of Poles questioned felt threatened by their Ukrainian neighbours.[19] The absence of such fears is most likely a result of the wide-spread belief (84% of all respondents) in the possibility of good relations with Ukraine. Indeed, only 7% of respondents expressed a different opinion.[20]

The success of the official Polish-Ukrainian cooperation at state level is also replicated on the regional level and a number of bilateral educational, cultural, academic and economic initiatives have also been launched in the border regions.[21] Relations are especially close between Ukrainian and Polish schools, cultural institutions, museums and even small and medium-sized businesses in the Przemyśl and Mościska regions. The cultural centre in Przemyśl maintains close and active relations to the concert hall, philharmonic orchestra and theatre in Lemberg.[22] The majority of these initiatives were developed within the framework of the countless Euroregions, structures of transnational cooperation established by the European Union during the course of the 1990s.[23]

Despite the excellent nature of official relations between the two governments, this has had only a limited effect on the quality and intensity of local contacts in the border region. Prejudices and animosities at the local level still remain. The low levels of Polish-Ukrainian investment are in the main, a result of the high level of fear and insecurity on the Polish side of the border regarding their Ukrainian neighbours. The value of official exports from Poland to Ukraine represents only a fraction of its exports to EU countries.[24]

Traditionally, cross-border contacts have long been restricted to those occurring within the framework of local trade and smuggling; such activities represented the most important source of income for many border settlements. Indeed, the main reason for both Poles and Ukrainians to cross the border before 2003 was a shopping trip.[25] This already low level of cross-border contact was further reduced by the introduction of a visa system in October 2003.[26] Ukrainians generally view the one-sided nature of this requirement (Ukrainians require a visa, Poles do not) as being unfair and a number of Ukrainians organized a protest on the day of its introduction by trying to prevent Polish traders from crossing the border.[27]

A survey of 2000 Ukrainians conducted in 2010 showed that the level of Ukrainian interest in Poland is not as large as was in 1990. A similar lack of interest is to be found in the media. Ten years ago, many Ukrainian journalists had at least a reading knowledge of Polish and were well-informed about events in Poland. They viewed Poland as being a model for a successful transition from Communism to a market economy. Today, many young Ukrainians consider Poland a second class Western nation. Nevertheless, many of those living on the Ukrainian side of the border still find the Polish-Ukrainian border region attractive. 35% of the Ukrainian inhabitants of the border area attach a high level of significance to relations with Poland and 92% even believe that these bilateral relations are very good.[28]

Polish perceptions of Ukrainians are highly negative, often referring to them as "Ruskis." In contrast, the popular Ukrainian conception of Poland and Poles is more favourable, with 89% of those questioned responding in a positive or at least neutral fashion; only 11% exhibited a negative attitude.[29] The Polish attitude towards Ukraine and Ukrainians is the worst of all their direct neighbours.[30]

THE POLISH-RUSSIAN BORDER REGION: CROSS-BORDER TRADE AS A MEANS OF ECONOMIC SURVIVAL

The Polish border with Russia, only 209 km long has a political and economic significance which far outweighs its size. Polish foreign policy-makers view the Kaliningrad area principally from the standpoint of relations with Russia, international cooperation in the Baltic area and in conjunction with their responsibilities within NATO and the EU. Nevertheless, distracted by the priority of realizing her integration into the enlarged EU, they neglected to develop the situation on their Eastern borders, especially that of the Kaliningrad district.[31]

The first to recognize the necessity of developing Polish-Russian contacts on the regional level following the collapse of the Soviet Union were the respective Presidents Boris Yeltsin and Lech Wałęsa. A Polish-Russian conference held in May 1992 produced an agreement regulating cooperation between the North-Easterly Voivodships of Poland and the Kaliningrad district. The signatories of the treaty sought to improve and intensify mutual relations in the areas of culture, education and the economy.[32]

Whilst a steadily growing proportion of Polish public opinion believes that relations with their Ukrainian neighbour display scope for improvement, the opposite is the case for Russia. Ever-fewer Poles believe in the possibility of a rapprochement with their Russian neighbour.[33] Attitudes towards Russia exhibit a direct relationship to the level of politicization and political affiliation: those declaring an interest in politics are more optimistic than the politically uninterested.[34] Voters for the liberal *Platforma Obywatelska* (citizens platform) and the Left-wing *Sojusz Lewicy Demokratycznej* exhibit a more positive attitude towards Russia than the supporters of the Right-wing *Prawo i Sprawiedliwość* (Law and Justice). Indeed, attitudes towards Russia are dependent to a great extent on the level of education and material status: those with a university education and a higher standard of living have a more positive appreciation of relations with Russia than those with a low income and standard of living.[35]

A further factor is religion: practising Catholics fear that Russia is seeking to regain its lost influence.[36] Above all, the predominantly negative Polish attitude towards Russia is fed by fear and prejudice. 59% of the Poles questioned conceded that they were afraid of Russia.[37] When asked what they associate with Russia, many Poles list Katyń und Smoleńsk. The first refers to the location of the massacre by the NKVD of a number of Polish officers in April 1940. 67% of Poles surveyed in 2008 believed that this event still exercises a strong and negative influence on current Polish-Russian relations.[38] The aeroplane crash in Smoleńsk in April 2010 in which a number of the Polish political and economic elite – including the state President – died, has even been transformed into a Russian conspiracy against Poland by the political party Law and Justice. The absurdity of the scenario becomes clear when we remember that the aeroplane crashed following interference on the part of the Polish President himself.

Today, the situation in the Polish-Russian border region is characterized by a residual level of "coexistence." This is to be explained by a number of factors, the first being the distances involved. The two closest Russian and Polish settlements (Bezledy and Kaliningrad) are some 45 km apart; even if residents of the border area were able to cross the frontier (which they are not), contact between Russians and Poles would be difficult to bring about. This situation of physical (and thus mental distance) is maintained by the difficulty of crossing the border. Those actually wishing to cross are forced to spend many hours waiting at the crossing point, unless they are prepared to bribe officials in return for a swifter passage.[39]

Despite these difficulties, cross-border traffic has registered a steady increase since the 1990s. The greatest increase took place during the period of visa-free travel: whilst a mere 5000 people crossed the border in 1980, the statistics for 1991 registered over 232.000 people. Following the opening of an additional border crossing in Bezledy and the resumption of cross-border rail traffic via Branevo (both in 1993) the figures reached 1.1 million travellers. 1996 saw this figure increase to 4.2 million.[40] Before the accession of Poland to the EU in 2004, the main reason for border crossings for both Poles and Russians was economic in nature – either to trade or to smuggle goods. Indeed, the area was to a large extent economically dependent on cross-border trade.[41]

The number of border markets represented a significant source of income for the inhabitants of Poland's North-Eastern regions which themselves exhibit the highest levels of unemployment in the country. Indeed, many thousands of people on both sides of the border survived thanks to a number of small businesses, shops and market stands. The Eastwards expansion of the EU changed this situation, something which did not go unnoticed by the inhabitants of this border region. In addition to large-scale traders, a further factor in the cross-border economy is the group of people commonly referred to as "ants," who make a living from transporting small amounts of goods entirely legally across the border.[42] Smuggling concentrates on the transport of alcohol, cigarettes, petrol, gold, electronic devices, clothes and foodstuffs.[43] These trading activities, both legal and illegal, represent almost the only form of Polish-Russian contact in the border area. This probably explains why the vast majority of Poles view their border with Russia exclusively as a haven for smugglers and other criminals.[44] The only form of migration occurring in this region is that for the purposes of illegal trade undertaken by the otherwise unemployed.

Indeed, the similarity of the situation prevalent on both sides of the border has bound both the Russian and Polish inhabitants of the border region into a peculiar community of fate, united by their common experiences and their attempt to take advantage of the opportunities provided by the characteristic form of cross-border trade. Regional policy makers in Brussels would be well advised to ensure that the Kaliningrad district does not become further isolated. This was the effect of the introduction of the visa requirement in October 2003.

CONCLUSION

The necessity of improved relations between Poland and her Eastern neighbours requires further urgent reforms aimed at increasing cross-border cooperation. Concentrating on strengthened border controls to combat smuggling and other forms of criminality can only be counter-productive. Indeed, it is highly doubtful whether measures imposed from above will suffice to eradicate the "grey zone" in the border area. Instead, policy makers should concentrate on strengthening Poland's Eastern border regions through the pursuit of initiatives in culture, education and economic stimulation. Moreover, such cooperation can only succeed if all those involved enjoy the same level of political and economic development. Dependence does not make for good partnerships. Cross-border cooperation should be conceived as a joint venture: initiatives cannot function if designed and implemented on a one-sided basis.

The greatest single challenge posed by the situation on the Polish Eastern border is the necessity of improving communications. This includes improvements in infrastructure, especially the construction of motorways and border crossings. The poor infrastructural connection between Poland's North Eastern area and the rest of the country (and hence the centres of European finance and industry) makes it difficult for Eastern Poland to compete with the more prosperous Western regions. Linguistic competence also represents a further key point in any development strategy. The readiness on the part of Poles to address the one-sided linguistic situation (Polish is largely the lingua franca in the Eastern border regions) and learn (if only a little) Russian or Ukrainian would greatly assist cross-border cooperation. Only through improved infrastructural and linguistic communication is it possible to overcome the stifling prejudice currently hindering cross-border development.

REFERENCES

1 Andrea Chandler, Institutions of Isolation. Border Controls in the Soviet Union and its Successor States 1917–1993, Montreal-Kingston-London-Buffalo 1998, 83; Katarzyna Stokłosa, Grenzstädte in Ostmitteleuropa. Guben und Gubin 1945–1995, Berlin 2003, 55; Stanisław Stępień, "Die polnisch-ukrainische Grenze in den zurückliegenden fünfzig Jahren", in: Helga Schultz (ed.), Grenzen im Ostblock und ihre Überwindung, Berlin 2001, 259–271; here: 265.

2 Tomasz Komornicki, Granice Polski. Analiza zmian przenikalności w latach 1990–1996, Warsaw 1999, 163; Andrzej Sakson, "Pogranicze polsko-rosyjskie w świadomości społecznej", in: Lubuskie Towarzystwo Naukowe (ed.), Transgraniczność w perspektywie socjologicznej. Kontynuacje i wyzwania, Tom 2, Zielona Góra 2001, 31–42; here: 37.

3 Stokłosa, Grenzstädte, Loc. Cit. (Note 1), 52–56.

4 Arkadiusz Żukowski, Pogranicze północno-wschodnie Polski a polska polityka zagraniczna, in: Polskie pogranicza a polityka zagraniczna u progu XXI wieku, (eds.) Polski Instytut Spraw Międzynarodowych, Warsaw 2002, 323-345; here: 332; Edmund Wojnowski, "Die Zusammenarbeit an der Grenze zwischen Polen und dem Kaliningrader Gebiet", in: Helga Schultz (ed.), Grenzen im Ostblock, Loc. Cit. (Note 1), 201–215; here: 201.

5 Edmund Wojnowski, "Granica polsko-kaliningradzka 1944–1997", in: Zbigniew Kurcz (ed.), Pogranicze z Niemcami a inne pogranicza Polski, Wrocław 1999, 247–271; here: 255.

6 Stokłosa, Grenzstädte, Loc. Cit. (Note 1), 61–63.

7 Roman Szul, "Pogranicza a polityka zagraniczna. Komentarz", in: Polski Instytut Spraw Międzynarodowych (ed.), Polskie pogranicza a polityka zagraniczna u progu XXI wieku, 381–391; here: 382.

8 Andrzej Miszczuk, Pogranicze polsko-ukraińskie a polityka zagraniczna III RP , [The Polish-Russian Border Area and the Foreign Policy of the Third People's Republic], Warszawa 2002, 265.

9 Klaus Ziemer, "Osten ist nicht gleich Osten. Die Beziehungen Polens zur Ukraine, zu Weißrußland und Litauen", in: Klaus Ziemer (ed.), Schwierige Nachbarschaften. Die Ostpolitik der Staaten Ostmitteleuropas, Marburg 2001, 57–75; here: 60.

10 Marian Malikowski/Dariusz Wojakowski, "Polska polityka wobec Ukrainy i mniejszości ukraińskiej a stosunki etniczne na pograniczu polsko-ukraińskim", in: Polski Instytut Spraw Międzynarodowych (ed.), Polskie pogranicza a polityka zagraniczna u progu XXI wieku, Warszawa 2002, 235–261 here: 238.

11 "Bronić – ale nie do śmierci" [Defend – but not to the Death], in: Gazeta Wyborcza, 24/2 (2004).

12 See Centrum Badania Opinii Społecznej (CBOS), Ocena stosunków Polski z Rosją, Ukrainą i Niemcami [Estimation of Poland's Relations with Russia, Ukraine and Germany], July 2009, 6.

13 CBOS: Opinie o stosunkach z Rosją, Niemcami i Ukrainą. Na kim Polacy mogą polegać, a kogo się obawiać. Komunikat z badań [Popular Opinion Regarding Relations with Russia, Germany and Ukraine. Who can the Poles Trust and Who Should they Fear? A Report], June 2006, 5.

14 See CBOS, Ocena stosunków Polski z Rosją, Ukrainą i Niemcami [Polish Relations with Russia, Ukrine and Germany], July 2009, 8.

15 See CBOS, Ocena stosunków Polski, Loc. Cit. (Note 14), 8.

16 CBOS, Opinie o stosunkach z Rosją, Loc. Cit. (Note 13), 6.

17 Ibid., 6.

18 CBOS, Ocena stosunków Polski, Loc. Cit. (Note 14), 8.

19 CBOS, Opinie o stosunkach z Rosją, Loc. Cit. (Note 13), 8.

20 CBOS, Ocena stosunków Polski, Loc. Cit. (Note 14), 8.

21 Olga Mrinska, "The Impact of EU Enlargement on the External and Internal Borders of the New neighbors: the Case of Ukraine", in James Wesley Scott (ed.), EU Enlargement, Region Building and Shifting Borders of Inclusion and Exclusion, Aldershot 2006, 81–93; Katarzyna Krok/Maciej Smętkowski, "Local and Regional Cross/Border Co-operation between Poland and Ukraine", in: James Wesley Scott (ed.), EU Enlargement, Region Building and Shifting Borders of Inclusion and Exclusion, Aldershot 2006, 177–191.

22 Dariusz Wojakowski, "Granica państwowa – recepcja zjawiska i tworzenie nowej struktury społecznej", in: Lubuskie Towarzystwo Naukowe (ed.), Transgraniczność w perspektywie socjologicznej, Zielona Góra 2001, 367–378; here: 372; Hanna Bojar: "Przybysze ze Wschodu w społecznościach lokalnych pogranicza polsko-ukraińskiego – stereotypy i realia", in: Lubuskie Towarzystwo Naukowe (ed.), Transgraniczność w perspektywie socjologicznej, Zielona Góra 2001, 451–462; here: 460; Stokłosa, Grenzstädte, Loc. Cit. (Note 1), 65.

23 The Euroregions have already generated a considerable literature. For a description of the development and function of the Euroregions on the Polish Eastern border see Marcin Rościszewski, Polska granica wschodnia, Warsaw 1997; Tadeusz Kowalewski, "Społeczne uwarunkowania współpracy Euroregionów w Polsce. Doświadczenia wschodnie", in Lubuskie Towarzystwo Naukowe (ed.), Transgraniczność w perspektywie socjologicznej, Zielona Góra 200, 103–112.

24 Krystyna Leśniak-Moczuk, "Wybrane obszary współpracy polsko-ukraińskiej na przykładzie transgranicznych kontaktów województwa podkarpackiego i obwodu tarnopolskiego", in: Lubuskie Towarzystwo Naukowe (ed.), Transgraniczność w perspektywie socjologicznej, Zielona Góra 2001, 113–123; here: 119.

25 Andrzej Miszczuk, Pogranicze polsko-ukraińskie a polityka zagraniczna III RP, in: Polskie pogranicza a polityka zagraniczna u progu XXI wieku, eds. Polski Instytut Spraw Międzynarodowych, Warsaw 2002, 263-280; here: 268; Jerzy Mikułowski-Pomorski, Pogranicza a polityka zagraniczna, in: Polskie pogranicza a polityka zagraniczna u progu XXI wieku, eds. Polski Instytut Spraw Międzynarodowych, Warsaw 2002, 349-370; here: 361.

26 "Ruch na przejściach granicznych mniejszy niż zwykle", in: PAP [Polish Press Agency], 02.10.2003; "Po wprowadzeniu wiz ruch zmniejszył się od 70 do 90 procent" in PAP, 04.10.2003; "Wizy wstrzymały ruch", in: Rzeczpospolita 08.10.2003; "Polskie konsulaty na wschodzie wydały ponad 44 tys. Wiz" in PAP, 09.10.2003; "Wizy w działaniu", in Gazeta Wyborcza, 20.10.2003.

27 "Ukrainiki blokowały granicę w Szeginiach" in PAP, 09.10.2003.

28 See Jacek Kucharczyk/Joanna Konieczna-Sałamatin/Joanna Fomina/Natalja Rjabińska (eds.), Report „Coraz dalsi sąsiedzi. Wizerunek Polski i Polaków na Ukrainie" [Ever-more unfamiliar neighbours. Conceptions of Poland in Ukraine], Warszawa 2010.

29 Aleksandra Jawornicka, "Mariusz Kwiatkowski: Przywracanie pamięci a granice zaufania. Spory wokół miejsc upamiętnienia na pograniczach polsko-ukraińskich", in: Lubuskie Towarzystwo Naukowe (ed.), Transgraniczność w perspektywie socjologicznej, Zielona Góra 2001, 463–480; here: 467.

30 Krzysztof Zagórski, "Stosunek do sąsiednich narodów i Integracji Europejskiej na pograniczu i w pozostałych regionach kraju", in: Lubuskie Towarzystwo Naukowe (ed.), Transgraniczność w perspektywie socjologicznej, Zielona Góra 2001, 161–175.

31 Żukowski, Pogranicze północno-wschodnie Polski a polska polityka zagraniczna, Loc. Cit. (Note 4), 329.

32 Wojnowski, Granica polsko-kaliningradzka 1944–1997, Loc. Cit. (Note 5), 260–262.

33 See CBOS, Ocena stosunków Polski, Loc. Cit. (Note 14), 1.

34 Ibid., 2.

35 Ibid., 2.

36 Ibid., 5.

37 Ibid., 9.

38 CBOS: Pamięć o zbrodni katyńskiej i ocena jej znaczenia dla stosunków polsko-rosyjskich. Komunikat z badań [Commemorating the Katyń Massacre and Evaluating its Significance for Polish-Russian Relations. Report], May 2008, 4.

39 Zofia Kawczyńska-Butrym, "Handel na pograniczu z Obwodem Kaliningradzkim. Wartość czy zagrożenie – opinie młodzieży", in: Lubuskie Towarzystwo Naukowe (ed.), Transgraniczność w perspektywie socjologicznej, Zielona Góra 2001, 341–355; here 344.

40 Sakson, Pogranicze polsko-rosyjskie w świadomości społecznej, Loc. Cit. (Note 2), 34.

41 Guido Müntel, "Kaliningrads Weg aus der Isolation? Eine Analyse des Transitkompromisses zwischen der EU und Russland", in: OSTEUROPA, 2–3 (2003), 249–261, here: 250.

42 Wojnowski, Die Zusammenarbeit an der Grenze, Loc. Cit. (Note 5), 211–212.

43 Sakson, Pogranicze polsko-rosyjskie w świadomości społecznej, Loc. Cit. (Note 2), 39.

44 Ibid., 38.

GERHARD BESIER

GERMAN-POLISH NEIGHBOURHOOD RELATIONS ON THE SHARED BORDER: AN AMBIGUOUS STORY

It was the nineteenth century Polish national movement that first developed the idea of the Oder-Neiße line as a suitable border with Germany; the territory east of this line, as they argued, had a long history as an area of Slavic settlement.[1] Nevertheless, the possibility of realizing this "Western conception" of Poland first presented itself with the constitution of a Polish state in the wake of German defeat in the First World War. Despite establishing the fact of Polish statehood, the precise form which it was to assume was initially unclear[2] and first assumed its inter-war form at the Peace conference of 1919.[3] Opening to the fanfare of Wilson's 14 points,[4] – including the right of national and ethnic self-determination[5] – it soon became clear that the international delegates had arrived with a number of very different diplomatic conceptions. Ignoring the purported right to self-determination, the Polish plenipotentiaries based their argumentation on an old legal title[6] which ignored the demographic realities of the areas to which they laid claim.[7]

The *Rzeczpospolita* conception held by the majority of the Polish elite (a return to the borders of 1772) around which they hoped to establish the newly-constituted Polish nation was even more unrealistic, ignoring as it did, the claims and existence of a whole host of Eastern peoples, including the Lithuanians[8], Ukrainians[9] and Byelorussians.[10] Polish and Soviet interests also led to their rejection of a further notable proposal contained in the Curzon line (named after the British Foreign Secretary, Lord Curzon), which based on majority vernacular self-determination, sought to establish Poland on something approaching its current Eastern border.[11] Indeed, disappointed by the fruits of diplomacy, the new Polish government made recourse to force to achieve its territorial aims – the ensuing peace treaty of Riga (March 1921) established Poland's Northern and Eastern borders in accordance with her maximalist aims.[12] As a result, Lithuania had to submit to permanent Polish occupation of what had been proclaimed as its Capital, Vilnius.[13] Polish territorial expansion also brought further challenges; the possession of new lands launched a long-term conflict with the Soviet Union and brought a number of ethnic minorities into what had originally been intended as an ethnically homogenous state. Furthermore, in view of the thin cultural heritage of the newly annexed territories, the Polandization of these new territories met with only limited success. The Ukrainians of

Eastern Galicia for example mounted considerable resistance to this unfolding cultural imperialism.

Encouraged by their success in the East, Polish nationalists now sought to apply the same logic to their Western borders.[14] Eyeing what actually represented the heartland of Prussia, they argued that the inhabitants of this area were in fact, Germanized Poles ruled by a very small upper class of German immigrants. One particular representative of this line of argument was the Polish General Staff officer Henryk Bagiński. In a wide range of pamphlets and books published between 1914 and the 1940s, he reemphasized the "necessity" of regaining what he saw as "lost Polish territory in the West".[15] A member of a working group chaired by the Polish foreign minister Józef Beck, he and his associates developed a theory of a "Third Europe" or "Intermarium" to serve as the geostrategic foundation of Polish foreign policy. This policy foresaw the division of Europe into three separate spheres of influence. Just as French power stretched from the Mediterranean to the Atlantic, Germany should rule the area between the North Sea and the Adriatic, whilst the third European Great Power, Poland, was to hold sway between the Baltic and the Black Sea. Working within this tripartite conception, Poland then developed her claim to what at the time, represented German territory. The most restrained of these conceptions foresaw Poland extending to what Bagiński referred to as the "Great Slavic river", the Oder. One of his books setting out these claims even contained a foreword by Marian Kukiel, the Polish foreign minister in London exile.

Viewed in terms of such conceptions, it soon becomes apparent that Poland could not be content with the extent of her Western border in the interwar period. Indeed, this was given clear expression in the number of plans to employ military means to extend her border westwards.[16] This position was mirrored in Berlin, where the *Reich* government never accepted the Versailles settlement, involving as it did the loss of formerly German lands to Poland. Such revanchist sentiments led to official support for and encouragement of German minority resistance to the new Polish state, and hindered the integration of German-speaking minorities in the republic.[17] Moreover, feeling their rights (guaranteed by international treaty) to have been violated, and having lost much land in the course of land reform,[18] hundreds of thousands of Germans left Poland in the interwar period to resettle in the *Reich*.

The latent conflict between the two states came to a head with the ban on exporting to Poland (1920–1922) and the nine-year "customs war" beginning in 1925, which acted as an effective boycott of Polish exports.[19] This policy met with considerable protest from German economy and industry of the border areas, as it brought extensive damage to these regions without achieving the desired political result. Seeking to defuse this situation,

German merchants and industrialists – especially those from lower Silesia – pressed for the normalization of German-Polish economic relations and to this end, founded the German Industrial Federation for Poland (*Deutsche Wirtschaftsbund für Polen*) which was renamed in 1930 as the German-Polish Chamber of Commerce (*Deutsch-Polnischen Handelskammer*). Joint meetings of the *Silesian merchants circle* and *Greater Poland* planned improvements to the German-Polish infrastructure as part of a greater attempt to "transform the Silesian-greater Polish connection into a bridge for global East-West traffic".[20] Both sides used a variety of means, including publications to push for a German-Polish trade treaty which would have necessitated an improvement in bilateral economic relations. This was eventually concluded in mid-March 1930, although it was never ratified by the Reichstag.

The German success at Locarno (October 1925) for which the German Foreign Minister Gustav Streseman was feted, consisted in dividing the question regarding Germany's borders into two. Having guaranteed the status quo in the West, he managed to obtain an agreement with the French which did not stipulate the nature of Germany's Eastern border, a question which remained open for further revision.[21] Indeed, Germany vehemently rejected any form of "Eastern Locarno" involving recognition of the Versailles border settlement in the East. Viewed from a Polish perspective, the situation appeared bleak, as Germany also began developing closer ties with the Soviet Union, which represented an alliance between Poland's principal enemies.[22]

The National Socialist rise to power in 1933 and the subsequent German-Polish non-aggression pact (January 1934) brought an improvement in German-Polish relations. The economic conflict was brought to an end, but the trade agreement signed on 11 October fell very much short of the draft of 1930, especially in terms of its much shorter duration. Nevertheless, the normalization of economic relations resulted in greater economic prosperity in the border area, and the *Breslau Trade Fair* and the *International Poznan Trade Fair* developed into two hubs of German-Polish trade relations. Germany even made an appearance at the June 1939 Poznan Trade fair, only two months before the German invasion of Poland on 1 September 1939. This event, followed by the Soviet invasion on 17 September effectively put an end to the twenty-year existence of the Second Polish Republic.[23] Both occupiers began immediate implementation of their aims: the destruction of the Polish state and the destruction of the Polish nation.[24] The West Polish Voivodship was annexed by the Reich and renamed as the *Warthegau*, an area which was to function as a central part of the German war economy and a testing ground for National Socialist ideology.[25] The Polish population was expelled, to be "resettled" in the General Government of Warsaw.[26]

THE POST-WAR SETTLEMENT AND THE EXPULSION OF THE GERMANS AND POLES

The establishment of the Oder-Neiße line as the German Eastern border in 1945 was a political decision taken at the conferences of Yalta and Potsdam lacking all historical foundation.[27] Indeed, the circumstances and genesis of this decision was to burden German-Polish relations for many years to come. The conference of Tehran (28 November–1 December 1943) established the Curzon line as the Polish-Soviet border[28] and added the provision that the Polish population East of this line (and indeed in other areas) was to be resettled in other formerly German territories in the West and East, the population of which was also to be forcibly moved. From this point on, the fate of Poles and Germans were inextricably tied.[29]

The conference of Yalta (4–11 February 1945) finally established the Polish Eastern border in accordance with Stalin's wishes. Losing an area of around 179.000 square kilometres (almost half of its former area), Poland was to be re-established in the West, but the exact nature of the reconstituted Polish state was to be decided upon at a future peace conference. Territory which was to be transferred from German to Polish sovereignty (established in negotiations between the USSR and the provisional Polish government) was however treated almost as war booty by the Red Army. Machines, industrial plant and kilometres of railway track were dismantled and shipped to Russia, followed by supplies and livestock. Ten thousands of Germans and Poles – such as the 15.000 miners from Silesia – were imprisoned in holding camps and later deported to the USSR. The policy of organized plunder of (formerly) German property continued until into the autumn of 1945.[30]

Concerned as they were to establish ethnically homogenous nation states and thereby minimize the potential for post-war conflict, when considering the problem at the beginning of 1945, the allies soon realized that the number of Poles and Germans which would be subject to a "population transfer" would be much larger than originally planned. The Yalta accords left an important aspect of the coming territorial re-ordering open: whether the German-Polish border was to proceed along a line through Glatz-Neiße or Görlitz-Neiße. Seeking to present the Western allies with a *fait acompli*, the Soviet Union and Poland simply expelled the German populations from all areas which they claimed without the faintest of legal foundation. The Poles in the Polish-Ukrainian border area did not fare any better: expulsions had been organized in this area since 1944 in order to lay the foundations for a later Greater Ukraine within the Soviet Union.[31] The expulsion of both the Germans from the formerly Eastern territories and the Poles from their Eastern areas was soon underway and assumed a rapid pace even before the Potsdam conference. Far from being conducted in a "humane and orderly" fashion, the early programme of expulsion was badly prepared, violent and ruthless. The Polish government hoped to alter the ethnic composition of the formerly German Eastern territories so as to present an ethnically-homogenous Poland at the Potsdam conference and in this way stake a claim to retaining their new "Western" territories. During the Potsdam negotiations, Stalin was now able to claim that the population East of the Oder and Neiße was now entirely Polish in composition – the Germans expelled from these areas had been replaced by Poles expelled from their Eastern homelands and transported many miles Westwards in an equally inhumane fashion.[32] The Germans and Poles affected by these actions bore no responsibility for their fate; decided by Stalin and executed by the Red Army, other Eastern army units and local militias it was tolerated (however grudgingly) by the Western Allies.

The decision taken at Yalta to postpone the final demarcation of Poland's Western border until a future peace conference was reaffirmed at Potsdam (17 July–2 August 1945). At the same time, it was decided that the area between the pre-war Polish border and the Oder-Lausitz-Neiße line, Southern East-Prussia and the territory of the former free city of Danzig was to remain under Polish administration and should not fall under the Soviet Zone of Occupation. In essence, this decision represented the de facto establishment of the new Polish-German border; the resolution to reach a definitive decision at a future peace conference came to nothing, as the peace conference never took place.[33]

The big three seemed to be in agreement at Potsdam: German responsibility for the outbreak and conduct of the Second World War justified a sacrifice through which it could hope to atone for its crimes.[34] Poland's new Western border on the Oder and Neiße was not only to serve as compensation for the loss of its Eastern territories, but in constituting a strategic barrier against Germany was to satisfy the security needs of the Soviet Union. This interpretation is confirmed by the predominantly military character of the border until the end of the 1940s.[35]

The mass exodus of Germans and Poles underway at the very time at which Churchill, Stalin and Roosevelt opened preceding in Potsdam shows that the expulsions were not decided upon or initiated at Potsdam; the big three merely reacted to their development and attempted to bring them under some vestiges of control and order.[36] The declared allied aim – the creation of ethnically homogenous national states – which they pursued consistently, involved great upheaval for both Poland and Germany, both in terms of loss of territory and mass population movement.[37]

In fashioning its Eastern border in this way, Poland confronted the big three with a *fait acompli*. In the period between Yalta and Potsdam, the allies had already decided that Poland should forfeit Polish territory to the East, but had reached no decision on the level of compensation to be offered to her in the West. Moreover, the demographic planning of the new Polish state went further than this: not only were Poles deported from their former Eastern homelands, but non-Poles were expelled from former Central-Poland and resettled in the Soviet Union. This decision predominantly affected ethnic Ukrainians, who were given until the end of 1946 to leave Poland. In this way, Poland was to be transformed into an "ideal" homogenous nation state free of any ethnic minorities. The "orderly and humane" organization of the expulsion also remained a fiction in Central Poland.[38]

Both the situations faced by expelled Poles and Germans and the societies which were forced to accommodate them displayed striking similarities.[39] The expulsion of the Germans was experienced in three phases: flight, wild expulsion and their "resettlement" in accordance with the Potsdam accords. The flight from the advancing Red Army began in the Reich's Eastern provinces and the particularly exposed Eastern German settlements as early as 1944. As party officials forbade any civilian evacuation in the face of the Russian advance, indeed, expected that the inhabitants mount resistance, the evacuations usually began far too late and the civilian populations often left at the very last possible moment. The disorganized, last-minute rush to escape resulted in terrible congestion on the roads and railways. The hard winter 1944–1945 also increased the number of victims of the refugee chaos.[40]

The arrival of the Red Army was followed in early 1945 by the phase of "wild expulsions", lasting around a month. Anti-German sentiment latent in the Czech and Polish populations was vented on the refugees. Between June – mid-July 1945, the entire German population was expelled from the border strip between Oder and Neiße.[41] The deportations followed in a number of stages. May 1945 saw the deportation of Germans from a strip of land 100–200 kilometres in extent East of the Oder and Neiße. The eviction of Germans from Danzig followed in June; Eastern Pomerania, West Prussia, the Southern area of East Prussia and Upper Silesia followed in the autumn of 1945. After a short pause for winter, the action was resumed in early 1946.[42]

The Potsdam agreement should have put an end to the chaos, averted atrocities and ensured the "orderly implementation" of the population transfer. Yet the implementation of this intention failed in the face of extensive anti-German sentiment and serious transport problems. A Polish administration was established only in the course of 1945 and only then barely functioned. Only a year after the Potsdam agreement did the situation become more bearable and the deportations better organized. Despite this improvement, many of those expelled in the winter of 1947 froze to death in the unheated trains in which they were transported.[43] Almost three million Germans had been expelled from the territory of the new Polish state. The subsequent years saw the flight of hundreds of thousands of more German Poles.[44]

In a manner similar to the expulsions of Germans, the deportation of ethnic Poles was conducted in several stages. The "evacuation" of Polish land owners, former military settlers, foresters and their families began in February 1940. In this way, the German occupiers removed the leading social classes and political elite. The second wave of deportation beginning in April 1940 affected the urban elites: teachers, soldiers, local government officials and businessmen. The third wave of deportation from May and June 1940 included many Poles and Jews who had fled from the General Government. The NKVD launched the last round of deportation in June 1941 to remove all those who had escaped the previous waves of expulsion.[45] 63% of all those deported were ethnic Poles.[46]

The second wave of Polish deportation began – this time under German organization – in the Polish Eastern territories at the end of 1942. As the Germans succeeded in playing off the ethnic Ukrainian inhabitants against their Polish neighbours, this wave of deportation culminated in bitter fighting between Polish and Ukrainian volunteer groups. In 1942, the Ukrainian insurgent Army UPA (*Ukrainskaja Povstanskaja Armija*) began a murderous campaign directed against Polish settlements in Wolhynien.[47] In response, the Poles organized units within the Polish Underground army AK (*Armia Krajowa*) to carry out acts of retaliation in areas of predominantly Ukrainian settlement.[48]

The internationally agreed expulsion of Poles began following an agreement between the Committee of National Liberation (PKWN) and the Soviet republics in September 1944. This measure primarily affected Poles and Ukrainians, and to a lesser extent, Byelorussians and Lithuanians.[49] In the years 1945–1946, the Poles expelled 480.000 Ukrainians, 36.000 Byelorussians and 2000 Lithuanians into the Soviet Union. Many of these people settled directly on the Eastern border; others were deported into the heart of the Soviet Union.[50]

The Polish deportations present a similar picture of violent chaos. With the collapse of all vestiges of government, those determining events sought to use the situation of upheaval to create new, unalterable circumstances. The material destruction, poorly functioning distribution network and damaged transport infrastructure made the task of deporting 1.5 million people almost impossible.[51] The expulsion by the Red Army of ethnic Poles from Western Ukraine to South East Poland had begun in October 1944. The mass of Poles moved in this action initially had nowhere to go until early 1945, when the Red Army advanced deeper into Germany. Despite experiencing a slight improvement in their situation, the modalities of the deportation (a lack of supplies and poor transport links) brought suffering upon the refugees who were forced to travel for more than two weeks.[52] The single largest wave of expulsion occurred 1945–1946; by the time it was completed in 1948, around 810.500 people had been forced to leave Western Ukraine.[53]

GERMAN-POLISH RELATIONS IN THE DIVIDED CITIES ON THE COMMON BORDER

At Potsdam, it was decided that German towns straddling the new border should be divided. The result was a series of "divided towns" including Görlitz-Zgorzelec, Guben-Gubin, Frankfurt an der Oder-Słubice, Bad Muskau-Łęknica[54] where an atmosphere of hate and fear pervaded in the post-war years. After the Second World War, the word "German" and its derivates became unwords. Germans were "criminals" or "executioners". Now was the hour of ideology, not understanding. The accusation of collective German guilt made by the anti-German government in Warsaw soon attained widespread popular acceptance, fuelling an almost universal and blind hatred of all things German.[55] This hatred simmering in the Polish inhabitants of the new border towns was accompanied by fear that the Germans would one day return to reclaim their old homes.[56] On the other side of the border, the Germans long nursed hopes that one day they would be allowed to return. This aspiration was especially strong in Guben, as Wilhelm Pieck, himself a son of East Guben made frequent visits to his home town and spoke openly of the prospects of a return.[57] Playing with the emotions of the inhabitants, he referred to the newly Polish part of the Guben, known for its attractive blossom trees as the "prettiest part of the town".[58] The Chairman of the SED and "son of Guben" promised the return of the Polish district.[59]

German hopes of revising the Oder Neiße border and returning to their old homes were kept alive until July 1950, when the Treaty of Zgorzelec established the irrevocable nature of the new border. This development put an end to discussions within the SED of a possible border revision[60] and established a taboo around the now defunct question.[61] Despite its dictated nature, this treaty acted to bring calm into the German-Polish border area, which in turn acted as a catalyst for the distrust against Germany.[62]

For the Polish inhabitants of the Northern and Western areas, the treaty had much more than a merely symbolic significance, as it put an end, albeit slowly to more than a decade of fear that they would once again be uprooted and forced to leave their new homes. Instead, with a new feeling of security, the Polish settlers began to feel increasingly at home.[63] These developments also helped to ease relations between the GDR and Poland. Despite the new atmosphere, the border remained closed, as the nature of the Communist system forbade any change. The sparse level of cross-border contacts was restricted to exchanges between firms, organizations, schools and the two Communist parties. The hermetically sealed border remained closed for ordinary people and the German expellees were not able to visit their old homes and meet their new inhabitants.[64] This dream had to wait 21 years to become reality, with the first border crossings taking place on New Year's

Eve 1971 following the establishment of passport and visa-free travel. The people of both Poland and the GDR greeted this development and many in the divided towns took advantage of the opportunity to cross the border.[66]5

The majority of German expellees also took advantage of this new opportunity to visit their old homes. Reports to the GDR security apparatus give a largely positive impression of the visits of GDR citizens to their former houses and the largely warm welcome with which their unexpected visit was received. The Poles in the Western and Northern Polish areas were initially surprised by these unexpected visitors, but after the initial shock often invited their German guests to a small meal. There is also information pertaining to the disappointment of the German visitors at the neglect to which their former houses were subject. Nevertheless, they often showed understanding for the difficult financial situation in Poland and some even offered help, for instance in bringing paint from the GDR with which to paint a weather-beaten fence.[66]

In general, the visits by GDR citizens to their former possessions assumed a positive course, as long as the Poles involved understood that the visit was merely a temporary affair and that Germans did not seek to regain their lost property. Allusions to the need to maintain the houses in a better state of repair were on the other hand, not taken with any gratitude. If the German visitors started to look around to see if the household installations were still in the same location, the new owners were often nonplussed. In contrast to the older GDR citizens, members of the younger generation were not concerned about the condition of their parents' former houses. They were much more interested in the plans and interests of the younger Poles, or the possibility of spending leisure time on the Polish side of the border.[67] Parents often reminded their children that it was "also their home from which the Poles had driven them".[68] Visits by GDR families to their former properties often occurred within the first months of the border being opened. On the whole, the short initial visits were either not repeated, or they developed into friendships, with each side inviting the other to attend birthdays, weddings, baptisms and other similar events.[69]

Following the spread of the *Solidarność* movement in Poland and the economic difficulties in both countries, the GDR authorities arranged for the border to be closed and travel once again required a passport and a visa.[70] In the early period of the *Solidarność* campaign, GDR citizens followed the political developments with some sympathy. After a while however, deterioration of the economic situation in Poland led to mounting criticism and the majority of GDR citizens were of the opinion that *Solidarność* served to destabilize the Polish economy.[71] Contact between Germans and Poles in the 1980s became increasingly difficult, as the closed border was impassable for ordinary citizens who required special permission or a visa. The personal contacts and cross-border co-operation initiatives in the divided towns forged in the 1970s came under threat from the new visa requirement. Nevertheless, despite the stagnation of the 1980s, the curiosity and openness characterizing the majority of ordinary people in the 1970s remained undiminished.[72] Countless acquaintances and friendships survived the difficult period of the closed border (1980–1991) and thrived again after 1991.

The 1990s brought fundamental changes for the East Central European border regions. Whilst many borders disappeared or became increasingly permeable, other regions witnessed an intensification of the conditions of division. The German-Polish border numbers amongst the benefactors of the collapse of Communism and the transformation process of the immediate post-Communist era, seeing the re-introduction of a visa-free border crossing.[73] Following the conclusion of the treaty confirming the existing German-Polish border (signed on 14 November 1990) and the German-Polish friendship agreement (17 June 1991) a number of agreements between individual border towns and regions cemented this process on the local level.[74] The first agreement in this process of local diplomacy was that between the towns of Gubin, Guben and Laatzen, signed on 19 January 1991 and thus before the opening of the border. This process either reactivated existing agreements or brought them up to date. Formed at the beginning of the 1990s, the German Polish border region constituted the first of several Euroregions.[75]

In 1991, five boroughs of the Polish Voivodship Zielona Góra and the forest authorities of the German side of the border seized the initiative and began with the construction of a Euroregion. Despite the early nature of this move, the resulting agreement was not signed until 21 September 1993. The current area of the Euroregion Spree-Neiße-Bober extends over an area of 10.000 km^2; its headquarters is located in the divided city Guben/Gubin. This Euroregion was founded with the aim of improving the economic potential of the region, harmonizing the regional infrastructure, improving co-operation in hazard prevention and intensifying contacts in culture, education, tourism and health. Four working groups were formed to implement these plans, divided according to their activity: 1) the economy, communications and tourism, 2) agriculture, forestry and environmental protection, 3) youth, sport, education and culture and 4) information. Their activities all aim at reducing existing barriers and restrictions.[76]

A further Euroregion on the Polish-German border area is the Euroregion pro-Europe Viadrina, founded on 21 December 1993 as a joint undertaking between *The Residents' Association of the Lubser Land "Border Region"* (Poland) and the German borough "Mittlere Oder". As with the Euroregion Spree-Neiße-Bober, this Euroregion also comprises over 10.000 km^2; its administrative head quarters is located in Dąbroszyn on the Polish side of the border. One of the most important tasks of the Euroregion includes promotion of good neighbourhood relations, the improvement of the quality of life of the residents and cross-border co-operation in the areas of education, culture and the economy.[77]

Since their foundation, the Euroregions have completed a great number of projects, mostly funded by the programmes *Interreg* and *Phare*. A very important area of cross-border co-operation is education. Sixth-form pupils in the Spree-Neiße-Bober can attend the Guben Comprehensive, whose "A" levels are valid in both countries and all children in the Euroregion have the opportunity of visiting the great number of language camps in the region which teach both Polish and German. Moreover, a number of bilingual further training programmes are offered to nurses, fire fighters and the members of other professions.[78] The Euroregion Pomerania has also established a number of German-Polish schools and the Euroregion form of the European school clubs, comprising 100 clubs, organizes training programmes, seminars, conferences, educational travel schemes and discussion meetings, all with the aim of spreading knowledge about the EU. The German-Polish youth organization is also very active in the Euroregion Pomerania, providing support and financing for numerous German-Polish youth meetings.[79] The Viadrina University at Frankfurt (Oder) and the *Collegium Polonicum* in Słubice also play a significant role in the Euroregion pro-Europa Viadrina, providing a forum for education and cultural exchange for students from across the world (including Germany, Poland, the Czech Republic, Russia, Byelorussia, Ukraine, the USA and South America). A former cloister in Neuzelle was converted into a German-Polish grammar and boarding school. Frankfurt (Oder) also boasts a German-Polish Kindergarten.[80] The Euroregion Neiße was selected as the location for the International Institute of Universities, located in Zittau, an institution similar to a University, responsible for the specialist teaching of German, Polish and Czech economics. German applicants to the institute must have passed their mid-diploma exams; Polish and Czech aspirants must have completed at least four semesters in a university in their homelands.[81]

All the Euroregions in the German-Polish border area are very active in the area of culture and sport, a sector in which the *German-Polish Jugendwerk* also plays an active part by promoting joint German-Polish exhibitions, concerts, seminars and sporting events in the Euroregions.[82] Cultural co-operation in the Euroregion is of especial significance for the development of good relations as it is highly effective in bringing together members of different cultures and mentalities, making a decisive contribution to reducing prejudice and stereotypes.[83]

A long-term aim of the Euroregions is the strengthening of the regional identity of the inhabitants of this border region.[84] One characteristic of the regional identities is a cross-border identity drawn from a sense of solidarity with those on the other side of a border. Such feelings are often especially pronounced in border regions due to the close proximity of cross-border neighbours. With the exception of a small minority, the German-Polish border area has yet to develop such an identity, and the populations continue to exhibit a singularly national affiliation apart from the usual assortment of prejudices, stereotypes and insecurities, the violent history of expulsion and the redrawing of borders can provide the explanation for the relatively weak formation of a border identity. Recent events prevent many from sharing a common history with their fellow inhabitants of the German-Polish border region.[85] These hurdles constitute a particular challenge for the work of the Euroregions and the further development of the German-Polish border region as a whole. Research into migration and practices of commemoration in Germany in Poland can make an important contribution to the establishment and propagation of good neighbourhood relations in Germany and Poland.[86]

CONCLUSION

The attempts to establish a permanent territorial settlement after the two world wars largely ignored both the Polish and the European perspective. Both exercises in post-war European cartography sought to establish Poland as part of a *Cordon sanitaire*. The Versailles settlement arranged a number of small East European states between the newly-emerged Soviet Union and Germany, designed to protect Western Europe from the former and contain the latter. The Potsdam settlement re-established Poland to serve Soviet security interests against any future threat from the West. Having gone to war to save Poland from German aggression, France and Great Britain (and now the USA) abandoned their former ally to Soviet domination. Poland was never included in important revisions of either post-war settlements, either in Locarno (1925) or the two plus four negotiations in 1990. This litany of affronts, broken promises and attempts to undermine the existence of an independent Poland has made Poland react with exceptional sensitivity to questions of its territorial and national integrity.

REFERENCES

1 See Roland Gehrke, Der polnische Westgedanke bis zur Wiedererrichtung des polnischen Staates nach Ende des Ersten Weltkrieges, Marburg 2000. Also Stefan Scheil, Fünf plus Zwei. Die europäischen Nationalstaaten, die Weltmächte und die vereinte Entfesselung des Zweiten Weltkrieges, Berlin [3]2006, 84 ff. The revanchist nature of many of the interpretations in this book makes this book somewhat problematic.

2 See Adam Krzemiński, Polen im 20. Jahrhundert. Ein historischer Essay, Munich [2]1998, 54; Margaret MacMillan, Paris 1919, New York 2002, 207–228; esp. 216–219.

3 Cf. to the following Grzegorz Gorzelak, "Normalizing Polish-German Relations: Cross-Border Cooperation in Regional Development", in: James Wesley Scott (ed.), EU Enlargement, Region Building and Shifting Borders of Inclusion and Exclusion, Aldershot 2006, 195–205; Hans-Joachim Bürkner, "Regional Development in Times of Economic Crisis and Population Loss: The Case of Germany's Eastern Border Region", in: James Wesley Scott (ed.), EU Enlargement, Region Building and Shifting Borders of Inclusion and Exclusion, Aldershot 2006, 207–215, and, in a broader perspective, Ann Kennard, "The Institutionalization of Borders in Central Eastern Europe. A Means to What End?", in: Eiki Berg/Henk van Houtum (eds.), Routing Borders Between Territories, Discourses and Practices, Aldershot 2002, 193–210.

4 Point XIII: "An independent Polish state should be erected which should include the territories inhabited by indisputably Polish populations, which should be assured a free and secure access to the sea, and whose political and economic independence and territorial integrity should be guaranteed by international covenant". Quoted in MacMillan, Paris 1919, 496.

5 See John M. Cooper (ed.), Reconsidering Woodrow Wilson. Progressivism, Internationalism, War, and Peace, Baltimore 2008, 238, 227.

6 See Krzysztof Ruchniewicz, "Noch ist Polen nicht verloren." Das historische Denken der Polen, Berlin 2007, esp. 11–31.

7 See Bernard Linek, "Deutsche und polnische nationale Politik in Oberschlesien 1922–1989", in: Kai Struve/Philipp Ther (eds.), Die Grenzen der Nationen. Identitätswandel in Oberschlesien in der Neuzeit, Marburg 2002, 137–168.

8 See Zigmantas Kiaupa, The History of Lithuania, Vilna 2005, 227 ff.

9 See Cornelia Schenke, Nationalstaat und nationale Frage. Polen und die Ukrainer 1921–1939, Hamburg-Munich 2004.

10 See Werner Benecke, "Kresy. Die weißrussischen Territorien in der Polnischen Republik (1921–1939)", in: Dietrich Beyrau/Rainer Lindner (eds.), Handbuch der Geschichte Weißrusslands, Göttingen 2001, 153–165.

11 See Gotthold Rhode, Kleine Geschichte Polens, Darmstadt 1964, 466 ff.

12 See Józef Szaniawski, Marszałek Piłsudski I Polacy. W Obronie Europy – Cud Nad Wislą 1920, Warsaw 2007. Vol 2 of the memoirs and documents of Josef Piłsudskis, Essen 1935, for which the German Minister of War General Werner von Blomberg wrote a foreword, concentrates on the year 1920.

13 See Kai von Jena, Polnische Ostpolitik nach dem Ersten Weltkrieg. Das Problem der Beziehungen zu Sowjetrussland nach dem Rigaer Frieden von 1921, Stuttgart 1980; Werner Benecke, Die Ostgebiete der Zweiten Polnischen Republik. Staatsmacht und öffentliche Ordnung in einer Minderheitenregion 1918–1939, Cologne-Weimar-Vienna 1999.

14 Regarding the Polish national-democratic propaganda directed toward "regaining traditional Polish lands," see Albert S. Kotowski, Hitlers Bewegung im Urteil der polnischen Nationaldemokratie, Wiesbaden 2000, 158 ff.

15 See Henryk Bagiński, Poland and the Baltic. The Problem of Poland's Access to the Sea, (Polish original 1927), Edinburgh 1942; Henryk Bagiński Poland's Freedom of the Sea, (Polish original 1931), Kirkcaldy 1942.

16 See G. Besier, "Die Hypothek von 1918/19: Das neue Polen und das geschrumpfte Reich. Ein Plädoyer zur Historisierung des Piłsudski-Kults", in: Mike Schmeitzner/Katarzyna Stokłosa (eds.), Partner oder Kontrahenten? Deutsch-polnische Nachbarschaft im Jahrhundert der Diktaturen, Berlin 2008, 27–37.

17 See Gerhard Besier/Katarzyna Stokłosa, Europa Dyktatur. Nova historia XX wieku, Warsaw 2009, 113 ff.

18 On 28 June 1919 Poland signed a treaty guaranteeing the rights of the minorities in her newly-won territories as a pre-condition to the territorial settlement. The treaty included a number of measures designed to protect the German and other minorities from rash and violent assimilation (Minderheitenschutzvertrag zwischen Alliierten und Assoziierten Hauptmächten und Polen. Versailles, 28. Juni 1919, in: Themenportal Europäische Geschichte (2007), URL: http://www.europa.clio-online.de/2007/Article=219. Accessed 24.10.2010. Despite the proviso of the treaty, the Polish state initiated a comprehensive programme of Polandization in the former German areas, which prompted a total of 700.000 Germans to leave Poznan alone. See Albert S. Kotowski, Polens Politik gegenüber seiner deutschen Minderheit 1919–1939, Wiesbaden 1998; Martin Scheuermann, Minderheitenschutz contra Konfliktverhütung? Die Minderheitenpolitik des Völkerbundes in den zwanziger Jahren, Marburg 2000, 22 ff.; 88 ff.; Ralph Schattkowsky, "Deutsch-polnischer Minderheitenstreit nach dem Ersten Weltkrieg", in: Zeitschrift für Ostmitteleuropa-Forschung 48 (1999), 524–554; Dieter Blumenwitz, "Minderheitenschutz nach dem Ersten und dem Zweiten Weltkrieg. Ein Rechtsvergleich unter besonderer Berücksichtigung der deutschen Minderheit in Polen", in: Dieter Blumenwitz et al., (eds.), Ein Jahrhundert Minderheiten- und Volksgruppenschutz, Cologne 2001, 49–61; Dariusz Matelski, "Legal Protection of the German Minority in the Second and Third Polish Republics" in Studia Historica Slavo-Germanica, 24 (2003), 193–205; Dietmar Müller, "Staatsbürgerschaft und Minderheitenschutz. 'Managing diversity' im östlichen und westlichen Europa", in: Themenportal Europäische Geschichte (2006), URL: http://www.europa.clio-online.de/2006/Article=172. Accessed 24. 10.2010. Regarding the various conflicts, see the Archives of the League of Nations (LON Archives), Geneva, R 1619; 1639–46; 1671–79; 1687–89; 1693.

19 See Stefan Kowal (Poznań) and Helga Schultz (Frankfurt/Oder), "Neue Grenzen – alte Nachbarn – Deutsche und Polen im Widerstreit von großer Politik und regionaler Kooperation (1919–1990)", in: Hans-Jürgen Wagener (ed.), Im Osten was Neues: Aspekte der EU-Osterweiterung, Bonn 1998, 174–195. see also: Karol J. Błahut, Polsko-niemieckie stosunki gospodarcze w latach 1919–1939 [Polish-german economic relations 1919–1939], Wrocław-Warsaw-Danzig 1975; Stefan Kowal, Partnerstwo czy uzależnienie? Niemieckie postawy wobec stosunków gospodarczych z Polską w czasach Republiki Weimarskiej [Partnership or Dependence? German Attitudes to Economic Relations with Poland during the Weimar Republic], Poznan 1995.

20 Quoted according to Kowal/Schultz, Neue Grenzen – alte Nachbarn, Loc. Cit. (Note 19), 177.

21 See Eberhard Kolb, Deutschland 1918–1933. Eine Geschichte der Weimarer Republik, Munich 2010, 101 f.

22 On 16 April 1922, Germany and the Soviet Union signed the Treaty of Rapallo, followed in 1926 by the German-Soviet Treaty of Berlin. See Kolb, Deutschland 1918–1933, Loc. Cit. (Note 21), 69–71. Speaking in the context of the treaty of Rapallo, the head of the Reichswehr, Hans v. Seeckt forecast the disappearance of Poland. "[...] following its own inner weakness and the workings of Russia supported by Germany". Quoted according to Jörg K. Hoensch, Geschichte Polens, Stuttgart 1983, 262. In July 1922, Reichskanzler Josef Wirth declared that "Poland must be eliminated. This is the aim of my policy [...]. I will not sign any treaty which could serve to strengthen Poland. Indeed, much has been undertaken in terms of our eastern border with my permission about which many are unaware. In this point, I find myself in complete agreement with our army, especially General von Seeckt". Quoted according to Joachim Rogall (ed.), Deutsche Geschichte im Osten Europas. Land der großen Ströme. Von Polen nach Litauen, Berlin 1996, 376.

23 Regarding the situation in 1939 see Rainer F. Schmidt, Die Außenpolitik des Dritten Reiches 1933–1939, Stuttgart 2002, 316 ff.; Werner Biermann, Sommer 1939, Berlin 2009; Richard Overy, Die letzten zehn Tage. Europa am Vorabend des Zweiten Weltkriegs. 24. August bis 3. September 1939, Munich 2009; Jochen Böhler, Der Überfall. Deutschlands Krieg gegen Polen, Frankfurt/M. 2009.

24 See Robert Seidel, Deutsche Besatzungspolitik in Polen. Der Distrikt Radom 1939–1945, Paderborn 2006; Peter Klein, "Die Gettoverwaltung Litzmannstadt" 1940–1944. Eine Dienststelle im Spannungsfeld von Kommunalbürokratie und staatlicher Verfolgungspolitik, Hamburg 2009.

25 See Markus Leniger, Nationalsozialistische "Volkstumsarbeit" und Umsiedlungspolitik 1933–1945: Von der Minderheitenbetreuung zur Siedlerauslese, Berlin 2006; Wilfried Schlau, Die Deutschbalten. Studienbuchreihe der „Stiftung Ostdeutscher Kulturrat", vol. 6, Munich 2001; Ortfried Kotzian, Die Umsiedler. Die Deutschen aus Bessarabien, der Bukowina, der Dobrudscha, Galizien, der Karpatenukraine und West-Wolhynien. Studienbuchreihe der "Stiftung Ostdeutscher Kulturrat", vol. 11, Munich 2004.

26 See Maria Rutowska, Wysiedlenia ludnosci polskiej z Kraju Warty do Generalnego Gubernatorstwa 1939–1941 (Prace Instytutu Zachodniego Nr. 71; Instytut Zachodni), Poznan 2003.

27 See Jörg-Detlef Kühne, Zu Veränderungsmöglichkeiten der Oder-Neiße-Linie nach 1945, Baden-Baden 2007.

28 See Kordan Bohdan, "Making Borders Stick. Population, Transfer and Resettlement in the Trans-Curzon Territories, 1944–1945" in: International Migration Review 31 (1997), 704–720.

29 See Krystyna Kersten, "Warianty polityki polskiej: rok 1944" [Variations of Polish Policy: the year 1944], in: Polska 1944/45–1989. Studia i materiały I [Poland 1944/45–1989. Studies and Materials I], Warsaw 1995, 29–61, here: 31.

30 See Carl Christoph Schweitzer/Hubert Feger (eds.), Das deutsch-polnische Konfliktverhältnis seit dem Zweiten Weltkrieg. Multidisziplinäre Studien über konfliktfördernde und konfliktmindernde Faktoren in den internationalen Beziehungen, Boppard am Rhein 1975, 34–36.

31 Serhy Yekelchyk, Ukraine. Birth of a Modern Nation, Oxford 2007, 146; Paul Robert Magocsi, A History of Ukraine, Toronto 1996, 648.

32 See Philipp Ther, Deutsche und polnische Vertriebene. Gesellschaft und Vertriebenenpolitik in der SBZ/DDR und in Polen 1945–1956, Göttingen 1998, 42–43.

33 See Andrzej Friszke, "Jałta i Poczdam w polskich koncepcjach politycznych (1945–1947)" [Yalta and Potsdam in Poland's political concepts (1945–1947)], in: Włodzimierz Borodziej/Artur Hajnicz (eds.), Kompleks wypędzenia [The expulsion complex], Cracow 1998, 328–358, here: 358; Andrzej Paczkowski, "Poczdam 1945 – zamiary, skutki i interpretacje" [Potsdam 1945 – Aims, Consequences, Interpretations], in: Basil Kerski/Zdzisław Owczarek (eds.), Czy możliwa jest wspólna pamięć? [Is Joint Commemoration Possible?], Berlin 2005, 119–134; Włodzimierz Borodziej, Od Poczdamu do Szklarskiej Poręby. Polska w stosunkach międzynarodowych 1945–1947 [From Potsdam to Szklarska Poręba. Poland and International Relations 1945–1947], London 1990.

34 See Hans Maretzki, "Die Potsdamer Beschlüsse und die DDR. Eine korrigierte ostdeutsche Sicht" in: Heiner Timmermann (ed.), Potsdam 1945. Konzept, Taktik, Irrtum?, Berlin 1997, 403–427, here: 421; Wolfgang Wagner, Die Entstehung der Oder-Neiße-Linie in den diplomatischen Verhandlungen während des Zweiten Weltkrieges, Marburg/Lahn 1968, 149–188.

35 See Mieczysław Tomala, Deutschland – von Polen gesehen. Zu den deutsch-polnischen Beziehungen 1945–1990, Marburg 2000, 39; Dagmara Jajeśniak-Quast/Katarzyna Stokłosa, Geteilte Städte an Oder und Neiße. Frankfurt (Oder) – Słubice, Guben – Gubin und Görlitz – Zgorzelec 1945–1995, Berlin 2000, 67–69.

36 See Ther, Deutsche und polnische Vertriebene, Loc. Cit. (Note 32), 43.

37 See Ther, Deutsche und polnische Vertriebene, Loc. Cit. (Note 32), 44.

38 See Ther, Deutsche und polnische Vertriebene, Loc. Cit. (Note 32), 48–50.

39 See Ther, Deutsche und polnische Vertriebene, Loc. Cit. (Note 32), 54; Jan Misztal, "Podobieństwa i różnice przymusowych wysiedleń Polaków i Niemców" [Similarities and differences between the expulsions of the Poles and Germans], in: Borodziej/Hajnicz (eds.), Kompleks wypędzenia, Loc. Cit. (Note 34), 179–184; Thomas Urban, Der Verlust. Die Vertreibung der Deutschen und Polen im 20. Jahrhundert, Munich 2004, 12–14. A good recent account of the German popular memory, both past and present, of the expulsions is provided by Eva Hahn/Hans Henning Hahn (eds.), Die Vertreibung im deutschen Erinnern. Legenden, Mythos, Geschichte, Paderborn-Munich-Vienna-Zurich 2010.

40 Ther, Deutsche und polnische Vertriebene, Loc. Cit. (Note 33), 54–55. Also: Włodzimierz Borodziej, "Die Katastrophe. Schlesien nach dem Zweiten Weltkrieg", in: Ulla Lachauer (ed.), Als die Deutschen weg waren: was nach der Vertreibung geschah: Ostpreussen, Schlesien, Sudetenland, Berlin [2]2006, 84–114.

41 Andreas Kossert, Kalte Heimat. Die Geschichte der deutschen Vertriebenen nach 1945, Bonn 2008, 30. Small numbers of the German population were able to maintain their presence – for instance in Lower Silesia – until the autumn of 1947. See Gerhard Besier, "Gehen oder Bleiben? Die evangelische Kirche und die Vertreibung der Deutschen aus Niederschlesien 1945/46", in Martina Pietsch (ed.), Heimat und Fremde. Migration und Stadtentwicklung in Görlitz und Zgorzelec seit 1933, Görlitz 2010, 47–68.

42 Kossert, Kalte Heimat, Loc. Cit. (Note 42), 33; Jan Misztal, "Przesunięcie Polski na Zachód" [The westwards displacement of Poland], in: Borodziej/Hajnicz (eds.), Kompleks wypędzenia, Loc. Cit. (Note 33), 70–112, here: 106.

43 Ther, Deutsche und polnische Vertriebene, Loc. Cit. (Note 32), 58–59; Bernadetta Nitschke, "Sytuacja niemieckiej ludności cywilnej na ziemiach polskich" [The situation of the German civil populations in the Polish territories], in: Borodziej/Hajnicz (eds.), Kompleks wypędzenia, Loc. Cit. (Note 33), 58–69, here: 68.

44 Andrzej Friszke, Polska. Losy państwa i narodu 1939–1989, Warszawa 2003, 136.

45 Ther, Deutsche und polnische Vertriebene, Loc. Cit. (Note 32), 71.

46 Piotr Eberhardt, Polska granica wschodnia 1939–1945 [The Polish Eastern border 1939–1945], Warsaw 1993, 73.

47 Piotr Eberhardt, Polska ludność kresowa. Rodowód, liczebność, rozmieszczenie [The Polish population of Kresy. Origins, Numbers, Expulsion], Warsaw 1998, 198; Serhy Yekelchyk, Ukraine. Birth of a Modern Nation, Oxford 2007, 148; Paul Robert Magocsi, A History of Ukraine, Toronto 1996, 648–649.

48 Serhy Yekelchyk, Ukraine. Birth of a Modern Nation, Oxford 2007, 148; Magocsi, A History of Ukraine, Loc. Cit. (Note 47), 648–649.

49 Ther, Deutsche und polnische Vertriebene, Loc. Cit. (Note 32), 78.

50 Zbigniew Kurcz, "Aussiedlungen und Umsiedlungen in den östlichen und westlichen Grenzgebieten Polens", in: Helga Schultz" (ed.), Bevölkerungstransfer und Systemwandel. Ostmitteleuropäische Grenzen nach dem Zweiten Weltkrieg, Berlin 1998, 39–54, here: 47.

51 Eberhardt, Polska ludność kresowa, Loc. Cit. (Note 47), 199; Andrzej Kwilecki, Łemkowie. Zagadnienie migracji i asymilacji [The Lemkos. Problems of Migration and Assimilation], Warsaw 1974, 77.

52 Ther, Deutsche und polnische Vertriebene, Loc. Cit. (Note 32), 78–80; Friszke, Polska. Losy państwa i narodu, Loc. Cit. (Note 45), 136–140.

53 Eberhardt, Polska ludność kresowa, Loc. Cit. (Note 47), 199; Stanisław Ciesielski/Grzegorz Hryciuk/Aleksander Srebrakowski, Masowe deportacje radzieckie w okresie II Wojny Światowej [Soviet Mass Deportations During the Second World War], Wrocław [2]1994.

54 Dagmara Jajeśniak-Quast/Katarzyna Stokłosa, Geteilte Städte an Oder und Neiße. Frankfurt (Oder) – Słubice, Guben – Gubin und Görlitz – Zgorzelec 1945–1995, Berlin 2000, 34–38; Katarzyna Stokłosa, "Görlitz Ost wird Zgorzelec. Ankunft und Integration der polnischen Ansiedler", in: Pietsch, Heimat und Fremde, Loc. Cit. (Note 41), 69–77.

55 Tomala, Deutschland – von Polen gesehen, Loc. Cit. (Note 35), 22–23.

56 Katarzyna Stokłosa, "Die Oder-Neiße-Grenze im Bewusstsein der Einwohner von Guben und Gubin (1945 bis 1972)", in: Helga Schultz (ed.), Grenzen im Ostblock und ihre Überwindung, Berlin 2001, 113–134, here: 128.

57 See Katarzyna Stokłosa, Grenzstädte in Ostmitteleuropa. Guben – Gubin 1945–1995, Berlin 2003, 139.

58 Quoted according to Stokłosa, "Die Oder-Neiße-Grenze im Bewusstsein", in: Schultz (ed.), Grenzen im Ostblock, Loc. Cit. (Note 56), 123.

59 Ibid.

60 Beate Ihme-Tuchel, "Fakten schaffen. Das Görlitzer Abkommen 1950", in: Information für die Truppe, 44 (7), 2000, 40–45, here: 41.

61 Andreas Malycha, "Wir haben erkannt, dass die Oder-Neiße-Grenze die Friedensgrenze ist!" Die SED und die neue Ostgrenze 1945 bis 1951", in: Deutschland Archiv 2/2000, 193–207, here: 205–206.

62 Stokłosa, Grenzstädte in Ostmitteleuropa, Loc. Cit. (Note 57), 143–144.

63 Stokłosa, Grenzstädte in Ostmitteleuropa, Loc. Cit. (Note 57), 160–161.

64 Stokłosa, "Die Oder-Neiße-Grenze im Bewusstsein", Loc. Cit. (Note 58), 132.

65 Katarzyna Stokłosa, "VR Polen und die DDR: Die Bedeutung der Grenze für das 'Freundschaftstheater'", in: Mike Schmeitzner/Katarzyna Stokłosa (eds.), Partner oder Kontrahenten? Deutsch-polnische Nachbarschaft im Jahrhundert der Diktaturen, Berlin 2008, 193–203, here: 195.

66 Stokłosa, Grenzstädte in Ostmitteleuropa, Loc. Cit. (Note 57), 209–213.

67 Ibid., 211.

68 Instytut Pamięci Narodowej (IPN) BU 0365/102/1, Notatka służbowa [Official notice].

69 Stokłosa, Grenzstädte in Ostmitteleuropa, Loc. Cit. (Note 57), 212.

70 G. Besier/K. Stokłosa, "Solidarność – nur ein polnischer Traum von der Freiheit?", in: TD 4 (2007), 267–284.

71 Stokłosa, "VR Polen und die DDR", in: Schmeitzner/Stokłosa (eds.), Partner oder Kontrahenten?, Loc. Cit. (Note 65), 200.

72 Stokłosa, Grenzstädte in Ostmitteleuropa, Loc. Cit. (Note 57), 237–244.

73 Stanisław Lisiecki, "Der Bewusstseinswandel der Grenzbewohner in den Forschungen in Słubice und Frankfurt (Oder)", in: Helga Schultz/Alan Nothnagle (eds.), Grenze der Hoffnung. Geschichte und Perspektiven der Grenzregion an der Oder, Potsdam 1996, 259; Czesław Osękowski/Hieronim Szczegóła, Pogranicze polsko-niemieckie w okresie transformacji (1989–1997) [The German-Polish Border Region in the Period of Transformation (1989–1997)], Zielona Góra 1999, 73.

74 Jajeśniak-Quast/Stokłosa, Geteilte Städte, Loc. Cit. (Note 54), 95–109.

75 Jajeśniak-Quast/Stokłosa, Geteilte Städte, Loc. Cit. (Note 54), 95–109.

76 Katarzyna Stokłosa, "Opportunities and Problems of Euroregions along the Polish-German Border", in: Josef Langer (ed.), Euroregions – The Alps-Adriatic Context, Frankfurt am Main 2007, 233–242, here: 236–237.

77 Ibid., 237.

78 Beata Trzop, "Transgraniczna współpraca regionalna – Euroregion Sprewa-Nysa-Bóbr" [Cross-border regional co-operation – the Euroregion Spree-Neiße-Bober], in: Leszek Gołdyka (ed.), Transgraniczność w perspektywie socjologicznej – kontynuacje [Cross-border co-operation from the sociological perspective – a continuation], Zielona Góra 1999, 523–533, here: 527–528.

79 See Urząd Statystyczny we Wrocławiu (ed.), Euroregiony na granicach Polski [Euroregions on the Polish Border], Wrocław 2004, 100.

80 Ibid.

81 Ibid., 157.

82 Trzop, Transgraniczna współpraca regionalna, Loc. Cit. (Note 78), 528–529.

83 Jajeśniak-Quast/Stokłosa, Geteilte Städte, Loc. Cit. (Note 54), 199–220.

84 See Lesław Koćwin, "Transgraniczne aspekty ekorozwoju w strategiach euroregionów z obszaru środkowego Nadodrza" [Cross-border Aspects of Ecological Development in Euroregion Strategy From the Area of the mid-Oder], in: Jerzy Leszkowicz-Baczyński (ed.), Transgraniczność w perspektywie socjologicznej. Kontynuacje i wyzwania. Tom 1 [Cross-border Co-operation from the Sociological Perspective – Continuations and Challenges Vol 1], Zielona Góra 2001, 185–207, here: 198.

85 See Katarzyna Stokłosa, "Identitäten in Bewegung: die deutsch-polnische und die ukrainisch-slowakische Grenzregion im Vergleich" in: Christian Pletzing/Peter Oliver Loew/Thomas Serrier (eds.), Wiedergewonnene Geschichte. Zur Aneignung von Vergangenheit in den Zwischenräumen Mitteleuropas, Wiesbaden 2006, 205–224, here: 224.

86 See Gerhard Besier/Katarzyna Stokłosa (eds.), Geschichtsbilder in den postdiktatorischen Ländern Europas. Auf der Suche nach historisch-politischen Identitäten, Berlin 2009; Martin Aust/Krzysztof Ruchniewicz/Stefan Troebst (eds.), Verflochtene Erinnerungen. Polen und seine Nachbarn im 19. und 20. Jahrhundert, Cologne-Weimar-Vienna 2009. Bill Niven/Chloe Paver (eds.), Memorialization in Germany since 1945, Basingstoke 2010; Mareike König/Rainer Ohliger (eds.), Enlarging European Memory. Migration Movements in Historical Perspective, Ostfildern 2006.

MONICA ANDRIESCU

THE POLITICS OF IDENTITY: HUNGARIAN LANGUAGE AND AUTONOMY CLAIMS IN POST-COMMUNIST ROMANIA

After 1918, the legitimacy of the Romanian state was secured through an infusion of norms and rules that did not follow a neutral, non-ethnic rationale. They were, in fact, more or less visibly constructed in accordance with the ethnic, cultural, linguistic and religious particularities of the Romanian titular nation. In the century that has passed since then, Romania's national minorities have been politically shaped through various factors influenced by historical events and phenomena such as migration, the geographical spread and the historical context. The Hungarian minority has emerged with an active political profile, putting forward an alternative political project for reorganizing the society, which has involved radical and moderate positions over the twentieth century. Other minorities in general have not put forward alternative ways to reorganize the state and have abided by the general societal rules, focusing on the preservation of their cultural and religious identity: the Turkish and Tatar minorities are only two such examples. The case of the Roma minority can be considered separately, as defined by the indirect rejection of many of the components of the social establishment through the preservation of the traditional axes of their community life.

As regards the post-communist timeframe, the most significant developments in the field of interethnic relations have occurred during 1997–2009. This entailed the establishment of a complex institutional and legal framework, which aimed to integrate minority groups in the post-communist Romanian state. The regulations, public policies and measures that were adopted and the institutions which were created during this period have highlighted several areas of prime importance for the management of diversity: education, public administration, judiciary and mass media. The demand for the use of mother tongue was the key element that linked these social and political spheres. In addition, national and local political representation of minorities has also played an important role. The minority rights framework was used to provide recognition to the specific elements of the identity of persons belonging to ethnic communities at various levels – ethnic, cultural, linguistic and religious – and was developed with the direct participation of the political representatives of these groups in the decision-making process.

Currently, the challenges of implementing the legal provisions are those that define the interethnic relations agenda in Romania. This study does not set itself the task of entering into the details of this debate, but does recognize the importance of coordinating the national, regional and local levels and stakeholders in this field to achieve effective governance. The purpose of this approach is, however, to look beyond the legal and institutional aspects, trying to offer a possible answer the following question: What is the social purpose of managing ethno-cultural diversity in post-communist Romania? Clearly, such an approach sees the granting and implementation of minority rights not as an end in itself but as an interim target of a process whose completion will result in the creation of a *political community* of citizens of Romania. The emphasis will fall on Romanian-Hungarian relations due to the critical importance and active role of the Hungarian minority representatives in advancing the minority rights protection framework in the analysed timeframe.

During the past two decades, there has been remarkable progress in Romanian-Hungarian relations, especially when looked at from the viewpoint of the extension of the minorities' rights framework. However, for those interested in upgrading these relations to the next level, another type of inquiry presents itself as necessary. While the Hungarians claim that the implementation of many minority rights provisions is still deficient and further steps ought to be taken in extending the minorities' rights regime, the Romanian authorities, regardless of their political affiliation, emphasize that enough "concessions" have been made. In this view, one could argue "Romanians and Hungarians were, and continue to be, equally insensitive to the distress of the other and to the representation of their distress".[1]

The deadlock can be succinctly portrayed as the *unitary state vision* versus the *autonomy seeking vision* of Romanian-Hungarian relations. In the former outlook, Romanians view Hungarians as challenging the authority of the state whose citizens they are, while in the latter, the Hungarians express their malaise concerning their perceived inferior status. Framed as either anti-Romanian or anti-Hungarian attitudes, these arguments can only strengthen the existing inter-community separating lines. In this logic, neither side's interests are genuinely served. Moreover, one is left to wonder why the leading political representatives of the Hungarian minority in Romania have yet to present a very detailed and articulate plan for implementing the long-claimed *autonomy* for the Székely region.

The present article identifies the key markers of the Hungarians' political identity – as indicated by Democratic Union of Hungarians in Romania (UDMR) discourse – and their evolution throughout the period that has led to the most significant increase in minority rights in Romania: 1996–2009. Far from being unswerving throughout the aforementioned time span, UDMR discourse has been influenced by the domestic and international political context. This resulted in the periodic emphasis or neglect of certain discursive elements.

The present approach analyzes the discursive means employed by the Hungarian political elites in delineating roles, knowledge systems, and the features and attributes of the Hungarian community as a collective entity in relation to state institutions. During the period that falls under the scope of this article (1996–2009), the discourse of the key political representative of the Hungarian community (the Democratic Union of Hungarians in Romania – UDMR) has configured Hungarian identity in essentially political terms. In other words, UDMR claims have outlined the importance of *internal self-determination* for the preservation of the identity of the Hungarians in Romania. The subsequent analysis is based on discourses that have been selected according to their relevance for the intra and/or extra-parliamentary debates concerning language use in education, local public administration and autonomy demands.

Throughout the early post-communist period (1990–1996), Romanian-Hungarian relations were predisposed to an increase in conflict and a virtual absence of cooperation. The Romanian parties generally viewed UDMR as a fringe element on the political scene, especially since it challenged the instated political and social organization of the post-communist Romanian state. Excluded from the negotiation table, UDMR demands escalated and revolved around the demand for *autonomy*. Sequentially, the emphasis on such claims radicalized Romanian opposition to granting extensive rights for minorities. This included education and language rights.

After 1996, due to a convergence of internal and external factors the Romanian and Hungarian political elites entered a new stage in their relations: *cooperation*. The discursive shift undertaken by UDMR after 1996 is relevant from the following viewpoints: firstly, UDMR was willing to compromise, and secondly, accepting a role in the governing coalition also implied a series of responsibilities, not only in what regarded the Hungarian minority, but the entire population of Romanian citizens. Once being part of the Government, UDMR found it more difficult to challenge the very foundations of the Romanian state – namely its national, unitary and indivisible character.[2] It may also be inferred as a generally valid assertion that the inclusion of ethnic parties in the governing coalition has the tendency to reduce their claims, while their non-inclusion has a tendency to provoke the opposite phenomenon. This assumption is testable in the Romanian case.

UDMR discourse has, since 1990 onwards, set several key objectives that had to be attained and which were vital to the defence of Hungarian identity: state-supported mother tongue education at all levels, linguistic rights in local public administration, the media and the judiciary, the return of property confiscated by the communist regime from the religious denominations, and the attainment of cultural and territorial autonomy. If looked at from the normative angle, the only rights yet to be attained are those referring to *autonomy*. This includes the creation of a state-funded Hungarian university since this regards university autonomy. If looked at from the implementation angle, the existing regulations are still partially deficient in practical terms.

Although various rhetoric elements have been more or less emphasized by UDMR discourse, what is noticeable is the consistency with which the party's elites have argued their position and bargained for the extension of the minority rights' framework. This consistency, regardless of occasional relapses, has determined a high mobilizing potential for the Hungarian voters. Although criticized for its compromises with the Romanian political elites and the alleged flexibility of its rhetoric, UDMR has delivered on many of its promises. Evidence for that stand the 175 normative items containing minority rights provisions[3], which have triggered substantial positive changes for all Romania's twenty national minorities, not only for the Hungarian one. It is evident that without the cooperation of its Romanian coalition partners, UDMR alone could never have been able to pass the aforementioned normative acts through Parliament or Government. It is also true that the Romanian-Hungarian dialogue was strongly encouraged by international pressures, especially in view of Romania's NATO and EU integration.

The following two sections analyze the key elements of UDMR rhetoric regarding language rights and autonomy, which are illustrative for the way in which Hungarian identity has been shaped during the post-communist period in Romania.

LINGUISTIC RIGHTS IN EDUCATION AND LOCAL PUBLIC ADMINISTRATION

The antagonism between the Romanians and Hungarians during post-communism was framed by the actions of their representative elites in political and institutional terms. UDMR claims were constructed in a way that challenged the post-communist ethnocentric and centralist state-building project. Through its claims on minority rights, UDMR has helped shape the Romanian institutional system in matters concerning the education, administration, justice and audiovisual fields. Converging with the EU-imposed regulations, the impact has been significant in terms of legislation, but still with significant delays in terms of implementation. The following two subsections will consider claims related to the use of minority languages in education and in relation to local authorities as being highly relevant to the political nature of Hungarian identity.

Mother tongue education

The claim to language use in education and in relation to local public administration authorities carries a weighty relevance for the political nature of Hungarian identity. These claims have represented the unvarying and comprehensive pillars around which the UDMR programs and discourses have been constructed.

One of the most important moments in the Romanian-Hungarians relations from the viewpoint of the articulation and clarification of demands was represented by the debates concerning the revision of the 1995 Law on Education.[4] The 1995 Law on Education had been opposed in Parliament by UDMR, due to its constraining character in what concerned minority mother tongue education. Following UDMR bargaining potential – acquired after the 1996 general elections – the Education Law was modified in 1997 and 1999, and integrated relevant provisions for minority mother tongue education.

UDMR has argued that in the form adopted in 1995, the Education Law "consolidates the unitary, etatist, centralized character of the educational system"[5] and disregards the interests of the Hungarian community and disposes of its "constitutional right of being educated in our native-language".[6] Condemning the fact that "the provisions of the law are formulated in the spirit of the unitary national state and national exclusivism"[7], UDMR maintained that the educational process was more difficult for children whose mother tongue was not Romanian.

If mother tongue tuition at lower levels represented less of a bone of contention for the Romanian-Hungarian dialogue, views concerning higher education in the Hungarian language remain locked in fierce opposition to this day. The initial major discursive confrontation was placed in 1997–1998, to be continued occasionally afterward, and to peak again in 2006. The basic UDMR contention is that the objective of cultural reproduction of Hungarian elites can only be fully satisfied by the existence of a separate state Hungarian university benefiting from autonomy in decision-making and the use of finances. The establishment of a Hungarian independent state university has aimed at acquiring "decision-making, structural and financial independence of the already exiting higher education Hungarian lines, the strengthening of existing structures, the creation of internal autonomy, the creation of the system of Hungarian faculties at the Babeş-Bolyai University […]".[8]

When defending its claims to higher education in the Hungarian language, UDMR has evoked the right to use minority languages as epitomizing "a factor of the right to preserve identity, […] a universal human right in states where native ethnic minorities live. This right meets the basic requirements of democratic states, appears as a constitutional right and denotes a means against assimilation".[9] As such, the reestablishment of a separate and independent Bolyai University is deemed by UDMR as "historical reparation"[10], a right "the Hungarian community will never abandon".[11] Apart from its historical justification, UDMR has deemed the reestablishment of the Hungarian independent university as a right to equal opportunities. Education represents in the most recent examples of UDMR discourse "the will for independence, in view of the objective of creating an educational system in the mother tongue, based on self-government".[12] The mediation of the two opposing stances was impossible, since both sides – politicians and representatives of the Babeş-Bolyai University – were unwavering. This resulted in the very hopelessness of carrying out dialogue on this issue.

The reluctance of the Romanian side to compromise can be accounted for by the demands the Hungarians put forward in that instance: it crossed the boundaries of education into those of politics. *Autonomous decision-making in the field of higher education* represented a challenge to the political order of the Romanian state, one that it has proved unable to overcome. On the other hand, UDMR unwillingness to settle for a shared decision-making in higher education marks the reluctance to come to terms with a Romanian-Hungarian co-decision-making conflict-mediation method.

A new step in the general direction proposed by the UDMR is the recently adopted law on education, which makes several substantial changes in mother tongue education. I refer only to three of them, whose importance is measured by the continuity they have had on UDMR's list of claims, since the early 1990s. The first one allows Romanian language and literature to be taught "throughout undergraduate education levels according to a curricula and textbooks specifically designed for that minority".[13] The second relates to the teaching of the geography and history of Romania in the national minorities' mother tongue at primary and secondary levels with "curricula and textbooks [that] are identical to those for classes taught in Romanian, with the obligation to learn the transcription of place names and proper names in Romanian also".[14] Finally, the law provides for an increased role for the local education management component, in fact leading to an increased autonomy in decision making at this level: "In the case of educational institutions with classes taught in minority languages [...] the director is appointed following consultation with organizations representing that minority in the Romanian Parliament [...]".[15] Moreover, the school director "fulfils its executive management"[16], while "the educational units at lower or upper secondary level with teaching in minority languages that are singular in the city, town or village are granted legal personality, regardless of the number of students". [17]

Taking into account these important changes, currently, the only major goal of mother tongue education that remains unfulfilled is the establishment of a separate Hungarian state university. In the current education law, the mother tongue state university education can be organised only as faculties, departments, lines or programs.[18]

The general conclusion that can be drawn from these developments is the importance of the political context in achieving the demands of a national minority with a strong political project. In this case, the party system configuration in Romania and their spectral arrangement has enabled the Hungarians to cast a balancing game in the last two decades has led to a substantial change in interethnic relations. The UDMR game on the political scene has been called by some "bargaining capacity" and by others "blackmail" of the governing coalition partners[19] who depended on UDMR support in Parliament.

Language use in relations with local public administration authorities

In what concerns language rights in local public administration, a relevant aspect is that the Law on Local Public Administration was initially adopted in 1991. At that moment, it hardly contained reference to the use of minority languages in the relations with the local administration, which raised the vocal opposition of UDMR. In terms of language use in the dealings with administrative authorities, Romanian remained the only option (Article 54). The revised version of the Local Public Administration Law was adopted in 2001.[20] It was accompanied by a contiguous normative item – *Government Decision regarding the approval of the Norms of Application* of the dispositions regarding the right of citizens belonging to a national minority to use their mother tongue in local public administration, included in the Law on Local Public Administration.[21]

With regard to Article 17 (2001) – which stated that language rights were granted "[i]n the administrative-territorial units in which the citizens belonging to national minorities are in a proportion that exceeds 20% of the number of inhabitants"[22] – Senator József Csapó noted that it "regulates the exercise of a fundamental right: the free use of mother tongue in public"[23]. The Hungarians have deemed this as a constitutional right, endorsed by the international conventions or documents that Romania signed and ratified and therefore committed to.

UDMR representatives in Parliament have argued that the revision of the Local Public Administration Law and the inclusion of minority-relevant provisions is a "basic principle of local autonomy"[24] and that this "meant the discovery of the European path toward decentralization".[25] UDMR brought forth other discursive items in its discourse, namely decentralization, regionalization, and the strengthening of local communities.

Senator Francisc Bárányi has argued that UDMR "actively participate[s] in the realization of all reforms set out in the governing programme, [it] share[s] daily hardships with our Romanian co-citizens: still, many times [Hungarians] are treated as second rank citizens, as sub-tenants in our common country".[26] Thus, UDMR rhetoric emphasized its will for integration in the Romanian society and its willingness to engage in consolidating the Romanian state in a relation of *equal partnership*.

The reference to the European Union has been a key component of UDMR discourse in what concerns administrative decentralization and regionalization. It represents an escape from the nation-state type of organization, since its core values – such as pluralism, dialogue, mutual respect and tolerance – encourages the "elimination of barriers separating Europe's peoples".[27]

In this sense, the discourse has two defining elements for UDMR claims, which are not entirely overlapping: *regionalization* and *autonomy*. The former is used as a softener for the latter. While being fully aware that autonomy, especially in its territorial format, will continue to stir the same unyielding opposition from all the Romanian political parties, UDMR often appeases them by using the rhetoric of decentralization and regionalization. Avowed as the most important goal, the *safeguarding of the national identity* of the Hungarians in Romania calls for the *decentralization* of state administrative organization, in such a way that "local administrations can operate as self-governments".[28] The degree of decentralization supported by UDMR would entail *self-governance rights* granted to the local communities, a mechanism which strengthens democratic consolidation. It is such institutional constructions that would – in the UDMR outlook – fully enable the development and reproduction of Hungarian identity in all its components: culture, education and politics.

AUTONOMY CLAIMS

Autonomy – sometimes referred to as *internal self-determination*[29] – has been a constantly exhibited principle beginning with the early 1990s. The UDMR third party congress represented a key moment, since that was the moment when an *autonomy* model was first (rather vaguely) conceptualized and inserted in a structured form in the party's program. This conception of autonomy defined the Hungarian minority as a "political community",[30] that "reflected a state in a state minority society organization model, which, starting out from the mobilizing capabilities of a movement profiting from identity ideology, presented the demand for autonomy strategy".[31] Gradually, as this representation of the desired autonomy came into pronounced antagonism with the participation in government of UDMR, it was relinquished to the background, while other remarkable elements took precedence: education, language use in the local administration and the media etc.

Two important stages in the development of claims to *autonomy* can be identified: one that can generally be placed during 1990–2002 and the later which extends beyond this period, until the present moment. During the former, the concept of autonomy evolved as a constitutive part of UDMR behaviour on the Romanian political stage. After 2002, however, autonomy claims are not entirely related with UDMR actions, but also with those of the factions within UDMR which formed subsequently opposing Hungarians' organizations: the National Hungarian Council in Transylvania, the National Szeklar Council and the Hungarian Civic Party (PCM).

The inclusion in the 1993 political program of the idiom partner nation (*társnemzet*) was a key event in the process of evolution of the meaning ascribed to autonomy in UDMR outlook. This implied that the Hungarians, through the political party that represents them, were claiming the political status of a state-constitutive community, with the rights and obligations that resulted from it. *Internal self-determination (belső önrendelkezés)* that is also integrated in the 1993 programme was derived from the political status that the UDMR claimed for the Hungarians. This outlook on autonomy emerged as a possibility during the debates on the adoption of the Romanian Constitution (1991).

Nevertheless, the three-fold conception of autonomy presented in the 1993 program is far from being a concrete definition of personal, local and territorial autonomy. As it was, it invited manifold interpretations, particularly from the Romanian political counterpart. Inevitably, although avowedly meant to challenge it from an administrative viewpoint, UDMR vision of autonomy has unwillingly been restrained by the confines prescribed by the Fundamental Act. Following from that, UDMR approach shifts to demanding *minority rights*. Many of these claims – right to language use in education, public administration, the media and the judiciary proceedings, representation, participation and cultural rights – are based on the principle of autonomous decision-making.

Another important period is marked by the years 1993–1996. During that time, two trends that are equally influential leave their mark on the evolution of autonomy claims. On one side, the deficient Romanian-Hungarian dialogue encouraged a more radical attitude on the part of UDMR. On the other hand, another trend acting from inside Romania, namely the formation of the Democratic Convention of Romania (CDR) and its rapprochement toward UDMR results in pressures made on the Hungarian party to diminish its autonomy claims. The result of the 1996 elections in Romania and the decision of the winners and UDMR to form a governing coalition resulted in the second trend having the upper hand. As a result, an opposing faction began to take shape inside UDMR, made up of those that were unwilling to discard autonomy as the short-term objective.

After 2000, UDMR no longer held governmental positions, but supported the ruling party in the Parliament: the Party of Social Democracy in Romania, which later became the Social Democratic Party (PDSR/PSD). Autonomy remained rather marginal in the UDMR official discourse, but the situation changes after 2002, when the internal dissentions increased and led to the separation of the strongest group that opposes Markó's discourse, led by László Tőkés. Following the 2003 UDMR Congress, Tőkés sets the basis for the *National Hungarian Council in Transylvania* (CNMA).[32] The party programme adopted at the 7th Congress (Satu Mare, 31 January–2 February 2003) reaffirmed that the protection of the identity and the rights of the Hungarians in Romania is "possible only through the institutions of autonomy established within the framework of the rule of law".[33]

The "autonomy of local administrations with special status" is described as a status that is to be bestowed onto those administrative units where significant minority populations dwell and who acknowledge the afore-mentioned status by means of a referendum.[34] *Territorial autonomy* is the third layer of UDMR outlook on the institutionalization of autonomous spheres of decision-making for the Hungarians, and is described as an "association of local public administrations".[35] Autonomy does not gain in clarity of definition in this program either, but several changes are noticeable, especially in relation with the discursive creation of an interconnected network between autonomy, decentralization, subsidiary, and *regionalization*.

Analyzing UDMR discourse on autonomy, one infers that autonomy-talk lies within the field of symbolic politics rather than in that of pragmatic and sustained action designed to lead to the accomplishment of the set goals. In the case of UDMR, symbolic talk of the definitive aspiration of the Hungarian minority – achieving its *autonomy* – has not been substantiated by pragmatic, focused and continuous endeavours to uphold a valid dialogue with the Hungarian community, or to appeal to the majority population to understand and perhaps even eventually support the Hungarians' need for self-management. Moreover, UDMR has also failed to put forward to public and political debate a concrete plan for the rapprochement of the Hungarian and Romanian communities.

A recent development, however, has triggered questions about the concrete steps that will be taken on the question of autonomy. In March 2011 the ruling coalition partners have signed a parliamentary and governing cooperation protocol that has brought in the public debate the autonomy demand by its references to two priority draft regulations of great interest to the UDMR: the Law on the Status of National Minorities in Romania and the reform of the regions. The minority status law is – as proposed – a framework law on managing ethnic diversity in Romania, which includes a separate chapter on cultural autonomy: institutional decision-making powers in areas related to development and protection of ethnic and cultural, linguistic and religious identity. This protocol is not the first in which coalition partners have identified the minority status law as a priority. A similar commitment was made in the 2005–2008 mandate. Although the previous attempt failed, there is the possibility for the UDMR coalition partners to reconsider their stances on local autonomy. However, the chances remain low due to the significant institutional-administrative changes that the adoption of this law would entail. There are also questions concerning the ability of UDMR and of the representatives of other national minorities to implement the legal provisions of autonomy, which remain unclear in the wording proposed by the above mentioned draft law.

CONCLUDING REMARKS

More than the UDMR leaders have been willing to admit, the support – electoral or otherwise – offered by the Hungarian community for the Union has dropped. Responsible for this are various factors, such as the natural corrosion of the support for a political party that is part of the Government and fails to accomplish part of its goals, the creation of two competing formations that avow to represent the interests of the Hungarian minority (The *Hungarian Civic Party* and the *National Hungarian Council in Transylvania*). Moreover, the decrease in the numbers of Hungarians in Romania has also represented one of the factors responsible for UDMR decrease in support. Among the highest-ranking causes of the aforementioned population decline are migration, assimilation (including mixed marriages), life expectancy etc. According to recent quantitative analyses, the decline in population due to emigration registered a peak at the end of the 1980s and the beginning of the 1990s, it continued on a steady course during 1992–2002 and registered a new increase after 2002.[36] Operationalizing the distinction between demographic and ethno cultural reproduction in the case of the ethnic Hungarians in Romania, the same research forecasts a continued tendency for population drop – to reach a 29.6% drop within the next 30 years.[37] Population decrease obviously also implies identity shifts.

For the researcher interested in Romanian-Hungarian relations, the obstinate refusal of politicians on both sides to take a step outside their own mental and cultural framework is staggering. Although they have managed to cooperate time and again due to their short-term interests and they have established a generous framework for minority protection, both sides' argumentative schemes present little inclination for adaptation and genuine compromise. The designing of a long-term plan aimed at triggering authentic societal changes comes into conflict with short-term political interests. As a result, less interest has been given to drafting strategies and public policies in the field of interethnic relations that overrun the life-span of transitory governmental coalitions.

The completion of such a desideratum is, however, impossible without a revision of both sides' identity-producing discourse in such a way that the organization of the majority and minority societies are interlinked in a mutually beneficial way. Despite the almost constant minority-majority strife caused by minority demands, the Romanian society has experienced no enduring debates concerning interethnic relations that would involve representatives of the political, cultural and social spheres. For cooperation to be enacted, the two societies need not become one, but on the contrary, their specific identity markers are to be preserved. Nevertheless, this present *status quo* indicates the "lacking tradition and institutions of consensus-making"[38], a situation which ought to be remedied.

In this sense, it is important to note the fact that the discourse of the Hungarian elites has marked that community as a political one, not just cultural. This meant that the Hungarian minority required political, as well as cultural rights, namely the right to be represented at the level of political institutions. Discourse has educated this political expression of the Hungarian identity, which contributed significantly to the shaping of Hungarian minority nation-building process throughout the last ninety years. The demand for autonomy represents the highest peak of the aspiration to be represented at a political echelon, since an autonomous framework would allow for political, administrative and cultural decisions in several spheres to be made without the intervention of the Romanian authorities. This expresses a marked divergence from the constraints imposed by the Romanian nation-building process to the identity of the national minorities living on its territory. This feature – in ethno-psychological terms – has been defined as "conflict of identification".[39] However, by claiming its rights and also achieving many of them, the Hungarian minority has contributed to the partial reformation of Romania's socio-political and cultural structure and can continue to be a factor with the potential to induce socio-political change.

Although aware of the fact that Romania's present legal conditions make territorial autonomies impossible' and that the Romanian officials, regardless of the party they belong to, will not concede to changing it, UDMR chose to continue to use this rhetorical political claim for the following purpose: abandoning this claim would have meant to abandon the legacy of the interwar period and to reject the historical justifications for which autonomy was deemed as necessary to begin with. Since many of the rights demanded by UDMR for the Hungarian minority, as well as for the other national minority groups in Romania, have been inscribed in various normative acts issued in the last two decades, the claim for *autonomy* remains the boundary marker around which the mobilization process can function most successfully.

In this article's interpretation, UDMR has three grand alternatives: the first is to continue the present course of action, which proposes autonomy as the decisive aim of the Hungarian minority in terms of rights but fails to clearly define it, offer a structured action plan and explain whether the requested decision-making powers are full or shared with the Romanian authorities; the second is to back the current autonomy-talk with a set of articulate plans necessary for its implementation, and thereby acknowledge its desire to separate itself from the Romanian state/ society; the third is to adapt the underlying principles of autonomy in such a way that the Romanian-Hungarian political and social cooperation are included. In all three variants, one is compelled that the first necessary benchmarks that has to exist is the will of the Romanian authorities to grant the rights to autonomy, and the determination and capability of the Hungarians to implement it and assure the manpower and expertise needed to make such an endeavour successful. On either of these two counts, evidence thus far suggests a negative answer.

For the Hungarians, as well as the Romanians, one feature of political identity the discourse deeply engraved has been the consciousness that the two communities have irredeemably separate and conflictual identities. However, once constructed, identity can also be deconstructed and replaced. It is in this reversal that political discourse plays a most significant role. In this article's approach, the reconfiguration through discursive practices of the Hungarian and Romanian political identities has to occur *consensually* and *gradually* and aim at achieving a transformation in values that guide the workings of state institutions. These elements are key coordinates of a genuine, multi-layered process of identity change, a process that needs to unfold regardless of changing political incumbents. The post-communist political, social and international conditions are favourable for allowing such a significant process of change to occur. However, the will of the Romanian and Hungarian political elites still lingers.

REFERENCES

1 Irina Culic, Dilemmas of Belonging: Hungarians from Romania, in: Nationalities Papers 34 (2006) 2, 184.

2 Article 1, Constitution of Romania, amended and completed by Law No. 429/2003: http://www.cdep.ro/pls/dic/site.page?den=act2_2&par1=1#t1c0s0a1, Accessed 15.06.2009.

3 According to the list made available in Levente Salat (ed.), Politici de integrare a minoritatilor nationale din Romania. Aspecte legale si institutionale intro perspectiva comparata [Policies of Integration of the National Minorities in Romania], Ethnocultural Diversity Resource Center, Cluj-Napoca 2008, 262–272.

4 The law was revised in 1997 (Government Decision No. 36/1997) and 1999 (Law No. 84/1995, republished in December 1999).

5 Legal Framework on the Education of National Minorities (The Law on Education), Cluj, June 16th, 1995, published in UDMR Documents 1989–1999, Bucharest 1999.

6 Ibid.

7 2008 UDMR Program, Chapter VI: http://www.udmr.ro/programalegeri.php?programalegeri=9, Accessed 15.05.2009.

8 Plans for the Distribution of the Hungarian Higher Educational Institutions in Romania: Hungarian Higher Education in Romania. Past-Present-Future, József Kötô/Sándor Tonk (eds.), Cluj-Napoca, 1998.

9 Jozsef Kötô, UDMR member, discourse held at the Chamber of Deputies' Session on 17 March 2009, on the occasion of the 50 year anniversary of the revocation of the independent and separate statute of the Hungarian Bolyai University in Cluj: http://www.cdep.ro/pls/steno/steno.stenogram a?ids=6604&idm=1,13&idl=1, Accessed 15.05.2009.

10 Ibid.

11 Ibid.

12 Ibid.

13 Art. 46, paragraph 2, Law on National Education No.1/2011, Official Journal No. 18/5 (2011).

14 Ibid., Art. 46, paragraph 8.

15 Ibid., Art. 97, paragraph 1, idem.

16 Ibid., Art. 97, paragraph 2.a.

17 Ibid., Art. 45, paragraph 6.

18 Ibid., Art. 135.

19 In the present case (2009–2012) the governing coalition is composed of the Democrat Liberal Party (PDL), UDMR, National Union for Romania's Progress (UNPR) and the Minorities' Parliamentary Group.

20 Law. No. 215/ 2001.

21 Government Decision No. 1206/ 2001.

22 Article 17, Law 215/ 2001 of the Local Public Administration, Official Journal No. 204/ 23: http:// www.cdep.ro/pls/legis/legis_pck.htp_act_text?idt=27123, Accessed 15.06.2009.

23 József Csapó (UDMR), discourse published in the "Official Journal" of Romania, 2nd Part, Year IX, No. 228 (1998), held during the debates in the Senate concerning the amendments brought to the Education Law and the Local Public Administration Law, 19.

24 Ibid.

25 Csaba-Tiberiu Kovács, discourse published in the "Official Journal "of Romania, 2nd Part, Year XII, No. 12 (2001), held during the Parliamentary Debates, 11.

26 Robert Kalman Ráduly, discourse published in the "Official Journal" of Romania, 2nd Part, Year XII, No. 41 (2001), held during the Parliamentary Debates, 22.

27 Senator Francisc Bárányi (UDMR), discourse published in the "Official Journal" of Romania, 2nd Part, Year X, No. 253 (1999), held during the debates in the reunited meetings of the Senate and the Chamber of Deputies, concerning the revision of the Local Public Administration Law, 8.

28 Document of the UDMR 9th Congress: Our Union, Our Europe, issued on 27 April 2009: http:// www.udmr.ro/stiri.php?hir=599, Accessed 15.05.2009.

29 Ibid.

30 UDMR Program, adopted at the party's 3rd Congress (Braşov, January 1993), in UDMR Documents 1989–1999, Bucharest 1999.

31 Levente Salat, "Visions of Minority Hungarians in Transylvania: Prospects and Obstacles", in: Kisebbségkutatás – Minorities Research 6, no details concerning the year of publication: http:// www.hhrf.org/kisebbsegkutatas/mr_06/cikk_nyomtatas.php?id=1245, Accessed 15.06.2009.

32 Ibid.

33 Erdélyi Magyar Nemzeti Tanácsot – EMNT.

34 2003 UDMR Programme, adopted at the party's 7th Congress.

35 Ibid.

36 Ibid.

37 Tamás Kiss and István Csata, Evoluţia populaţiei maghiare din România. Rezultate şi probleme metodologice [The Evolution of the Hungarian Population in Romania: Results and Methodological Problems], the Institute for the Study of National Minorities' Issues 2008.

38 Ibid., 16.

39 Salat, Visions, Loc. Cit. (Note 31).

LIST OF CONTRIBUTORS

MONICA ANDRIESCU (b. 1984), Master of Arts (Nationalism Studies and Comparative Politics), researcher in Babes-Bolyai University, Cluj-Napoca, Romania. Her main topics of research are minority integration and mobilization, political violence in non-democratic regimes, anti-immigration discourse and immigrant mobilization in Western and Southern Europe. Contact information: E-mail: Monica.andriescu@yahoo.com.

GERHARD BESIER (b. 1947), Dr. theol. habil., Dr. phil., Dipl.-Psych, Professor, Chair in European Studies at the University of Dresden, Germany. His main topics of research are religion, state and society in national and international perspectives, dictatorships in the 20th century and psychohistorical and neurobiological aspects of human being. Contact information: University of Dresden, Chair in European Studies, Chemnitzer Strasse 46, 01062 Dresden, Germany. E-mail: gbesier@aol.com.

OLGA ILYKHA (b. 1960), Cand (PhD) of History, senior researcher at the Institute of Karelian Language, Literature and History, Karelian Research Centre of the Russian Academy of Sciences, Russia. Her main topics of research are local history, schooling and national issues in Russian Karelia. Contact information: Institute of Karelian Language, Literature and History, Karelian Research Centre of the Russian Academy of Sciences, Pushkinskaya Str., Petrozavodsk 185610, Russia. E-mail: iljuha@krc.karelia.ru.

KIMMO KATAJALA (b. 1958), PhD, Professor of History at the Department of Geographical and Historical Studies, University of Eastern Finland, Finland. His main topics of research are history of borders, history of Eastern Finland and Karelia and the early modern peasant movements. Contact information: University of Eastern Finland, Department of Geographical and Historical Studies, P.O. Box 111, 80101 Joensuu, Finland. E-mail: kimmo.katajala@uef.fi.

JUKKA KOKKONEN (b. 1965), PhD, researcher fellow at the Karelian Institute, University of Eastern Finland, Finland. His main topics of research are history of borders and interaction relations between Sweden and Russia in the early modern times. Contact information: University of Eastern Finland, Karelian Institute, P.O. Box 111, FI-80101, Joensuu, Finland. E-mail: jukka.kokkonen@uef.fi.

MIKHAIL KROM (b. 1966), Dr. sc. in History, Professor of Comparative Studies in History at the European University at St. Petersburg, Russia. His main topics of research are early modern history of Russia and the Grand Duchy of Lithuania in comparative perspective, methods of historical research and historiography. Contact information: European University at St. Petersburg, 3, Gagarinskaya Str., St. Petersburg 191187, Russia. E-mail: krom@eu.spb.ru.

ANNA LAAKKONEN (b. 1983), Master of Arts (History) at the Department of Geographical and Historical Studies, University of Eastern Finland, Finland. Her main topics of research are Karelia, borders and Soviet press. Contact information: E-mail: annamaria.laakkonen@gmail.com.

JENS LERBOM (b. 1964), PhD, lecturer at the Department of Humanities, Halmstad University, Sweden. His main topics of research are integration, ethnicity, violence and migration in the early modern Scandinavia. Contact information: Department of Humanities, Halmstad University, P.O. Box 823, S-301 18, Halmstad, Sweden. E-mail: jens.lerbom@hh.se.

MARIA LÄHTEENMÄKI (b. 1957), PhD, Jutikkala Professor at the Department of Geographical and Historical Studies, University of Eastern Finland, Finland. Her main topics of research are regional history, gender studies and history of labour movement. Contact information: University of Eastern Finland, Department of Geographical and Historical Studies, PB 111, 80101 Joensuu, Finland. E-mail: maria.lahteenmaki@uef.fi.

JENS PETTER NIELSEN (b. 1949), Cand. philol., Professor at the Department of History and Religious Studies, University of Tromsø, Norway. His main topics of research are Russian and Soviet history and Norwegian-Russian relations. Contact information: IHR, University of Tromsø, NO-9037 Tromsø, Norway. E-mail: jens.petter.nielsen@uit.no.

KATARZYNA STOKŁOSA (b. 1974), Dr. phil. habil., Associate Professor at the Department of Border Region Studies, University of Southern Denmark, Denmark. Her main topics of research are border regions, European history, international relations and prejudices and stereotypes. Contact information: Alsion 2, DK-6400 Sønderborg, Denmark. E-mail stoklosa@sam.sdu.dk.

HALLVARD TJELMELAND (b. 1952), Cand. Philol., Professor at the Department of History and Religious Studies, University of Tromsø, Norway. His main topics of research are history of the labour movement, history of identities and international history of the 20th century. Contact information: Department of History and Religious Studies, University of Tromsø. 9037 Tromsø, Norway. E-mail: hallvard.tjelmeland@uit.no.

KONSTANTIN ZAIKOV (b. 1983), Candidate of Science, PhD student at the Department of History and Religious studies, University of Tromsø, Norway. His main topics or research are the history of Norwegian-Russian borderland and the Norwegian-Russian relations. Contact information: E-mail: konstantin.zaikov@uit.no.